Undercover Tales
of World War II

Undercover Tales
of World War II

William B. Breuer

CASTLE BOOKS

This edition published in 2005 by
CASTLE BOOKS ®
A division of Book Sales, Inc.
114 Northfield Avenue
Edison, NJ 08837

This edition published by arrangement with and permission of
John Wiley & Sons, Inc.
111 River Street
Hoboken, New Jersey 07030

This publication is designed to provide accurate and authoritative information in regard to the subject matter provided. It is sold with the understanding that the publisher is not engaged in rendering professional services. If professional advice or other expert assistance is required, the services of

Library of Congress Cataloging-in-Publication Data:

Breuer, William B.
Undercover tales of World War II / William B. Breuer.
p.   cm.
Includes bibliographical references and index.
World War, 1939-1945—Secret service. 2. Espionage—History—20th century. I. Title.

D810.S7B685   1999
940.54'86—dc21   98-24119

ISBN-13: 978-0-7858-1953-0
ISBN-10: 0-7858-1953-3

Dedicated to
Four-star General Edwin H. Burba, Jr. (Ret.),
who fought with great courage
and distinction as a junior
officer in Vietnam, was seriously
wounded, yet rose to the top
in his profession

Contents

Author's Note   xi

Part One — A Gathering Tempest

Black-Bag Jobs and Madam X   3

Hitler's Crony a U.S. Secret Agent   5

"Me No Here, No Movies!"   7

Hitler's "Mystery Spy" in London   9

Stealing a Supersecret Bombsight   13

Espionage Target: The Panama Canal   17

The Gestapo Comes to New York   21

Practicing "Nazi Psychology" in the United States   24

A Gentleman Farmer Flies to London   25

An "Unsportsmanlike" Murder Scheme   30

Part Two — Outbreak of War

"Take Possession of the [British Captives]"   33

Agent X Conspires with the Pope   36

The Spy Was a Clip Artist   41

Denmark's Patriotic Burglar   42

Deceit in the Desert   44

The Jewish Pal of the Nazis   46

The FBI Undercover in South America   49

"War of Nerves" against England   53

The Führer's Concrete Crocodiles   57

Tuned in to the Luftwaffe   57

Hosting a Boy Scout Official   60

"We Came to Blow Up America!"   61

The Bogus Traitor of Flekkefjord   65

A One-Man Cloak-and-Dagger Agency   70

Part Three—Conflict Spreads to the Pacific

One Briton's Revenge   79
Spies inside a U.S. Embassy   80
The "Evangelists" of New York Harbor   82
Confrontation at a Montana Airport   85
Clandestine Payoffs in Mexico   88
Urgent: Hide the Suez Canal   89
A Covert Cruise in the Pacific   93
Four Frogmen against Two Battleships   96
The Superspy at Pearl Harbor   100
An American Turncoat in Washington   106

Part Four—The Turning Tide

The World's Richest Spymaster   109
The Plot to Blow Up the Pan Am Clipper   112
Lady Luck Flies with the Führer   114
Rommel's Secret Informant   117
The Scientist Who Knew Too Much   120
The Dogs of Torigni   124
Conspiracy in Casablanca   126
Outfoxing the Desert Fox   129
Smuggling Two Men out of Morocco   134
The Creeps and the Atomic Scientists   136

Part Five—Beginning of the End

The Spy Who Refused to Die   143
Blowing Up a Locomotive Works   147
The Mystery Man of Algiers   150
Top Secret: Parachuting Mules   153
America's Fifteen Thousand Secret Snoopers   155
Coercing Surrender of the Italian Fleet   159
Deception Role for the Panjandrum   163
Bedeviling the Gestapo in Toulouse   166
An X-Craft Calls on the *Tirpitz*   169

A French Boy and His Music Teacher   172
An Atomic Alert on New Year's Eve   174
"Ghost Voices" over Europe   177
Close Call in a Secret Room   178
Masking the "Chicago Skyline"   179

Part Six—The Lights Go On Again
A U.S. Colonel's Private Airline   187
Kidnapping a German General   190
Blasting a Japanese Headquarters   195
Mad Dash in an Explosive-Laden Car   196
A Special Job for "Scarface Otto"   199
Sneaking onto Utah Beach   203
X2 Agents in Cherbourg   205
Covert Targets: Germany's Atomic Scientists   208
Alias Gregor and Igor   213
Dodging the Gestapo in the Ruhr   217
A Murder Job for Two "Specialists"   221
T Force Hunts for Chemical Weapons   224

Notes and Sources   227
Index   237

Author's Note

HARDLY HAD THE INK DRIED after the signing of the Treaty of Versailles that officially concluded World War I on June 28, 1919, than leaders of several nations began preparing for World War II.

Only months after Versailles, a flamboyant politician in Italy, Benito Mussolini, created an antidemocratic party, Fasci di Combattimento, dressed its members in black shirts, and seized control of the weak government two years later. Hoping to revive the glories of ancient Rome by expanding the Italian empire, Mussolini began building a modern army, navy, and air force.

Versailles restricted Germany to a Reichswehr (army) of only one hundred thousand civilian volunteers and prohibited it from having airplanes or tanks. In 1921, efforts were launched to circumvent these restraints. Instead of civilian volunteers, the ranks were filled with the cream of the wartime officer corps. A covert agreement was reached with the Soviet Union to manufacture tanks, aircraft, artillery, shells, and even poison gas for the Reichswehr.

In the late 1920s Japanese warlords, who had become the nation's dominant force, drew up the Tanaka Memorial, a grand design for widespread conquest in the Pacific and an eventual invasion of the United States.

Throughout the 1930s and during the six years of World War II, global powers sought to gain military, political, economic, and psychological advantage by a deluge of clandestine maneuvers, only some of which took place on the battlefield, but often reacted decisively on it. These secret actions involved spies, saboteurs, propagandists, traitors, thefts of plans, bribes, traps, code breaking, and plots to kidnap or murder persons in high places.

Most of these surreptitious events would have been rejected by Hollywood film producers as implausible—yet they happened, and they helped to shape the outcome of World War II.

During the past several years I have collected research materials from a wide variety of sources to re-create the intriguing, often baffling episodes that are told, generally in chronological order, in this book. Among these sources were personal and telephone interviews with participants or those who had been connected with a secret activity, official archives, media accounts, books and articles by responsible authors, declassified documents, and several amateur history buffs who have gathered a wealth of World War II information as a hobby.

WILLIAM B. BREUER
Chilhowee Mountain,
Tennessee
August 1998

xi

Part One

A Gathering Tempest

Black-Bag Jobs and Madam X

As FAR AS the outside world was concerned, the United States and Japan appeared to be on the friendliest of terms in the early 1930s. The two nations exchanged cultural missions, and a team of baseball all-stars from the United States, headed by the legendary Babe Ruth, each year played a series of exhibition games in Japan to packed stadiums. Behind the scenes, however, an ongoing undeclared war of wits between competing naval intelligence code-breakers was raging relentlessly.

In February 1933 a Japanese tailor, smiling and bowing graciously, called at the U.S. consulate at Kobe and explained that as a gesture of friendship between the two nations, he would be most happy to provide handmade suits at a quite low cost to those assigned to the diplomatic staff. After displaying cloth samples, the tailor took orders from several of the Americans, who knew a great value when they saw one.

In the weeks ahead, the pleasant, convivial tailor was a frequent visitor to the consulate, taking orders for suits and even doing odd jobs for the staff. He gained the Americans' total trust and no longer had to show his special pass to the guard at the front door. He even had free run of an office that contained a safe, which, he learned by judicious inquiry, held a secret U.S. code.

Actually, the "tailor" belonged to the *kempeitai*, Japan's secret police force. Cagey but cautious, he bribed a junior member of the consulate staff to "borrow" the key to the safe, after which the spy had a wax imprint made. From this imprint a key was fashioned.

On a Saturday night in late April 1933, when the "tailor" knew that the consul and a few of his staffers would be at a local geisha house, a squad of kempeitai men, thoroughly briefed in advance and provided with a detailed drawing of the consulate floor plan, pulled a "black-bag job," as a surreptitious entry is called in the espionage business. With ease, they pried open the office door, used the spy's key to open the safe, and removed a book containing the U.S. State Department's Gray Code.

Like a well-oiled machine, the burglars rapidly photographed each page, then replaced the book in the safe, being exceptionally careful to put it precisely where it had been lying. Then the intruders sneaked out of the building.

The venture had been conducted so skillfully that the Americans would not learn for several years that their Gray Code had been pilfered by the Japanese.

The ease and simplicity with which the U.S. consulate had been penetrated energized the kempeitai into organizing an entire division of safecrackers, photographers, and technicians to cooperate with Japanese naval intelligence in conducting black-bag jobs against other American diplomatic facilities and also other foreign consulates. These burglaries were painstakingly planned. While one squad was breaking into a consulate, some five or six other men would remain outside to create a noisy diversion should danger approach, thereby giving the burglars inside time to escape.

Soon, Tokyo intelligence was reading the British Foreign Office's messages being radioed in secret code not long after they had been sent from London. This situation, of which the British were unaware, resulted from a visit by a black-bag squad to His Majesty's consulate in Osaka.

Then the customarily meticulous Japanese break-in artists bungled. After burglarizing the office of the U.S. naval attaché in Tokyo, the intruders left behind telltale clues that disclosed the nocturnal visit. The Office of Naval Intelligence in Washington rightfully concluded that the navy's current secret code had been compromised by the Japanese.

Consequently, security at U.S. consulates in Japan was tightened, locks on safes were changed and upgraded, a system of visitors' passes was vastly improved, and a far more sophisticated and intricate code was adopted.

To confuse Japanese wireless eavesdroppers, the U.S. Navy continued to send occasional messages in the purloined code, information that was totally irrelevant or, in some instances, nonsensical. These wireless machinations presumably would send Japanese agents scurrying endlessly into dead end alleys in search of additional intelligence.

At the same time, because American operatives had not pulled any black-bag jobs, the Japanese never suspected that the U.S. Office of Naval Intelligence (ONI) cryptanalysts had broken the Imperial Navy's Blue Code and were reading top-secret communications. It had taken Agnes Meyer Driscoll, a cryptanalyst in the Code and Signal Section of the ONI in Washington, three years of mind-boggling effort, beginning in 1930, to crack the incredibly complex Blue Code.

In the U.S. Navy, Driscoll was without peer as a cryptanalyst, and she was held in the highest esteem by her uniformed colleagues at OP-20-G, the designation of their section of the ONI. Known affectionately as Madam X, she was highly sensitive to being the only woman in the otherwise all-male world of American code breakers. Because of that situation, she kept to herself as much as possible, and no one in her section was ever invited to socialize with her and her lawyer husband.

When Madam X had first been assigned the task of breaking the Blue Code, she was confronted by the seemingly impossible job of working out the meanings of a code made up of some eighty-five thousand basic groups. At the time, an interoffice feud was raging, and her boss, the director of naval communications, refused to ask the ONI for a black-bag job at a Japanese embassy to help her solve the intricate Blue Code.

Madam X was undaunted to know that she would have to solve the bewildering riddle by cryptanalysis alone. However, she received some assistance from the regular shipment of bags brought by courier from New York City. These bags were crammed with scraps of paper, many of which contained Blue Code jottings, that ONI undercover agents had obtained by rifling through the trash bin behind the Japanese consulate in New York.

American leaders would continue to read secret Blue Code radio traffic until November 1938, when the Japanese began using a new code. The change apparently had been made after an investigation of "leaks" by Japanese security officers indicated that the eight-year-old Blue Code had been compromised.[1]

Hitler's Crony a U.S. Secret Agent

SOON AFTER the onetime Austrian house painter Adolf Hitler seized power in Germany in early 1933, he appointed a longtime crony, Ernst Franz Hanfstaengl, to the prestigious and influential post of foreign press secretary for the National Socialist German Workers' Party, which came to be known as the Nazis. The hulking, six-foot, four-inch Hanfstaengl was called "Putzi," meaning Little Fellow.

A jovial individual, the Falstaffian Putzi was highly regarded by Hitler, who enjoyed having him around. That affection was not shared by other Nazi big shots, such as Hermann Goering, Rudolf Hess, and Heinrich Himmler, who thought of Putzi as an obnoxious loudmouth. His standing in the Nazi hierarchy (except with Hitler) plunged even deeper when, at a crowded reception attended by Berlin's elite, he thundered that Josef Paul Goebbels, the propaganda minister, was a *Schweinehund* (dirty dog).

Hanfstaengl, who had a German father and an American mother, had lived in Germany during his youth. He went to the United States after World War I to enroll at Harvard, earning a degree in business administration.

Soon after he returned to Germany in 1923, Putzi became enamored of the fast-rising, articulate politician named Adolf Hitler, who had changed his name from Schicklgruber, his unmarried mother's cognomen. Hitler was making firebrand speeches in Munich beer halls and trying to entice listeners to join his tiny Nazi Party.

Hanfstaengl eagerly linked up with Hitler, did his bidding, and remained loyal, even after the charismatic Nazi leader was arrested on November 8, 1923, for trying to take over the Bavarian government in Munich. Hitler and his assistant Rudolf Hess were tried in court, found guilty, and imprisoned for three years. When his idol was freed, the faithful Putzi was there to greet him.

Years later, in early 1937, Putzi became the target of unknown parties (no doubt those near Hitler) in a weird scenario apparently intended to get rid of the nuisance with the big mouth. He was handed sealed orders, reputedly signed by Hitler, and told that the führer wanted him to open the envelope only after Putzi was aloft in an airplane that was waiting for him at a Berlin airport.

It spoke eloquently of Putzi's deep devotion to the führer that, without question, he boarded the airplane. Nor apparently did he think it strange that the aircraft's windows had been blacked out.

Soon after the plane was in the sky, Putzi read the orders. They stated that he was to parachute into Spain, where a bloody civil war was raging. Then he was to report back to Hitler on the performance of the Condor Legion, the five thousand German "volunteers" the führer had sent to help Generalissimo Francisco Franco's Nationalists fight the Communist insurgents being backed by the Soviet Union.

Because the windows had been blacked out, Putzi could not tell that the airplane was flying in circles above Germany to simulate a flight over the towering Pyrenees along the Spanish-French border. Periodically, the pilot landed to refuel.

Gradually, Putzi concluded that he had been set up, that influential enemies in Berlin had orchestrated an intricate scheme to "eliminate" him, which may very well have been the case. So at one refueling stop, he bolted from the plane and made a dash for a railroad station a short distance away. No doubt he was astonished to find that he was still in Germany, not in France or Spain. He went on the run, not halting until he had made his way to England.

Putzi's defection soon became known to the Abwehr (secret service), and a few weeks after he reached England, General Hermann Goering, chief of the Luftwaffe and number two man on the Nazi totem pole, sent him a letter.

"We only wanted to give you an opportunity of thinking over some rather overaudacious utterances you [had] made," the rotund Goering stated. He assured the presumed defector that there were no hard feelings against him in Berlin, and that he had Goering's word of honor that he would be safe in the Third Reich.

Putzi had no intention of accepting Goering's word of honor and apparently decided to cast his lot in an undercover role with the Anglo-Americans. A few weeks later, he arrived in the United States escorted by secret agents, and was held incognito at Bush Hill, an estate in the Virginia countryside not far from Washington, where he lived quite comfortably.

After Adolf Hitler declared war on the United States three days after the Japanese launched a sneak attack against Pearl Harbor, Hawaii, on December 7, 1941, Hanfstaengl became deeply involved in an ongoing secret mission for his host country. Propaganda and psychological warfare specialists in Washington regularly called at Bush Hill to consult with the German on how their schemes against Hitler and the Third Reich might be improved or altered.

Putzi had become such an important cog in this propaganda campaign against his homeland that he was even taken to the White House and introduced to President Franklin D. Roosevelt. Thus he became one of the few individuals who was an acquaintance of the leaders of both Germany and the United States.

Putzi remained a "guest" of the U.S. government throughout the global war. His intelligence, his keen knowledge of the thinking processes of the Nazi hierarchy, and his media background enabled him to give sage advice on how best to utilize propaganda against his old pal Adolf Hitler.[2]

"Me No Here, No Movies!"

ONE DAY IN THE FALL OF 1934, while the U.S. battleship *Pennsylvania* was resting in a Southern California port, Lieutenant Commander Joseph J. Rochefort, assistant operations officer and chief of intelligence, called in Lieutenant Edwin T. Layton, who was in charge of the main gun turret.

"Ed, there's a navy doctor over at Long Beach who works with an ONI undercover squad," Rochefort said. "They're keeping track of what's going on in the Japanese community here. He just reported that the Japanese naval tanker that arrived today has some special film that they plan to show to a local Japanese association tomorrow night. We suspect the film is subversive."

A tall, lean man whose gentle manner and soft-spoken words belied a fierce competitiveness, the intelligence officer told Layton, "I'd like to have you help the undercover boys in this matter."

Sponsoring the film-showing would be a group calling itself the Japanese Citizens Patriotic Society. It had rented an auditorium in Long Beach from the Shell Oil Company, which, no doubt, was unaware of the propaganda nature of the film. Layton, in mulling over his task, realized that as a Caucasian he might be denied entry to the session.

On the night of the event, Lieutenant Layton put on coveralls bearing a phony commercial firm's name and posed as a fire insurance inspector. In one hand, he carried a fire extinguisher. As the naval officer had anticipated, he was denied entry at the front door. Playing his role to the hilt, Layton loudly declared that he was there to protect the property of Shell Oil, and he whipped out his false credentials to prove his affiliation. His job was to make certain there would be no smoking in the auditorium while the film was being shown, he declared.

Soon the local chairman of the Japanese Citizens Patriotic Society appeared, and while pretending not to speak a word of Japanese (he was fluent in the language), Layton flashed his fake papers and demanded that he be allowed to enter.

"Get out!" the chairman shouted.

"Me no here, no movies!" Layton exclaimed.

It was time for the film showing to begin, and some three hundred persons gathered in the auditorium were growing restless. With a scowl, the chairman waved Layton into the auditorium.

Layton moved about, telling people officiously to extinguish the cigarettes they were smoking. Between admonitions, he glanced at the movie being shown. The gist of the story line was that the Japanese emperor system had been made in heaven, and the U.S. democracy was decadent and designed to permit a few well-heeled men to keep citizens in poverty.

Clearly, the film's producers had hoped to stir Japanese patriotism. One part showed Japanese troops, after capturing an enemy position during the war against Russia in the early 1900s, atop a wall, waving a Japanese flag vigorously and shouting "Banzai!"

A cartoon part of the film depicted John Pierpont Morgan, one of the wealthiest men in U.S. history, pushing a wheelbarrow overflowing with thousand-dollar bills over the prostrate bodies of poor people.

While Ed Layton had been circulating through the crowd, his fire extinguisher rested in a corner. An inquisitive sailor from the Japanese tanker decided to examine the strange-looking apparatus and turned it upside down, receiving a faceful of foam. More foam spilled out onto the floor.

After the showing was completed, Layton, a good "company man" for Shell Oil, cleaned up the mess. When he had finished, the Japanese Citizens Patriotic Society chairman, perhaps embarrassed by the situation, handed Layton a five-dollar bill for his clean-up job.

A native of Nauvoo, Illinois, and a Naval Academy graduate, Layton had done such an outstanding job in his first undercover assignment that he was soon given another secret mission. Commander Rochefort told the thirty-year-old Layton that there was a Japanese spy operating in the Dutch Harbor region of the Aleutians, a chain of volcanic islands that extends more than nine hundred miles westward from the tip of the Alaskan Peninsula. Admiral Joseph M. Reeves, commander of the Pacific Fleet, wanted the spy "eliminated" so he could not observe and report on Reeves's ships, which would soon arrive for a fleet problem, Rochefort explained.

A U.S. naval base was located in the bay at Dutch Harbor (population, 47), which received its name from a story that a Dutch ship had been the first to enter the bay sometime in the early 1700s.

Two weeks later, Layton, wearing civilian clothes, debarked from the navy tanker Brazos, which had arrived in advance of the fleet, and sneaked ashore at Dutch Harbor. There the lieutenant contacted the postmaster in the civilian community Illilliuk, presented his credentials, and described his mission. The postmaster, who also was a federal judge, replied that there was only one Japanese, a Mr. Shimizu, in the region.

Layton soon turned up evidence that Shimizu and his Alaskan girlfriend, a prostitute, were engaged in espionage. However, convicting the pair could be a long, drawn-out procedure. So, working with the federal judge, Layton managed to have Shimizu and his girlfriend put in the tiny, dingy local jail, at least until the Pacific Fleet exercises in the Aleutians had been completed. The charge: illegally selling bootleg whiskey to Ed Layton.

The cost of "eliminating" the two Japanese spies had been meager: two dollars for the purchase of bad booze from Shimizu, and two dollars paid to an American sailor at the base for compromising the whore in the bootleg sale.

Layton's superiors praised him for his resourcefulness and a job well done. He would learn later, however, that not everyone in the Pacific Fleet was happy with him. During shore leave, a large number of sailors visited Illilliuk, and they became hostile after learning there was only one prostitute in town—and she was behind bars.

Two sailors, neither of whom was feeling any pain, hurried to the jailhouse and loudly demanded to go her bail for the relatively minor offense of selling a bottle of illegal booze. The plea fell on deaf ears.[3]

Hitler's "Mystery Spy" in London

ON FEBRUARY 11, 1936, Admiral Wilhelm Canaris, chief of the Abwehr, requested an immediate conference with Adolf Hitler, who held the title of president of Germany but in actuality had been an iron-fisted dictator since seizing power three years earlier. There was urgency in Canaris's tone, so the führer met with his espionage ace at 8:00 P.M. at the Reichskanzlei (Chancellery) in Berlin.

Canaris, a diminutive, nervous man with a slight lisp, had been one of Kaiser Wilhelm's most successful spies in World War I. Now he had agents planted in most governments around the world. Reaching into his briefcase, Canaris pulled out a document marked top secret in French, and said that one of his most capable operatives had just succeeded in "procuring" it from a high government official in Paris.

It was a stunning instrument—a transcript of a secret conference between high-level French and Soviet diplomats in which the two nations agreed to join with Czechoslovakia for an armed invasion of Germany to short-circuit Hitler's reported plans to grab territory in Europe.

Admiral Canaris had barely departed from his office when Hitler ordered General Werner von Blomberg, commander in chief of the Wehrmacht (armed forces), to report immediately and issued orders for him to prepare Operation Schulung (exercise) for execution at the earliest possible date.

Schulung had been drawn up by a staff of handpicked army officers. It called for German forces to march into and occupy the Rhineland, an area covering French, Belgian, and German soil that had been demilitarized and declared neutral by agreement of seven European powers back in 1925.

Ein Volk, ein Reich, ein Führer!

Drumbeat slogan: "One People, One Country, One Leader!" (U.S. Army)

To keep the true purpose of the Rhineland plan covered even from high-ranking German officers, it was said to be merely a training exercise (as its code name implied) to give the planning staffs something to do. That was the word that had been spread by General von Blomberg even to his closest confidants.

On February 27 Blomberg called on Hitler and told him that preliminary preparations had been completed. The führer set *X-Tag* (X-Day) for March 7, only nine days away.

Back at his headquarters the next day, Blomberg called in General Ludwig Beck, chief of the General Staff, and General Werner von Fritsch, commander in chief of the *Heer* (army). Blomberg dropped a blockbuster on the two officers: Schulung was not just a plan for a field exercise, as they had been led to believe, but rather Hitler had ordered the army to be ready to march in six days.

It was, Blomberg told his senior commanders, to be a "surprise move," and he said he expected it to be a "peaceful operation." Beck and Fritsch were shocked. Fritsch pointed out that the only force he had for such an adventurous action was thirty-five thousand men, and that only a single division could be mustered for combat. Beck reinforced Fritsch's qualms by arguing that the

French could rapidly bring up twenty superbly equipped and keenly trained divisions to hurl at Fritsch's little force. "The French will make mincemeat of us," Beck emphasized.

Meanwhile, alarming signals were being sent back to Germany from Admiral Canaris's Abwehr agents whom he had planted in the Rhineland for just such an operation as Hitler was now going to launch. Headquarters for the espionage penetration of the Rhineland was in Münster, a major German city east of the Rhine River. The Abwehr there operated under the cover of a phony civilian commercial company.

Spies reported to Münster that the French were manning fortifications all along the German border, with troops being brought there from throughout France. In a major intelligence coup, Canaris was able to show Hitler a precise copy of the actual order the French had drawn up to rapidly mobilize thirteen divisions in an emergency.

The Forschungsant, the Luftwaffe's electronic monitoring branch that had earlier cracked the French diplomatic code, was steadily intercepting messages of deep concern that André François-Poncet, the French ambassador to Germany, was sending to Paris from Berlin. He warned that Hitler was going to occupy the Rhineland, so Hitler's hope for secrecy would be lost.

At the same time, German military attachés in London were sending Berlin gloomy assessments of the mood of the British government. One of the attachés stated that "a good friend of mine in the [British] War Office" had told him that England would plunge into the conflict alongside France if Hitler had the temerity to try to take over the Rhineland by force.

Now, at the grim conference among the three senior German commanders in Berlin, General von Blomberg, fully aware of the flood of intelligence reports declaring that France and Britain would fight, confided to Fritsch and Beck a countermeasure to be activated in case Schulung ran into heavy armed resistance from the French army: beat a hasty retreat back over the Rhine bridges.

Blomberg knew that Beck and Fritsch were demoralized, that they were convinced Schulung would trigger a disaster, perhaps result in Germany again being fully occupied by France and England, as it had been after the 1914–1918 war, to prevent future military adventures. At the insistence of Fritsch and Beck, Blomberg took them to see the führer and articulate their serious forebodings.

As was his pattern when dealing with reluctant generals, Hitler responded in a bitter tone. "I have absolutely reliable information that the French and British will not move a single soldier!" he snapped. "You will see that!"

Beck and Fritsch, both of whom loathed the führer, had no choice. Under a thick coat of secrecy, elements of three battalions moved to jump-off points near the Rhine bridges under the cover of night. Only this weak spearhead would cross initially to cut losses in case the French struck.

Why had Adolf Hitler been so unyieldingly adamant in opposing the professional advice of his top military leaders and brushing off the stream of intelligence flowing from Abwehr agents in Paris and the Rhineland, intelligence that asserted the French and British would march side by side? The führer's firm stance had been taken because unbeknownst to his military chieftains or the Abwehr, he had an exceptional contact in England, his own personal "mystery spy."

This extraordinary agent was obtaining unimpeachable intelligence from the highest source—King Edward VIII, the former prince of Wales, who had acceded to the throne in early 1936 on the death of George V, his father. This intelligence contradicted the other reports that were pouring into Berlin.

Hitler's mystery spy was fifty-five-year-old Leopold Gustav Alexander von Hoesch, the German ambassador to the Court of St. James, who had close ties with the royal family. Queen Mary even referred to the suave, impeccably garbed career diplomat as "my favorite foreigner."

Before being crowned king, the prince of Wales and Hoesch had become fast friends and were frequent partners in golf and tennis. The prince addressed the German as "Leo" and the ambassador called the Briton "David." When the prince became deeply involved in a torrid romance with Wallis Warfield Simpson, an American divorcée, he was hammered by his family and by top government officials. In this personal crisis, the prince sought out his older German friend, "Leo," for advice and consolation. "Leo is the best friend I have," the emotionally racked prince told a confidant.

Meanwhile, there had been much grumbling among top bureaucrats in the Foreign Ministry in Berlin. They objected to the ambassador's cozying up to the heir to the throne of the British Empire. He was not being sufficiently "Nazi." There was talk of replacing Hoesch by those in the Ministry not privy to the fact that the ambassador was, in essence, Hitler's personal spy in England.

On the morning after the death of George V, Ambassador von Hoesch had sent a long message to Foreign Minister Baron von Neurath in Berlin. King Edward VIII resembled his father in some respects but differed greatly from him in others, Hoesch stated. "While the late king was certainly critical of Germany, King Edward feels warm sympathy for Germany," he added. "I have become convinced during frequent, often lengthy, talks with him that these sympathies are deep-rooted."

Hoesch concluded his message: "At any rate, we should be able to rely upon having on the British throne a ruler who is not lacking in understanding for Germany."

Now, as Hitler was preparing to occupy the Rhineland, an Abwehr mole in the French military high command in Paris informed Berlin that General Maurice Gamelin, commander in chief of the army, had informed government civilian leaders that he would be unable to send his divisions to oppose any Rhineland takeover by the Germans unless the British were marching at their side.

That left the crucial question of war or peace in Europe up to King Edward VIII. Consequently, Ambassador von Hoesch assured Berlin (presumably after a conversation with the new monarch) that the British would not join with the French to fight against Germany over the Rhineland. That was the green light for Operation Schulung to be launched.

At noon on March 7, Adolf Hitler was standing at the podium in the Reichstag (home of the rubber-stamp Parliament) before a wildly cheering audience. "Men of the Reichstag!" the führer roared, "in this historic hour, when, in the Reich's western provinces, German troops are, at this very moment, marching into their future peacetime garrisons . . . "

Thunderous cheers drowned out his subsequent words. It was news to the Reichstag that German soldiers were moving into the Rhineland. Members of the audience sprang to their feet, yelling and crying, their hands upraised in Nazi salutes.

Adolf Hitler, a consummate stage performer, played his role to the hilt. His head lowered, as if in all humbleness, he waited for silence. It would not arrive until fifteen minutes later.

By the time the führer concluded his oration, a token force of three battalions, ready to pull back at any sign of armed opposition, had crossed over the Rhine bridges and was deep into the Rhineland. As Ambassador von Hoesch had informed Hitler, neither the French nor the British lifted a finger to halt the operation.

Winteruebung (Schulung now called by its operational code name) had been a rousing success—thanks in a large part to the mystery spy.

Winteruebung had been a staggering victory for Adolf Hitler. In the *Vaterland* (Fatherland) it fortified his popularity and his power, elevating him to heights that no German ruler of the past—even the legendary Frederick II, called *stupor mundi* (the amazement of the world) in the twelfth century—had attained.

Of equal significance, the führer had seized an ascendancy over his generals, who had been jelly-kneed at a moment of crisis when he had held firm—thanks to his personal mystery spy, Ambassador von Hoesch. It impressed on German generals, rightly or wrongly, that his judgment in foreign policy and even in military affairs was superior to theirs.

Finally, and most important of all, the Rhineland venture emboldened Hitler to set his sights on other territories bordering the Third Reich.[4]

Stealing a Supersecret Bombsight

HOLDING A WALKING-CANE UMBRELLA in one hand and a briefcase in the other, Dr. Hans Rankin strolled down the gangplank of the German ocean liner *Bremen* at Pier 86 in New York. A stout, blond man of average height, he was the managing director of an export-import firm in Hamburg, and he had come to the United States on a business trip. It was the overcast morning of October 17, 1937.

On the dock, the customs inspector gave Rankin's suitcases the normal cursory scrutiny, but he was intrigued by the German's walking-cane umbrella. "How does it work?" the official asked curiously. The amiable Rankin gave a brief demonstration.

"A pretty slick trick for a spy!" the inspector quipped. Rankin joined the man in laughter over the joke.

Only the German passenger knew it was no joke. He was indeed a spy. The name Dr. Hans Rankin and his role at the Hamburg import-export firm were a "cover." Actually, he was a major in the Abwehr, Germany's secret service, and his real name was Nicholaus Ritter. He had been sent to the United States to steal one of that nation's most closely guarded secrets, the highly accurate Norden bombsight for military aircraft. It had become common knowledge in global aviation circles that such a sophisticated device had been developed separately by three U.S. scientists, Carl T. Norden and Elmer Sperry in association with Theodore H. Barth.

Major Ritter's espionage mission to the United States had its origin back in 1926, when Germany, in violation of the Versailles Treaty ending what came to be known as World War I, began to clandestinely create an illegal Schwarz Luftwaffe (black air force). Progress was handicapped because modern aviation designs were sorely lacking. German industry, severely limited by Versailles, could not provide the sophisticated technology.

So "scouts" were sent abroad to purchase whatever aviation items were available on the open market. However, in the United States, such things as aircraft designs, automatic bombsights, and retractable landing gear were classified as U.S. military secrets and not available at any price.

Undaunted, leaders of the Black Luftwaffe decided that what they could not buy, they would steal. Efforts to pilfer needed new aircraft developments intensified after Adolf Hitler publicly denounced the disarmament clauses of the Versailles Treaty on March 16, 1935, and promptly established high commands of the Heer (army), Kriegsmarine (navy), and Luftwaffe. Then the führer, as he called himself, openly began to build the Wehrmacht (armed forces).

Two years later, Major Nicholaus Ritter was sent on his crucial espionage mission to the United States to steal the design for the Norden bombsight. Until being recruited by the Abwehr in Hamburg early in 1937, Ritter had no experience in clandestine operations. But he did have two highly important qualifications for his task: he had spent ten years in the United States as a textile manufacturer, and he spoke American English fluently and without a trace of an accent.

Ritter's textile firm in the United States had collapsed (as had countless other companies during the Great Depression) in December 1936. Broke and desperate, he had been approached by General Friedrich von Boetticher, the German military attaché in Washington, who suggested that Ritter return to his homeland and join Adolf Hitler's rapidly expanding army. So the bankrupt busi-

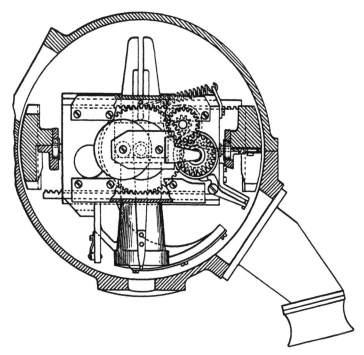

Part of the insides of the supersecret Norden bombsight stolen by German spies. (Author's collection)

nessman sailed to Germany, received a major's commission, and was assigned to the Abwehr in Hamburg as chief of Ast X, the air intelligence section.

Soon after Ritter reported for duty at Ast X, high officials in Berlin began bombarding him with demands that the Norden bombsight designs be pilfered and brought back for incorporation into existing Luftwaffe planes by German scientists. Because of the heavy pressure, Ritter decided to assign himself to the seemingly impossible task.

Now, after clearing customs in New York, Ritter lugged his suitcase and a briefcase to the Taft Hotel, north of Times Square, and checked in. He stashed his walking-cane umbrella in the closet. Only Ritter and a few Abwehr men in Hamburg knew that the umbrella had a hollow center for carrying secret messages.

Two days after his arrival, Ritter took a yellow cab to a drab apartment at 245 Monitor Street in the borough of Brooklyn. He alighted from the taxi, glanced around to see if he were being followed, then walked to the door and rang the bell. A heavyset, middle-aged man in a soiled blue shirt and with several days' stubble on his chin responded.

"*Herr Soehn?*" Ritter inquired.

"*Ja,* I am Soehn," the man replied cautiously in a German accent.

"Well, I'm pleased to meet you, Pops. I bring greetings from Roland."

"Pops" was Ast X's code name for its agent Heinrich Soehn, and "Roland" was the prearranged cover name for his *Treff* (secret rendezvous).

Soehn was a bumbling, low-level operative, so Ritter was not interested in him. What the major wanted to know was whether Soehn could arrange a meeting for him with "Paul." "Of course," Pops replied.

When Ritter returned in forty-eight hours as planned, Soehn introduced him to blond, thirty-five-year-old Hermann W. Lang, whose code name was Paul. Lang had come to the United States in 1927 but had not yet been naturalized. He worked at the Norden factory (at 80 Lafayette Street in Manhattan) that produced the secret bombsight for the U.S. Army Air Corps. He had been leading the comfortable life of a middle-class citizen with his wife and young daughter in a New York suburb.

Seated in Soehn's living room, Major Ritter casually sized up Lang and found him to be quiet and reserved: a man who, through hard work and intelligence, had been promoted to inspector at the Norden plant.

Lang explained to the Abwehr officer that while the United States had been good to him, he wanted the "New Germany" under Adolf Hitler to have the bombsight, too. "I can never forget the Fatherland," he declared emotionally. He stressed time and again that he had no interest in money for his espionage activities.

Ritter was deeply impressed by Lang's patriotism. "Herr Lang, you are a fine German," the Abwehr officer exclaimed. "On behalf of Adolf Hitler, I congratulate you and I thank you. Now, how many blueprints of the Norden bombsight can you get me?"

Perhaps Ritter would not have been so impressed with Lang's "patriotism" had he known that a few months later, Lang would deposit five thousand dollars into his New York bank account—courtesy of the treasury of the Third Reich.

Lang proved to be a slick espionage agent. He had no trouble removing top secret blueprints of the Norden bombsight from files at the plant and then sneaking them out under his clothing. His wife was kept uninformed about his double life. When the couple retired for the night, Lang waited until she was asleep, then slipped downstairs and traced the blueprints on the kitchen table. After gaining a few hours' sleep, he went to work and put the blueprints back into their files.

When his tracing task was completed a week later, Lang held another treff with Major Ritter and handed him all the blueprint copies of portions of the bombsight. Ritter was exhilarated and arranged to get the tracings to an Abwehr courier whose cover was as an attendant on the *Bremen*, which sailed for Hamburg the next day.

For two more weeks, Lang copied every blueprint he could get his hands on—which was nearly all of them. On the eve of Ritter's departure for home, Lang, Heinrich Soehn, and Ritter met for a farewell drink, which included toasts to Adolf Hitler. Then Lang handed over the remainder of the blueprint tracings.

In Berlin, Admiral Wilhelm Canaris, the cagey chief of the Abwehr whose espionage career preceded World War I, was astounded by the top secret plans Major Ritter had managed to acquire. A scientist told Canaris: "This is what we have been looking for. . . . This will revolutionize our whole bombing strategy!"

A few weeks after Major Ritter returned to Germany, the Abwehr invited "Paul" (Hermann Lang) to Berlin—all expenses paid—to thank him personally for his enormous contribution to the führer. Lang spent a mind-spinning week being feted by high-ranking Nazi officials and having a private audience with General Hermann Goering, chief of the Luftwaffe.

Conspicuous by his absence from the Lang activities was Major Ritter, who had engineered the espionage coup at the risk of a prison term in the United States. Much later, Ritter learned that a conniving officer in Admiral Canaris's headquarters in Berlin had schemed to receive full credit for stealing the Norden bombsight.[5]

Espionage Target: The Panama Canal

SNOW HAD COVERED Manhattan with a blanket of crisp white on the night of December 12, 1937, when Wilhelm Böning, a machinist and father of four children, spoke the praises of Adolf Hitler and the "New Germany" at a meeting of the German-American Bund in the Grand Central Palace in the Yorkville section of the borough. A burly, loud-voiced man, Böning was leader of the fifteen hundred men of the Ordnung Dienst, the U.S. version of Hitler's Nazi storm troopers.

After the meeting, the rough-hewn Böning and ten of his men gathered in a corner tavern to hoist a few beers and to boast of their escapades while fighting with the Kaiser's army in what was then known as the Great War. All were clad in grayish-blue tunics with black cuffs and neckbands, black forage caps with silver braid, and black trousers and boots.

Listening to the tales was John Baptiste Unkel, an officer of the Bund branch in New Rochelle, a New York City suburb. Born in Linz on the Rhine River, Unkel was fifty-one years of age. Perhaps he felt out of tune with his beer-guzzling comrades because he had come to the United States at an early age, enlisted in the U.S. Army, and was stationed in the Panama Canal Zone.

Resenting military discipline, Unkel deserted in 1914, was caught, and served eighteen months in prison. Despite his criminal record, he reenlisted in the U.S. Army in 1917 and spent two years during the Great War at Fort Slocum, New York.

Not to be outdone by Wilhelm Böning and his pals, Unkel began bragging about his own military experiences. He related how he had helped to build fortifications in the Panama Canal Zone, and said that he had a complete set of the plans at his home.

A group of U.S. Nazis gives the "Heil Hitler!" salute in suburban New York City. (National Archives)

Böning's ears perked up. Here was a chance to strike a mighty blow for the fatherland: the Panama Canal, he knew, was one of the United States' most crucial—and vulnerable—overseas outposts.

This artificial waterway, built by the United States and completed in 1914, cuts across the Isthmus of Panama in Central America for fifty-one miles, linking the Atlantic and Pacific Oceans. The canal shortened a ship's voyage between New York City and San Francisco to fewer than fifty-two hundred miles. Previously, a ship making this trip had to sail around the tip of South America, a distance of thirteen thousand miles.

Panama and its canal were especially vital to the U.S. armed forces. In the event of war in the East or the West, warships and troop transports could move to the Atlantic or the Pacific, whichever region was being threatened, in far less time than had earlier been the case.

Early in the morning after the beer-drinking session in Yorkville, a predominantly German-American neighborhood, Wilhelm Böning rushed to see Fritz Ewald Rossberg, who was reputed to be the assistant Gestapo chief in New York City, at the Franz Siegel Tavern. Böning was bursting with excitement about the Panama Canal plans.

Then Rossberg became enthusiastic. "Arrange to get those plans," he ordered. "We must have them!"

Böning caught up with John Unkel at the headquarters of the German-American Bund, at 178 East 85th Street. "Those plans you spoke about the other night, they are of great value," the storm trooper chief declared. "You must produce them."

Unkel balked. Was Böning an undercover agent for the Federal Bureau of Investigation (FBI)? Was he hoping to make a financial killing by selling the canal fortifications plans to some foreign power other than Germany? It was known that Panama was thick with spies for the Soviet Union, Japan, Italy, and other nations.

Unkel insisted that he would not turn over the plans unless he knew specifically with whom he was dealing. So Böning looked up the reputed Gestapo leader, Rossberg, and told him of Unkel's obstinance. Rossberg exploded: "We must get them—by force if necessary!"

Böning then told Unkel that he would put him in touch with the man who wanted the plans. A few nights later, at a Bund meeting in New Rochelle, a mystery man—he gave a phony name—approached Unkel and asked: "Are you a loyal German?"

Unkel was on guard and told the stranger he was a U.S. citizen. The man kept asking if Unkel was a loyal German, and finally he demanded that the Panama Canal fortifications plans be turned over to him. Suddenly the stranger's tone turned menacing, even threatening. Where in the hell were the plans? Unkel said he didn't have them.

Whoever the mystery man was, he promptly went to Böning and told him Unkel refused to turn over the documents. Böning then contacted Rossberg: "Unkel's a lying son of a bitch!" the reputed Gestapo leader barked. "If we can't get them any other way, we'll break into his house and get them. If Unkel tries to stop us, kill him!"

A few days later, the FBI, perhaps acting on a tip from a mole planted in the German-American Bund in New York, picked up Wilhelm Böning and John Unkel for questioning. Severely shaken, both men told all they knew about reputed Gestapo leader Fritz Rossberg's efforts to secure the Panama Canal fortifications plans that Unkel once had claimed he possessed. Now Unkel denied that he had ever had such documents, although he admitted that Rossberg had tried to get them from him. Böning vehemently denied that he had been involved in Rossberg's plot to break into Unkel's house and steal the Panama Canal materials.

On the morning of March 29, 1938, the FBI took Rossberg into custody and confronted him with Unkel's and Böning's statements implicating him in spying. "They're liars!" Rossberg snapped angrily. Questioned for many hours, Rossberg repeated time and again that he was but a simple working man, that he knew nothing about Gestapo or Abwehr operations in the United States.

With no firm evidence on which to charge or hold Rossberg, the FBI gave him a strict warning not to leave New York City and released him for the time being.

Early the next morning, the FBI received a tip that Rossberg had fled the country on the North German Lloyd Line's *St. Louis*, which had just sailed for Germany. Agents rushed to Pier 86 and demanded that the steamship line office radio the *St. Louis* to ask if Rossberg was aboard. The inquiry was dispatched, but no reply was received. It was clear to the FBI men: the Gestapo agent had abandoned his young wife and child to fend for themselves to protect his own skin by fleeing to Germany.

For ten days, the U.S. Department of Justice angrily protested the failure of the North German Lloyd Line to reply. Then came a cable from the firm's home office in Bremen. It stated that one Fritz Rossberg, a German national, had been discovered as a stowaway aboard the *St. Louis* when the ship was more than halfway to Europe. He had paid a half fare, the cable concluded, so was permitted to disembark at Bremerhaven, just like any other passenger.

Had Rossberg actually carried with him to Germany the secret plans of the Panama Canal fortifications, having obtained them from Unkel by threats, coercion, or a heavy cash payment? Had Unkel truly had these documents in his possession? The FBI would never know for certain.

A month after he had fled, however, the FBI intercepted a letter that Rossberg had written to a friend, Ernst Ramm, who lived in Manhattan. Rossberg gloated, "I received a hero's welcome in Berlin [presumably from the Gestapo]." He added that he was "extremely proud" of what he had achieved for Nazi Germany in the United States. The letter closed with: "Heil Hitler!"

Meanwhile, two thousand miles south of New York City, a network of German spies also was trying vigorously to steal Panama Canal secrets. This high-priority mission of the Abwehr was code-named Project 14, and its goal was how best to cripple the vital lifeline in the event of war with the United States.

Earlier in 1939, the Abwehr in Berlin had been ordered to develop a topographical and technical report on the canal, the ships moving through it, and its defenses, along with conducting ongoing surveillance of U.S. military personnel and military installations there.

Making certain that the all-inclusive espionage order was carried out, the Abwehr dispatched Wolfgang Blaum, an experienced and imaginative operative, to orchestrate Project 14. He would work under Karl Lindberg, who had been in Panama since 1935 and using his job as manager of the Hamburg-American Steamship Line as cover. Recruiting agents from the German colony in the canal region, Blaum soon had a network of informants planted at each key location.

Most of the espionage ring's members were working men in modest but important jobs—mechanics, machinists, stevedores, a locksmith, and a crane operator. All were longtime residents of Panama, highly regarded by their superiors, respected in their workplaces. They knew their way in the maze of the Canal Zone, and, because of their jobs, had free access to even off-limits installations that bored soldiers in a somnolent U.S. Army were supposed to be guarding.

One of Blaum's most productive and innovative agents was Ernst Kuhrig, who had been in Panama off and on since 1931. As a typewriter repairman, he strolled in and out of Fort Randolph, the main U.S. military post in the Canal

Zone, without identifying himself. The sentries merely waved him on in without challenge, although a guard once joked, "How do we know you ain't an enemy spy?" Both men chuckled.

On one occasion, Kuhrig took with him to Fort Randolph two professional German spies, Hans Schackow, whose cover was a job at the Hapag-Lloyd Steamship Company in the Panamanian town of Balboa, and nineteen-year-old, attractive Ingeborg Waltraut Gutmann, the secretary of the German consul at Colón. Reaching the gate, Kuhrig told the sentry that he was taking his friends to lunch at the restaurant in the post exchange.

As he had been instructed, the guard asked, "Ya got any cameras on ya?"

"What on earth would I be doing with a camera?" Kuhrig replied pleasantly.

The German spies were waved on past.

Instead of going to the post exchange, Kuhrig and his companions strolled casually about the facility like sightseeing tourists. Periodically they would stop to photograph gun installations and other defensive positions with the Leica that had been hidden in Kuhrig's trademark typewriter repair kit.

A steady stream of intelligence about the supposedly closely guarded canal was collected from his undercover agents by the network chief, Wolfgang Blaum, who used the communications facilities at the German legation in Panama to transmit his reports to the Abwehr in Berlin.

If war were to erupt between Nazi Germany and the United States, Adolf Hitler and his Oberkommando der Wehrmacht (high command) would have available at their fingertips an amazing array of photographs and reports on gun batteries, dams, locks, military installations, and power stations, along with detailed maps of Uncle Sam's Achilles heel of his already weak defenses.[6]

The Gestapo Comes to New York

SLICK-HAIRED, DARK-EYED, lean Karl Friedrich Herrmann, who had bounced around as a waiter in ten places in Germany during the previous four years, was summoned to Hamburg and was awed to find himself in the presence of Herr Schleckenbag, the Geheime Staatzpolizei (Gestapo) chief in that city. For three years Herrmann had proven himself to be a Nazi zealot, ruthless and dedicated. It was early 1938.

For nearly two hours, Schleckenbag grilled Herrmann, probing for a chink in his Nazi armor. He found none. Then he announced that Herrmann was being sent to the United States as Gestapo chief in New York City.

A few weeks later, Herrmann arrived in the United States and easily melded into the American scene. He obtained "cover" jobs as a waiter, first at Longchamps Restaurant in Manhattan and then at the Brooklyn Club in the borough of Brooklyn.

At that time, the United States was a spy's paradise. Foreign agents roamed the country at will. No single federal agency was charged with countersubversive responsibility, and the United States was the only major nation in the world that had no secret service to ferret out the intentions of hostile powers.

Soon after the Gestapo chief settled down in New York, a courier posing as a steward on the German luxury liner *Europa* brought him his first major secret mission. His bosses in Germany had gotten it into their heads that a highly dangerous, anti-Nazi counterespionage ring was spying on German spies in the United States and seeking to disrupt their activities. Herrmann was told by Hamburg that the masterminds behind the anti-Nazi network were two prominent New York women, Mrs. Thomas Manville and Antonie "Astra" Strassmann, who had been born in Germany and lived there for many years.

Herrmann plunged into his investigative work, and within two weeks, he notified Hamburg that he had uncovered four other members of the anti-Nazi ring. All were German citizens: a man named Hassfurter, another named Aichner, a Fräulein Drachau, and a Fräulein Fichtner. Herrmann's report stated that they had been engaged in clandestine meetings with Mrs. Manville at Cherbourg, Southhampton, and other ports of call of German ocean liners in recent times.

Mrs. Manville was reputed to be the brains of the anti-Nazi network. An extremely wealthy woman, she lived in a spacious suite in the stylish Savoy-Plaza Hotel in Manhattan. She was known as the mother of Tommy Manville, a big-spending playboy who gained wide notoriety for his zany escapades and his twelve marriages, give or take a couple.

She traveled extensively, liked to take German ships, made friends easily, and on completion of a cruise, she gave gifts to those who had been especially nice to her—chefs, stewards, hairdressers, and waiters. Gracious almost to a fault, she invariably invited these passing acquaintances to visit her at the Savoy-Plaza whenever their ship docked in New York City.

Invariably, the ship employees usually accepted the offer, and Mrs. Manville entertained them royally. Word of this stream of German visitors traipsing in and out of the Savoy-Plaza suite had reached the ears of Karl Herrmann. Obviously, with her money, she had to be the brains and ringleader of the conspiracy, Herrmann concluded. For what other reason would she be entertaining and lavishing gifts on Germans of modest stations whom she barely knew? No doubt she was concealing secret messages in the gifts for delivery to some sinister plotter in Germany, he surmised.

The matriarch's coconspirator, the Gestapo in Hamburg believed, was Astra Strassmann, a close friend of Mrs. Manville's. She had been forced to flee Germany after Adolf Hitler had seized power because she was said to have had a trace of Jewish blood in her family tree. Vengeance against the Nazis was Strassmann's sinister motive, the Gestapo had become convinced.

Astra was a world-renowned figure. She had been a stage and radio star in Germany, became interested in flying, and in May 1932 she piloted the giant

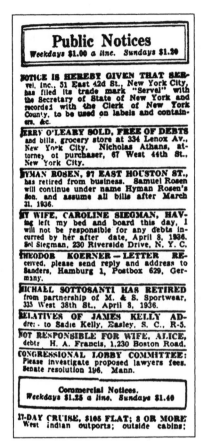

Public Notices
Weekdays $1.00 a line. Sundays $1.20

NOTICE IS HEREBY GIVEN THAT SER-
vel, Inc., 51 East 42d St., New York City,
has filed its trade mark "Servel" with
the Secretary of State of New York and
recorded with the Clerk of New York
County, to be used on labels and containers, &c.

JERRY O'LEARY SOLD, FREE OF DEBTS
and bills, grocery store at 334 Lenox Av.,
New York City. Nicholas Athans, attorney of purchaser, 67 West 44th St.,
New York City.

HYMAN ROSEN, 97 EAST HOUSTON ST.,
has retired from business. Samuel Rosen
will continue under name Hyman Rosen's
Son, and assume all bills after March
31, 1936.

MY WIFE, CAROLINE SIEGMAN, HAV-
ing left my bed and board this day, I
will not be responsible for any debts incurred by her after date, April 8, 1936.
Sol Siegman, 230 Riverside Drive, N. Y. C.

THEODOR KOERNER — LETTER RE-
ceived, please send reply and address to
Sanders, Hamburg 1, Postbox 629, Germany.

MICHAEL SOTTOSANTI HAS RETIRED
from partnership of M. & S. Sportwear,
335 West 38th St., April 8, 1936.

RELATIVES OF JAMES KELLY AD-
dress to Sadie Kelly, Easley, S. C., R-5.

NOT RESPONSIBLE FOR WIFE, ALICE,
debts H. A. Francis, 1,230 Boston Road.

CONGRESSIONAL LOBBY COMMITTEE:
Please investigate proposed lawyers fees.
Senate resolution 196. Mann.

Commercial Notices.
Weekdays $1.25 a line. Sundays $1.40

17-DAY CRUISE, $105 FLAT; 3 OR MORE
West Indian outports; outside cabins;

Gestapo in the United States communicated with Hamburg headquarters in the New York Times classified ad section. See fifth item from top.

airplane *Dorner DO-X* from the United States to Berlin, with refueling halts at Newfoundland and the Azores. The German *Herrenvolk* (people) showered adulation on the beautiful aviatrix.

After the Hitler regime took over about a year later, her physician father and her mother, both Christians, were expelled from their clubs and professional associations because of their alleged Jewish blood. So Astra moved to the United States, bringing along her principal assets—brains, beauty, charm, and wit, which launched her into a highly successful career buying and selling patents worldwide.

Astra became even more suspect in the eyes of the Gestapo when it was learned that she consorted with many influential Washington figures, including leaders in the Franklin D. Roosevelt administration, members of Congress, and high-ranking military officers.

Then, suddenly, the Gestapo investigation of the anti-Nazi counterespionage ring in the United States collapsed like a house of cards in a tornado.

There had never been such a network. Even the buffoon Karl Herrmann finally realized that the kindly, frail, elderly (charitably, in her late seventies) Mrs. Manville could hardly be a sinister cloak-and-dagger mastermind bent on destroying Adolf Hitler and his regime. Neither could thirty-six-year-old Astra Strassmann, who spent so much of her time globe-hopping on her thriving patent business that she could not have had time to hatch devious and complicated plots. Her numerous contacts with Washington bigwigs had all been social in nature.

Of the four German "accomplices" uncovered by the bumbling Herrmann, Aichner was a minor official in a tour agency, Hassfurter was a steward on the *Europa*, Drachau was a maid, and Fichtner was a stewardess on that same ship. Their only involvement with Mrs. Manville was serving her on her travels and visiting the kindly lady at the Savoy-Plaza.

Comic opera figures as they were during their early years, the Gestapo agents who infiltrated into the United States in the months ahead would be cagier, bolder, and far more dangerous.[7]

Practicing "Nazi Psychology" in the United States

WALTER BECK had long been widely known in Germany as a prominent psychologist at a major university. But in early 1938, he said he had grown disillusioned with the Nazi regime. So he fled to the United States, arriving there in April. It was not unusual for German intellectuals and scientists to follow that course: the noted physicist Albert Einstein also had left his homeland after Adolf Hitler had seized power.

Professor Beck was received with open arms by the U.S. academic community, and he accepted a teaching position at a prestigious university in the East. Articulate, friendly, and witty, Beck quickly made friends on campus.

No doubt his reception would have been much cooler had it been known that Beck was actually a spy for the Third Reich and was using his professional status as a cover for his secret mission. He had been sent by the Psychological Branch of the Oberkommando der Wehrmacht to collect information on which to base a composite portrait of the potentially militarily powerful nation.

Beck's clandestine assignment called for him to obtain detailed demographic data of the exactitude of the U.S. Census Bureau's inquiries, material on all strata of ethnic communities and their relations to one another, and intimate knowledge about the people's ideas, desires, ambitions, hopes, preferences, prejudices, frustrations, morale, and aptitudes.

This wealth of information on the people of the United States would be turned over to Propaganda Minister Josef Paul Goebbels. Since joining Hitler in 1933, Goebbels had gained total control over the German press, radio, and cultural life, as well as being the official designated to create and disseminate propaganda in foreign countries.

Professor Beck soon made arrangements with the administration at the U.S. university to take time off—at full pay—to visit all parts of the sprawling nation, presumably to collect data for the sociology class he taught. His true purpose, however, was to estimate what sort of soldiers young Americans would make if the traditionally peaceful and isolationist country were to go to war.

Astute as he was, Beck had trouble forming any conclusions. All the youths with whom he talked had different opinions on war and peace. Then one day, he viewed his first college football game, and grasped the elusive focus he had sought. When he compiled his voluminous report for the Nazi propaganda ministry, he represented all U.S. youths as football players.

Beck emphasized in the report that most Americans had a highly developed team spirit, that they were aggressive competitors in contests, had tenacity, and, above all, brought a scientific approach to everything they did—from football to war.

Unlike Adolf Hitler, who had long held Americans with scorn as weaklings whose sons and fathers would make poor soldiers, Beck was convinced that the spirit of the Old West frontier days was still very much alive among the people of the United States. And he cautioned against the tendency in high German circles—meaning Hitler—to regard all Americans as materialistic and decadent.

Beck concluded his study with the urgent recommendation that Germany refrain from provoking the United States into a war, not only because of its vast industrial potential, but also because of superior social factors that would come to the fore in any armed conflict.

Only two weeks before Hitler's powerful military juggernaut invaded neighboring Poland on September 1, 1939, and plunged Europe into World War II, Professor Beck returned to Germany. In the years ahead, he no doubt took great satisfaction in following Josef Goebbels's propaganda aimed at the United States, a campaign designed largely on the psychologist's undercover mission.[8]

A Gentleman Farmer
Flies to London

A BLACK-BODIED JUNKERS civilian airliner from Berlin glided to a landing at Croyden Airport outside London. Among the passengers debarking was Edwald von Kleist-Schmenzin, a wealthy German gentleman farmer. When he strolled

Top leaders in the Schwarze Kapelle conspiracy, Admiral Wilhelm Canaris (left) and General Ludwig Beck. (Author's collection)

into the terminal, he was approached by three men in civilian clothes who identified themselves as agents of MI-6, Britain's secret service responsible for offensive intelligence. It was mid-August 1938.

It had already been arranged for Kleist-Schmenzin to pass through customs and security controls without the customary inspections, because he was on a secret mission for the Schwarze Kapelle (Black Orchestra), a small, tightly knit group of prominent German military officers, government officials, and civic leaders whose goal was the "elimination" of Adolf Hitler and his regime.

Leaders of the Schwarze Kapelle were General Ludwig Beck, who, as chief of the General Staff, had directed the army's enormous expansion since 1935, and Admiral Wilhelm Canaris, head of the Abwehr, the secret service agency that had thousands of agents around the world.

Beck, a man of high moral courage and principle, resigned from his post and went into retirement in early August 1938, after Adolf Hitler refused to give assurances that he did not plan to ignite a war in Europe. Living quietly near Hanover, Beck began recruiting distinguished Germans to his anti-Hitler conspiracy. All were convinced that the führer was embarking on a campaign of conquest that would take Germany down the road to destruction.

Eventually the conspirators would develop an elaborate scheme to gain their goals. At the proper time they planned to have Hitler kidnapped, but not kill him and thereby convert him into a martyr. Rather, the führer would be put on public trial for "crimes against the German people." Then a yet unspecified illustrious civilian, respected by most of the *Herrenvolk* and foreign leaders, would be appointed to organize a new, democratic government.

The plot also called for the arrest of several of Hitler's top officials, including newly promoted Field Marshal Hermann Goering, Gestapo chief Heinrich Himmler, and thirty-five-year-old Obergruppenführer (General) Reinhard Heydrich, chief of the Sicherheitsdienst (SD), the intelligence branch of the Schutzstaffel (SS), Hitler's elite, black-uniformed private army. These Nazi bigwigs would be imprisoned in a castle in Bavaria, in mountainous southern Germany, and later be tried in open court.

Each tiny detail of the Schwarze Kapelle's scheme to rid Germany of the Nazi regime had been painstakingly crafted with military precision—except for one unknown component. Would Great Britain use strong words or oppose with her armed forces Adolf Hitler's plan to invade and seize Czechoslovakia?

British prime minister Neville Chamberlain, who had been trying to appease the führer for the past year, would have to be told by an informative anti-Hitler source inside Germany that if Britain took a strong hand, a bloody war in Europe might be prevented. In that case, the Schwarze Kapelle could move aggressively to get rid of Hitler and other top Nazis.

At General Beck's request, Edwald von Kleist-Schmenzin had agreed to carry the crucial message to London. It could be a perilous task. In the Third Reich, informers were everywhere, and Kleist-Schmenzin might well be arrested by the Gestapo and executed as a traitor. There also was the distinct possibility that the British, through careless talk or deliberate betrayal by Nazi moles planted in the British government, might tip off Berlin about the Schwarze Kapelle plot.

Before leaving for London, Kleist-Schmenzin had been told by Beck: "If you can bring me positive proof that the British will make war if [Hitler] invades Czechoslovakia, I will put an end to the [Nazi] regime!"

What would Beck regard as positive proof? "An open pledge to assist Czechoslovakia in the event of war," the general replied.

After his arrival at Croyden Airport in London, Kleist-Schmenzin was shielded from the public, the media, and any Nazi spies by the three MI-6 men. They bundled him into a limousine and escorted him to the plush Hyde Park Hotel, where he used a rear entrance. In his suite, the German held a private conversation with Lord Lloyd of Dolobran, who had high-level connections in the British military and government.

"Everything is decided [for the Czechoslovakian invasion], Lord Lloyd," Kleist said. "The mobilization plans are complete, zero day is fixed, the army group commanders have their orders. All will run according to plan at the end of September, and no one can stop it unless Britain speaks out in an open warning to Herr Hitler."

Then Kleist-Schmenzin spoke for nearly two hours on events transpiring in Germany behind the scenes, including the details of the Schwarze Kapelle plot against the führer. If Great Britain, along with France, were to take "a firm and positive stand" against Hitler, "there is a good hope that the [German] commanding generals would arrest him if he persisted in his [plan] and thus put an end to the Nazi regime."

Lord Lloyd listened intently and also without interruption to the briefing and was highly impressed by Kleist-Schmenzin's sincerity and intelligence.

On the following morning, Kleist-Schmenzin met with Robert Vansittart, an adviser on foreign affairs to the British government, and repeated what he had told Lloyd. Vansittart, however, was not favorably impressed. It seemed to him that the Schwarze Kapelle was as much interested in striking a deal about Germany's future frontiers after Hitler had been eliminated as it was in getting rid of the führer and establishing a democratic government.

A day later, Kleist-Schmenzin called on Winston Churchill, the first lord of the Admiralty, at his country estate outside London. Once more the German presented a briefing, while Churchill puffed on a long cigar and remained silent. When Kleist-Schmenzin started to leave, the British leader allegedly remarked, "You can have everything [from our government], but first bring us Herr Hitler's head!"

Churchill's terse comment reflected the divergent views of the British leaders and the Schwarze Kapelle. The German conspirators wanted a firm public pledge that the British would support the anti-Hitler conspiracy and oppose German aggression against Czechoslovakia. For their part, British leaders had no intention of taking a firm stand against Hitler's plan of conquest until the führer had been eliminated by the conspirators.

A dejected Kleist-Schmenzin sneaked back into Germany and went to see Admiral Canaris at Abwehr headquarters in Berlin. "I have found nobody in London who wishes to wage a preventative war," Kleist-Schmenzin said. "I have gained the impression that they wish to avoid war at almost any cost."

Kleist-Schmenzin's diagnosis of the British mood proved to be precisely on target. While Hitler continued preparations to invade nearly defenseless Czechoslovakia, appeasement, not firmness, was the order of the day in London. Britain's sixty-nine-year-old prime minister, Neville Chamberlain, was determined not to provoke the führer by strong words of protest or the threat of military action.

Instead, on September 13, Chamberlain sent an urgent message to Adolf Hitler:

Adolf Hitler and General Wilhelm Keitel welcome Neville Chamberlain to a "peace conference" at Berchtesgaden, Germany. (Author's collection)

In view of the increasingly critical situation, I propose to come over at once to see you with a view to try to find a peaceful solution. I propose to come by air and am ready to start tomorrow.

The führer was astounded and delighted that the head of the British Empire was going to come groveling to him. *"Ich bin vom Himmel gefallen!"* (Good heavens!), he exclaimed.

Hat in hand, Chamberlain met with Hitler at Munich, and on September 30 the two leaders signed a document that stated the "desire of our two peoples never to go to war with one another again." In return for what the naive Chamberlain called "peace in our time," Czechoslovakia had been sold out to the führer, who swore he had no farther "territorial claims" in Europe.

Edwald von Kleist-Schmenzin's hazardous secret mission to London had been in vain. Appeasement of Hitler by the British made it impossible for the Schwarze Kapelle to act. How could the conspirators kidnap and try the führer for "crimes against the German people" when he had just scored a stunning and completely bloodless victory and was being hailed in the Third Reich as one of the greatest figures in German history?[9]

An "Unsportsmanlike" Murder Scheme

New year's day 1939 brought with it a world fearful of an outbreak of another bloody war in Europe. The preparations for a conflict were visible in England, France, Belgium, Italy, and, most significantly, in Germany. No state secrets in history were as badly kept as Hitler's that last year of peace.

Major Francis Foley had been MI-6's agent in Berlin since 1920. Working in the British Consulate under the cover of His Britannic Majesty's Passport Control officer, Foley had been reporting regularly on the secrets of the strange set of men and weird events that had dominated Germany since Hitler had gained total control in early 1933. Now Foley was sending a stream of reports telling of preparations within the Third Reich for war.

In London, Alexander Cadogan, an Etonian who was the undersecretary of the Foreign Office, warned British leaders, "Hitler's mental condition, his insensate rage against Great Britain, and his megalomania, are entirely consistent with the execution of a desperate coup against the Western powers."

Translation: Expect the führer to launch a war in Europe despite his public pledge that he sought peace.

These were desperate times for Great Britain. It was militarily weak, while Germany's armed forces were growing more powerful every day. Desperation calls for desperate actions. So when Major General Frank Noel Mason-MacFarlane, the military attaché at the British embassy in Berlin, proposed a scheme to murder Hitler, the London leaders debated the idea.

Mason-MacFarlane, who had a distinguished record in World War I and who was the son of an army colonel, suggested that the führer could be felled by a bullet from a high-powered rifle equipped with a telescopic sight from an apartment overlooking the Reichskanzlei in Berlin. The assassin would lay in wait, and when Hitler appeared on a front balcony, either to greet crowds or for a breath of fresh air, he would be shot. It was not clear how the marksman was to escape from the highly congested area.

Hitler's death at this time would lead to the overthrow of the Nazi regime and save millions of lives in the war the führer was preparing to launch, Mason-MacFarlane declared.

On the basis that murdering Hitler was "unsportsmanlike," the British government vetoed the plot. There "is an antipathy on principle against murder in democratic states," British leaders declared.

With Great Britain facing extinction a year later, the British government, under a new leader, Winston Churchill, would largely drop its concern about scruples.[10]

Part Two

Outbreak of War

"Take Possession of the [British Captives]"

A FEW DAYS AFTER Germany went to war with England and France on September 3, 1939, Captain Hans Langsdorff was on the bridge of the battleship *Graf Spee* as it plowed through Atlantic waters off the coast of Brazil. A signals officer handed the skipper a decoded message from *Kriegsmarine* (navy) headquarters in the Third Reich. Langsdorff was ordered to commence operations against Allied merchant ships.

For ten weeks, the *Graf Spee*, one of the world's most powerful warships, marauded through the Atlantic, sending ten large cargo vessels carrying hundreds of tons of valuable war materials to the bottom. After each of the sinkings, Captain Langsdorff, a kindly officer, had his men pick up surviving British merchant seamen and put them in his supply ship, the *Altmark*.

At dawn on December 13, the *Graf Spee* was at the mouth of the Río de la Plata off Uruguay when the ship was spotted by a British cruiser squadron under Commodore Henry H. Harwood. Greatly outgunned and despite the heavy odds against him, Harwood ordered an immediate attack by cruisers *Ajax*, *Achilles*, and *Exeter*. Closing in from three directions, the British ships scored more than twenty damaging shell hits and caused more than one hundred German casualties in only twenty minutes.

Langsdorff, who had been severely dazed by a blow on the head during the British shelling, took the *Graf Spee* into the port of Montevideo in the hope of making repairs. But the government of the neutral country gave him seventy-two hours—the maximum under international law—to take the battleship out of Uruguayan waters.

Perhaps through the devious sowing of false intelligence over the airwaves by the British, Langsdorff had become convinced, albeit wrongly, that Harwood's cruiser squadron waiting for him outside Montevideo Harbor had been heavily reinforced by the Royal Navy aircraft carrier *Ark Royal* and battleship *Renown*. So to spare some twelve hundred crew members, Langsdorff ordered them to leave the ship and go into internment; then he had the *Graf Spee* scuttled in the shallow estuary.

That night, Langsdorff wrapped himself in the Nazi flag and committed suicide with a pistol shot to the head.

Royal Navy Captain Philip L. Vian of the Cossack. *(National Archives)*

Captain Hans Langsdorff, skipper of the Graf Spee. *(National Archives)*

Meanwhile, the *Graf Spee's* supply ship, the *Altmark*, had slipped away and was trying to sneak back to Germany. Intelligence sources had informed the Admiralty in London that there were 299 British merchant seamen on board. The *Altmark's* skipper, Captain Heinrich Dau, hid for nearly two months, and then was able to reach Norway on his way to northern Germany, aided by good luck and bad weather.

On February 4, 1940, the *Altmark* was spotted by British airplanes, and Dau took refuge in Jossing Fjord, within Norwegian territorial waters. At the same time, the destroyer *Cossack*, commanded by Royal Navy Captain Philip L. Vian, along with a cruiser and another destroyer, closed in on the *Altmark*. A tall, energetic man of demonstrated dash, Vian received orders to enter the fjord and establish the fact that the German ship was in violation of Norwegian neutrality by entering her waters with prisoners of war on board.

As Vian sailed into the mouth of the fjord, he was met by two Norwegian gunboats and told that the *Altmark* was unarmed, had been closely inspected by a boarding party that found no POWs, and had received permission to proceed through Norwegian territorial waters.

Vian pulled the *Cossack* back for new instructions. These orders came directly from First Lord of the Admiralty Winston Churchill: "Unless the Norwegians convoy *Altmark* to the port of Bergen with a joint British-Norwegian

With nearly three hundred British captives on board, the German ship Altmark *enters Norway's Jossing Fjord. (National Archives)*

guard on board, you should board *Altmark*, liberate the ship, and take possession of the [British captives]."

Waiting for darkness, Vian took the *Cossack* into the narrow fjord without a human pilot to guide the vessel. Using searchlights, Vian located one of the Norwegian gunboats and sent two officers to quiz the skipper. He again told the Britons that the *Altmark* had been carefully searched twice and that there were no POWs on board.

Captain Dau, meanwhile, got the *Altmark* under way and tried to ram the *Cossack*. Dau's aim was poor: his ship went aground. Vian was now thoroughly angry. He tied up alongside the *Altmark* and sent Lieutenant Commander Bradwell Turner and Petty Officer Norman Atkins to lead a boarding party. A shoot-out erupted in the dark, and four Germans were killed and five wounded.

When the shooting died down, Vian's men had control of the German ship. All was quiet. Somewhere belowdecks a distinctly British voice calmly called out, "Chaps, our ny-vee is 'ere!"

The 299 captives were found hidden on the *Altmark*. Also on board the "unarmed" vessel were four heavy machine guns and two antiaircraft guns.[1]

Agent X Conspires with the Pope

NOW THAT ADOLF HITLER'S SWORD of conquest had drawn blood in Poland, the Schwarze Kapelle conspirators intensified their efforts to get rid of the führer. A plan drawn up by Colonel Helmuth Groscurth, an aide to Admiral Wilhelm Canaris in the Abwehr, called for a march on Berlin to capture Hitler and overthrow the Nazi Party. Two army panzer divisions moving from Poland across Germany to the Western Front opposite French and British forces would be turned back to Berlin to secure the city against the SS, the elite private army fanatically loyal to the führer.

It was planned that after Hitler was taken into custody, he would be indicted for crimes against humanity, declared legally insane, and confined to an asylum. Killing him would only elevate him to martyr status and trigger endless turmoil inside the Third Reich. General Ludwig Beck, who had resigned as chief of the General Staff a few months earlier after a bitter dispute with the führer, would be proclaimed regent (caretaker), the army would establish a provisional government, and a Hohenzollern would be invited to return to the throne. Hohenzollern was the name of the famous royal family that had for centuries served as kings and emperors and was noted for establishing efficient, fair governments until Kaiser Wilhelm was exiled by the victorious Allies in World War I.

If the coup to rid the world of Adolf Hitler and Nazism was to succeed, however, the Schwarze Kapelle realized that the British government would have to be contacted, because the conspirators planned to seek an armistice with the Western Allies. Therefore it was essential to learn what conditions would be acceptable to Great Britain and France. Consequently, Admiral Canaris designated his top aide, Major General Hans Oster, to open a secret line of communication with London.

Oster was the son of a Protestant clergyman. As a lieutenant in World War I he had been awarded several decorations for valor. Remaining in the army, he began a long and close relationship with Canaris in 1931, two years before Hitler came to power.

Many military contemporaries regarded Oster as brash, cynical, volatile, and an inveterate womanizer. In 1932 Oster, then a lieutenant colonel, was brought before an army court of honor as the result of an adulterous affair and compelled to resign.

Soon he was back in the intelligence field as a civilian employee with the Abwehr, a small, incompetent agency at the time. When his old pal Wilhelm Canaris was appointed by Hitler to take over and rejuvenate the Abwehr in 1935, Oster was brought aboard and given the rank of major.

In the years ahead, Oster became contemptuous of the führer and the Nazi Party. As Canaris's number two man, he was in the position to stock key Abwehr posts with anti-Hitlerites. His role in the Abwehr provided Oster with an ideal cover for conspiratorial machinations.

Vatican City, one hundred nine acres surrounded by Rome, was the center of a conspiracy involving anti-Hitler German leaders. (Author's collection)

On October 9, 1939, only eight days after Poland had been crushed by the Wehrmacht, Hitler called in his generals and offered them a new conquest— "Case Yellow," the invasions of France, Belgium, and the Netherlands. That announcement energized the Schwarze Kapelle to take immediate action, and General Oster called to his office Josef Mueller, a forty-one-year-old Munich attorney.

Mueller, whose nickname was Ochsensepp (Oxen Joe) because he had driven a pair of the sturdy animals to pay his way through college, was a staunch Catholic. Most importantly to Oster, Mueller was known and regarded favorably by Pope Pius XII, and the lawyer also had friends in high places in the Vatican in Rome.

Knowing of Mueller's connections in the Vatican and of his anti-Hitler views, Oster asked him if he would take on the mission of establishing a line of communication between the British government in London and his friends in the Vatican, where the pope lived. Mueller, bright and energetic, knew the extreme danger involved, but he immediately accepted the assignment. If he were caught by the Gestapo, Mueller would go to the axman, the führer's favorite means for dealing with those he considered to be traitors.

Once Mueller had made contact with London, through his Vatican sources, Oster explained, the lawyer was to inform the British of Case Yellow and find out what terms would be demanded to bring about an armistice with Germany after Hitler's kidnapping.

Two weeks later, Mueller—known to the Abwehr as Agent X—was conferring with his good friend Monsignor Ludwig Kaas, the keeper of the fabric at St. Peter's Basilica inside the Vatican, at a small, secluded wine garden near the historic Appian Way.

Agent X reported to Oster that the pope had refused to grant him a private audience on the grounds that visits to him by outsiders were observed by and reported to the Gestapo. However, Mueller added, His Holiness had consented to serve the Schwarze Kapelle as an intermediary with the British government. Pius XII had accepted by declaring solemnly, "The German opposition [to Hitler] must be heard in Britain."

The pope had attached one demand to his intercession: A peace would have to be based on a promise by Great Britain and France not to try to take advantage of the chaos that would follow the incarceration of the führer to invade and occupy Germany, Mueller told Oster.

It was agreed that the Schwarze Kapelle's proposals would reach the pope from Monsignor Kaas and another good friend of Mueller's, Father Robert Leiber, the archivist at the Vatican. The pope would contact London through periodic conversations with D'Arcy Osborne, the British ambassador to the Vatican, a perfectly normal event that would not trigger the suspicion of Gestapo informants.

So the line of communication ran from the Abwehr offices of Canaris and Oster through Josef Mueller to Monsignor Kaas and Father Leiber; then to Pope Pius XII to Ambassador Osborne to Whitehall, a London street between Trafalgar Square and the Houses of Parliament and along which the principal British governmental offices are located.

As spiritual leader of some 350 million Roman Catholics in both warring camps, the sixty-three-year-old Pius XII (Eugenio Pacelli) found himself in a delicate position—that of a conspirator. A brilliant scholar and gifted linguist, he had earned doctorates in theology, philosophy, and law at Rome's Capranica College. Ordained a year later, the tall, lean Pacelli was well acquainted with Germany. In 1917, during World War I, he was nuncio to Bavaria, a *Länder* (state) in southern Germany. In 1920, when Germany was writhing in postwar chaos and economic depression, he was assigned to Berlin as nuncio for all of the nation.

By 1933, when Hitler was appointed chancellor, Pacelli was back in Rome as a cardinal and Vatican secretary of state. In that post he negotiated a concordat of mutual respect and understanding between the Vatican and Germany. Four years later, with the führer rearming the Third Reich and instituting widespread civil rights violations, especially against Jews, Cardinal Pacelli publicly condemned the Nazi regime. That act placed Pacelli on Hitler's enemies list.

In one of the Vatican's fastest elections—three ballots—Cardinal Pacelli was elected pope on his birthday, March 2, 1939. Pius XII announced that the theme of his reign would be peace in the world. For centuries the Vatican had been committed by tradition to be aloof from temporal disputes except when invited to be a peacemaker. So now, with war having erupted in Europe, Pius XII not only found himself as a peacemaker, but also a conspirator to achieve that lofty goal.

For more than two months the Schwarze Kapelle's Vatican connection remained somnolent, largely because Edward Halifax, the British foreign secretary, was fearful that Josef Mueller, Agent X, was an Abwehr plant. Assured personally by the pope that Mueller was a genuine anti-Nazi, Halifax gave the British ambassador, D'Arcy Osborne, permission to open talks with Pius XII.

In his study in the Vatican on January 12, 1940, the pope told Osborne that he had indisputable information that Hitler was preparing to launch Case Yellow, and that the "German generals" would act to forestall that major offensive "if they could be assured of peace," meaning an armistice with the Western Allies.

Osborne, reflecting the view held by British intelligence services in London, promptly splashed cold water on any hope for an armistice before Case Yellow erupted. Osborne told the pope that London considered the Schwarze Kapelle approach "so vague as to be useless."

Perhaps shocked by that blunt reaction from official London, the pope promptly terminated the conversation. However, the pontiff met again with Osborne on February 7. He told the Briton that he had "new information" that "part of the [German] army was prepared to act [against Hitler], if they could be reassured that the territorial integrity of Germany and Austria would be respected."

On February 17, Halifax informed Osborne that Britain could not take a definite stand on the Schwarze Kapelle armistice plan without France. However, in the same communication, he inferred that Britain would offer terms to "the German generals" if they were to provide a specific program "authoritatively vouched for."

In the meantime, "Oxen Joe" Mueller had been traveling back and forth between Berlin and Rome. He was aware that each trip increased the odds that he would be arrested by the Gestapo. So during each jaunt, he purchased, with a few cigars and a lighter, a frontier entry-and-exit rubber stamp from an Italian immigration official. Using this stamp, Mueller proceeded to make unrecognizable in his passport the dates on which he had entered and left Italy—a conundrum designed to thwart the Gestapo from placing him in Rome at any given time should he be arrested.

Early in February, Mueller returned to Berlin from Rome carrying a highly incriminating sheet of paper. On it was a message written by Mueller's good friend Father Robert Leiber and dictated to him by the pope. The writing was on the pope's personal stationery, and it contained details about peace terms Britain allegedly would offer to a post-Hitler regime in Germany.

Mueller translated the pope's message and put it in German military terminology. It came to twelve pages and was known as the X Report after Mueller, Agent X. Then it was covertly distributed among a few top generals who, while not belonging to the Schwarze Kapelle, were thought to be anti-Nazis. Apparently the goal was to trigger some action to thwart Case Yellow.

One of those given the X Report was General Heinrich von Brauchitsch, the *Oberfehlshaber des Heeres* (commander in chief of the army). Back in 1938, when Brauchitsch, a man of much culture who spoke several languages and

The London Daily Mirror *the day after Great Britain declared war on Germany. (Author's collection)*

was known for his interest in economics, was being considered for the army's top post, the aristocratic general was in dire need of money to settle a nasty divorce and marry Charlotte Rueffer, a captivating, statuesque woman with whom he had been involved for nearly twelve years. She was a staunch admirer of Adolf Hitler, who, in turn, found her most engaging.

At the time Brauchitsch had become head of the army, the führer gave him eighty thousand marks to settle his divorce. By this chicanery, Hitler had yet another compliant general in a key military post.

Now, perhaps, Brauchitsch repaid the führer's financial generosity. Privately, he branded the contents of the X Report treason and urged that the document be sent to the SD, the SS intelligence branch, for investigation. The army chief demanded that the "culprit" who brought the report from Rome be identified and arrested. However, Brauchitsch did not pursue the matter, perhaps fearful that he himself might be suspected by Hitler.

Brauchitsch's outburst was the death knell for the X Report. It was filed in a large safe where the Abwehr kept its most secret papers. There it would remain for many months—a ticking time bomb that could explode at any minute.[2]

The Spy Was a Clip Artist

ADMIRAL JAMES H. RICHARDSON, commander of the U.S. Pacific Fleet, was not a happy man. In April 1940 he had taken his warships and carriers from their permanent base at San Pedro, California, three thousand miles to the west for exercises in Hawaiian waters. At the conclusion of maneuvers on May 10 he expected to take his armada back to California. President Franklin Roosevelt, however, ordered the fleet to remain at Pearl Harbor.

Richardson was strongly opposed to the realignment. Tensions had been running high between Japan and the United States in the Pacific, and the fleet commander was fearful that "some fanatical, ill-advised [U.S.] officer in charge of a submarine or ship might attack on his own." Moreover, the admiral felt that his ships could be better prepared for war by being based on the West Coast.

Admiral Harold R. "Betty" Stark, the staid, white-haired chief of naval operations in Washington, told Richardson that the move was made as a bluff, to deter Japan from "going into the East Indies," meaning a vast region of southeastern Asia that included India, Burma, Thailand, Indochina, the Philippines, and the islands around the Malay Archipelago.

In Tokyo, the warlords who held Japan in an iron grip looked on the transfer of the U.S. Fleet as a possible threat to their planned campaign of conquest in the East Indies. Japanese spies had long been active in Hawaii, but to reinforce the intelligence they sent back, the Foreign Office directed Otojiro Okuda, the young consul general in Honolulu, to dispatch regular reports on the U.S. Navy, now based at Pearl Harbor.

Smart, sophisticated, and ambitious, Okuda plunged into his assigned mission. He was ideally located: the Japanese consulate was only seven miles from Pearl Harbor. Soon he began sending Tokyo a stream of highly detailed accounts that delighted and amazed the Foreign Office and naval intelligence. Without prior espionage experience and with no background in naval lore, the young diplomat regularly reported on the size, numbers, and movements of the U.S. Fleet, providing precise names and descriptions of the warships and aircraft carriers, along with their dates and times of arrival and departure, and the names of the skippers and their top aides.

This wealth of high-grade intelligence was classified top secret in Tokyo. But what officials at the Foreign Office and naval intelligence did not know was that Okuda was collecting it without leaving his office. Armed with a pair of sharp scissors, the consul general scanned the Honolulu newspapers each day and clipped the articles that provided voluminous information about the U.S. Fleet.

Okuda then put these data into diplomatic language and, without indicating how he had obtained it, fired the information on to Tokyo, where he was held in awe as an espionage genius.[3]

Denmark's Patriotic Burglar

DURING THE EARLY SPRING of 1940, Adolf Hitler's armies of 2.5 million men had been aligned along the French border for more than seven months, waiting for the signal to launch Case Yellow, the invasions of France, Belgium, and the Netherlands. The offensive had been postponed nineteen times, for various reasons.

Suddenly, on April 9, the führer diverted his attention from France and the Low Countries and sent his shock troops northward to seize tiny, defenseless Denmark in a single day.

For a period of time, the Germans allowed the Danes to manage their own affairs under what was termed "the protection of the Third Reich." But the Danes, a proud and stalwart people, worked secretly against their conquerors. Numerous underground cells were formed: "the Priests" acted against the harbors, "the Brewers" conducted raids against the electrical system, "the Painters" directed sabotage against the railroads, and "the Princes" attacked any likely target of value to the Germans.

A German captain was beaten to death in Odense, a German troop train exploded near Ålborg, Danish naval officers scuttled their ships in Copenhagen Harbor, and a truck filled with *Feldgrau* (field gray, the average German soldier) plunged into an abyss at night after a bridge had been dismantled secretly.

In the wake of these and many other instances of violence against the occupying force, the Germans dropped all pretense of cooperation and declared martial law. In August 1943 King Christian X, the symbol of Danish resistance to countless citizens, was arrested and placed under military guard, and Parliament ceased to function. Then the Danish police force was disarmed and its leaders sent to German concentration camps.

Not all the Danes were patriots. A tiny minority of them collaborated with the Germans. One of those currying favor and giving aid to the occupiers was Hans Petersen, who was about forty years of age and had spent half of his life serving a series of terms in prison.

Before the war, Petersen had been known as the country's "most dangerous burglar." H. P., as he became known to Danes, would burglarize a house,

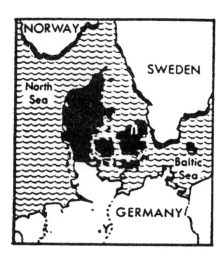

Location of Denmark, in black.

then send a detailed account of what he had taken and how much it was worth to the newspapers for publication.

On another occasion he broke into and spent a weekend in the home of a Danish chief of police, who was out of town with his family on a brief vacation. Petersen reported to the press that it was a nice house but that the bedsprings sagged. When the exploit was published, Danes, knowing that H. P. had never harmed anyone and was considered to be nonviolent, laughed uproariously.

Once H. P. had confessed that he had taken his loot to London, where he opened an antiques store and engaged a reliable man to manage it without letting him know how the merchandise had been acquired.

Soon after the Wehrmacht had seized Denmark, H. P. incurred the wrath of his countrymen when he was seen on a regular basis eating and drinking with German officers. The collaborator even wore a finely tailored German uniform, and made it a point to arrogantly snub any Dane he had known before the war. Members of the Danish underground plotted to kill the turncoat.

On Refshaleö, one of the many islands that make up Denmark, the Germans had taken over a factory and converted it to making airplane parts for the Luftwaffe. The Danish underground decided to blow up the plant. Planning was done in great detail. Specific resistance men were assigned to "eliminate" German guards outside the factory. Others were to smuggle dynamite and conceal it near the building. A night on which there would be no moon was selected for the action.

Now everything was in readiness—almost everything. The sabotage planners could not find a way to open the locks of the huge steel doors at the plant's entrance. Two days before the appointed time to blow up the plant, the underground chief in the region received a note in handwriting identical to that in messages that had been sent to him in the past by an unknown source, giving details of German plans. There had been much speculation on the identity of the sender, because all of the information in the notes had proven to be accurate. The latest message stated, "I will be at the factory at midnight two days from now. I will be in German uniform. I will open the locks on the gate."

Unlike previous messages, this one was signed—with the initials H. P.

Now an intense debate evolved among resistance leaders. Was Hans Petersen, who had been cozying up to the Germans, to be trusted? Was this note from him some kind of a machination by the Gestapo to kill or capture the saboteurs? It was finally decided to take a chance. But a provision had been made to make certain that Petersen was killed in the event the Germans set a trap at the factory.

At midnight, the underground struck, the plant sentries were silenced, and the hidden dynamite was lugged to the front gate. Minutes later, Petersen, wearing his German uniform, arrived. The resistance men tensed and tightly gripped their weapons. Any moment now, firing could erupt from the shadows.

Speaking in a hoarse whisper, the burglar said, "If anything happens to me, I want my name to be cleared." He began picking at the lock. Two minutes later, the gates swung open. Instead of departing, Petersen stole into the building with the saboteurs, groups of which went to designated areas to place dynamite. "I want to set a fuse myself," Petersen explained.

Minutes later, one by one or in pairs, the saboteurs sneaked out of the building and congregated at a safe distance to watch. Soon there was a loud *booommm!* Then another *booommm!* Then still another. The explosions lit up the black sky as pieces of brick, concrete, and wood spiraled into the air. Nothing was left of the factory except piles of rubble and twisted machinery.

All the saboteurs had emerged from the building before the blasts. But Hans Petersen, who had been masquerading as a German sympathizer, had not come out. Twenty-four hours later, resistance members gathered to hold a brief memorial service for the patriotic burglar who had sacrificed his life for his country.[4]

Deceit in the Desert

DURING THE NINE MONTHS FOLLOWING the outbreak of war between Nazi Germany and the Western Allies, a squat, middle-aged vegetarian named Benito Mussolini had been watching from Rome with mounting jealousy while the war machine of his pal Adolf Hitler overran much of Europe. Calling himself *Il Duce* and fancying himself as the last of the Caesars, the Italian dictator declared war on Great Britain on June 10, 1940.

Mussolini already had a quarter-million men in the vast desert of Libya, North Africa, under the command of fifty-eight-year-old Marshal Rudolfo

Graziani. Plans called for driving eastward to seize the great British naval base at Alexandria, Egypt, then push on and capture the Suez Canal, which connected the Red Sea on the south to the Mediterranean on the north.

Great Britain, meanwhile, had assembled in Egypt a force vaingloriously called the Army of the Nile, under the command of a one-eyed general, Archibald Wavell. There were only thirty-six thousand men in his force. Many of his troops were either untrained or administrative personnel. There was no hope of rapid reinforcement.

When Graziani struck, the British had to fall back, and Italian forces poured eastward into Egypt in the north in a sector along the Mediterranean coast on September 13, 1940. Halting the far larger Italian Army seemed remote. However, reinforcements for Wavell were on the way from England after British leaders learned from wireless intercepts that Adolf Hitler had called off Operation Sea Lion, the invasion of Great Britain.

Until these reinforcements arrived in Egypt, it was crucial that Wavell hoodwink Graziani on the true British strength and battlefield plans. That most difficult task was handed to a forty-one-year-old colonel on Wavell's staff, Dudley W. Clarke. While posted in London a few months earlier, Clarke had been responsible for energizing an official action that created the commandos—elite, heavily armed raiders whose main mission was to harass the Germans across the English Channel.

Now, in the North African desert, Clarke, energetic and decisive, quickly rounded up teams of men to implement the deception scheme. Soon he had fabricated a powerful force: hundreds of tanks made of rubber that were blown up like balloons, as were scores of artillery pieces, trucks, and prime movers.

To give the impression that this heavy force was preparing to encircle Graziani's forward elements along the Mediterranean coast, Clarke had dummy roads laid and tank tracks carved into the hard sand to the south. Italian reconnaissance planes would pick up these new developments, Clarke knew.

Then Clarke launched his *pièce de résistance*. Large numbers of Arabs were recruited to bring their camels and horses, which dragged large planks behind them, to stir up enormous clouds of dust. When seen from the air, these antics looked like long columns of tanks on the move.

All the while, British antiaircraft guns kept Italian reconnaissance planes high in the air so their photographs would not give away what was really happening down below.

From these photographs and reports of heavy British movements by Italian forces on the ground, Marshal Graziani concluded that Wavell was preparing to strike with formations of tanks and guns on his right flank. British cloak-and-dagger operatives also "permitted" the Italians to crack a code and learn from wireless intercepts that heavy British reinforcements were on the way to Egypt—which was true. This disclosure caused Graziani to be even more hesitant.

Fearing that he might be cut off by a powerful tank assault against his right flank, Graziani ordered his forces to halt and dig in. By the time the Italian marshal apparently realized that he had been bamboozled, it was too late. The tank and infantry reinforcements had arrived from England.[5]

The Jewish Pal of the Nazis

ADOLF HITLER, absolute ruler of 90 million Germans and commander in chief of the Wehrmacht, stood in a clearing in Compiègne Forest, just north of Paris, on the warm and beautiful day of June 22, 1940. With him was a galaxy of top Nazi leaders, including Field Marshal Hermann Goering, the Luftwaffe chief; beetle-browed Rudolf Hess, the deputy führer; and General Wilhelm Keitel, the tall, monocled chief of staff of the Wehrmacht.

Hitler could not conceal his jubilation. Only six weeks earlier he had launched Case Yellow, in which his armies of 2.5 million men, preceded by *Fallschirmjäger* (paratroopers) and Stuka dive bombers, plunged across the borders of France, Belgium, and the Netherlands. Now Hitler, who had been a decorated infantry corporal in World War I, was gaining revenge for the defeat of Kaiser Wilhelm's army.

Next to the Nazi leaders was the identical railway car, hitherto kept as a museum piece, in which French Marshal Ferdinand Foch had dictated terms to Germany on November 11, 1918, at the end of World War I. Led by the triumphant führer, the Nazi delegation boarded the coach that was serving as the parlor for France's funeral. Minutes later, French generals signed the surrender document.

Within a few days of the capitulation ceremony, Jacques Weil, a Swiss who had extensive business interests in France, approached an undercover British intelligence officer in Zurich, Switzerland, and offered to help the Allied cause in any way he could. After a cursory check of Weil's background, the businessman's offer was passed along to Whitehall.

Meanwhile, Adolf Hitler returned to Berlin and promptly offered peace terms to Great Britain. He thought the war was over. Winston Churchill, who had succeeded Neville Chamberlain as prime minister on the same day that Case Yellow had been launched, disdained even to reply.

Britain was in mortal danger. Churchill tried to divine Hitler's intentions. What would the führer do next? Would he leap the English Channel and invade the British Isles? Intelligence sources in France were almost nonexistent. The few agents who had been left behind when the British Army had been evacuated from Dunkirk in helter-skelter fashion shortly before the French surrender were in hiding. Some did not have any means of communication, or if they did, dared not use them.

So to help fill this critical intelligence vacuum, to gain even an inkling of what the Germans in France were intending to do next, British authorities accepted the services of Jacques Weil. He seemed to be in a perfect position to spy on the Germans because for years he had been making periodic business trips into France.

In a few weeks Weil began producing eagerly sought information from France. A tall, blond-haired man with an engaging personality, he had managed to infiltrate high German military circles in Paris and make friends with many Wehrmacht officers. On one occasion he was invited to visit the headquarters of the *Heer* (army), where he was treated deferentially as a friend of Nazi Germany.

What the Germans didn't know was that Jacques Weil was Jewish, a fact he had concealed by occasionally dropping a disparaging remark about his own race.

Weil, who was quite wealthy, also ingratiated himself with German officers by showing them the glittering and racy Paris nightlife. He shelled out large amounts of his own money to get the Germans drunk, and when they had passed out, he surreptitiously rifled their pockets and removed anything that resembled military information.

When returning to his base in Switzerland, Weil usually lugged two heavy suitcases. It was risky business, especially when his train reached the Swiss border and its passengers were inspected by Gestapo agents. One suitcase carried his clothing and personal items; the other was packed with secret papers he had obtained from the Germans.

Despite being nearly unmasked numerous times, Weil continued his espionage work. He was able to identify targets of military significance, which were either blasted by Royal Air Force bombers or sabotaged by the French underground.

In 1943, the Swiss businessman joined the French resistance network code-named Prosper, a widespread espionage apparatus that the British secret service was building to rise against the German occupiers when the Allies would one day invade France. He hooked up with an old friend and colleague, Jean Worms (code-named Robin), who was in command of Juggler, a *réseau* (subsection) of Prosper.

Back in October 1942, British Major Francis Suttill, who had been born of a French mother and English father thirty-one years earlier in Lille, France, had landed at night by parachute in a meadow near Vendôme, 110 miles southwest of Paris. He immediately assumed his cover identity: François Desprée, a Belgian traveling salesman in agricultural products.

At the same time, Suttill also assumed his assigned cryptonym—Prosper, from Prosper of Aquitaine, a fifth-century Christian writer and disciple of St. Augustine. The major's mission was to build réseaux in northern, central, and eastern France and bring them under his personal control in Paris.

Prosper rapidly plunged into his daunting task. In an incredibly short period of time he had put together the nuclei of some twenty réseaux, including Juggler. He established *courrier* (secret mail), clandestine communications, intelligence, action, finance, and medical branches. Eventually he would have ten thousand secret agents working for him.

*British major Francis Suttill,
whose code name was Prosper.
(Author's collection)*

Prosper's own sense of security was not always airtight. He had a streak of bravado, which sometimes resulted in carelessness. On one occasion he negotiated with German secret service agents in Paris for the release from jail of what he had been told were two attractive and highly productive members of one of his réseaux. He paid 1 million francs ($24,000 or £5,000) for their release. Prosper was dismayed to find two elderly whores who had been arrested for soliciting waiting for his men when they arrived at the designated rendezvous.

It was not Prosper's occasional security lapses that resulted in disaster for the far-flung espionage network, however. Rather, he was betrayed by French traitors in his organization. On the night of June 22–23, 1943, fifteen German secret service men charged into an old hotel on the rue Mazagran in a rundown district of Paris. Prosper was not in his dingy little room, but when he returned the next day, he was pounced on and seized by the German operatives.

Although grilled mercilessly, Prosper refused to disclose the identities of his lieutenants or the locations of his arms dumps. But some traitors in his underground did talk. The German secret service men sped to all parts of Prosper's vast region and collected some 470 tons of arms and ammunition. Then, in the days ahead, hundreds of Prosper's agents were captured. Suttill and his lieutenants were shot to death.

While the great roundup of Prosper *résistants* had been in full swing, Jacques Weil managed to escape and return to Switzerland. Soon he became aware, through clandestine connections in France, that the entire network had collapsed. It was leaderless, and the survivors had gone into hiding.

Angered by the tragedy that befell Prosper, Weil was more than ever determined to strike a blow at Adolf Hitler. So he shed his business suit and commercial connections and became leader of an active underground group operating in southeastern France. He and his résistants were still bedeviling the Germans when U.S. and French armies overran the region in late 1944.[6]

The FBI Undercover in South America

WAR CLOUDS FROM EUROPE were drifting toward the United States in early 1940 when President Franklin Roosevelt and key leaders in his administration became aware that Nazi agents had established a string of bases from Mexico City to the tip of South America. Clandestine radio stations beamed on Hamburg, Cologne, and Brussels were funneling military, political, and economic reports received from Nazi spies in the United States to the Abwehr (secret service).

Years before Adolf Hitler came to power in Germany in early 1933, large numbers of Germans had immigrated to South America and settled in colonies. In the late 1930s an estimated 600,000 German nationals or native-born descendants lived in Brazil, Argentina, and Chile.

When Hitler began rearming Germany, the Nazi movement was embraced with great enthusiasm in those three countries. Germans and their offspring wore the uniforms of storm troopers and unfurled the Nazi flag on ceremonial occasions. There were German war veterans' organizations, a German youth movement, and a German labor front.

In early June 1940 President Roosevelt held a solemn conference to discuss the security threat from south of the border. Present were J. Edgar Hoover, the Federal Bureau of Investigation (FBI) chief, and the heads of army and navy intelligence. After extensive discussion it was decided that a Special Intelligence Service (SIS) would be created to operate overseas to secure information of activities detrimental to the security of the United States.

Roosevelt was enthusiastic about the new organization, mainly because the United States was the only major country in the world that did not have its own global intelligence agency. (It would be another year before what came to be known as the Office of Strategic Services [OSS] was established.) The president issued a directive setting forth the responsibilities in foreign intelligence.

FBI director Hoover and his agents would have jurisdiction over nonmilitary intelligence in the Western Hemisphere.

Acting with typical alacrity, Hoover organized an SIS operation in less than a month, and his agents were already slipping into several countries in South America. These men traveled under phony names and would work as undercover operatives. Later other agents were openly assigned to U.S. embassies and given misleading titles to mask their true missions.

All of this planning, organizing, and infiltrating of agents was carried out under a veil of strict secrecy. The stakes were enormous in this sophisticated program to wipe out the Nazi spy threat in South America, an operation in which FBI men often would risk their lives.

It also would be a delicate operation, and it could be successful only through cooperation with and by friendly governments in South America. Results would have to be achieved without public attention or embarrassing either the officially neutral United States or any of the cooperating regimes.

One undercover agent went to South America as a salesman for a U.S. soap manufacturer whose executives never suspected his secret role with the FBI. Within a few months the agent sold so much soap that his company had to expand its distribution facilities. In the meantime, the gung-ho salesman had established valuable contacts in business and governmental circles. These personal relationships provided the agent with invaluable leads into Nazi activities in the country.

In an Argentine city, a youthful-looking FBI agent arrived to work as a reporter. Soon he began sending articles to publications in the United States and attracted considerable attention from companies interested in South American affairs. His name was William Byers (a pseudonym). He often spent time around a small hotel operated by a man in his midthirties whose parents lived in a European country occupied by the German Army.

The innkeeper rebuffed Byers's subtle suggestions that he should become a spy for the United States. He was head of a civic organization whose members were in businesses, utilities, and government agencies across the city, and therefore, Byers had concluded, would be a highly productive asset to the FBI.

Byers settled on a new tack to coerce the innkeeper into cooperating. "I would like to do a series of articles on the various groups in the city," he said. "And I'd like your help in gathering the information."

Byers looked at the man intently to judge his reaction. The innkeeper stared at the young American for almost a minute. Clearly, he had suspected all along that Byers was actually a plant of the brutal Argentine secret police. Then the man said solemnly, "If I give you this information, will it reach the right people?"

At that moment Byers realized that the innkeeper had been wanting to get information to the United States but had not trusted the agent. "It certainly will reach the 'right people'!" Byers replied.

FBI Director J. Edgar Hoover (left) sent his G-men to hunt Nazi spies in South America. FBI Special Agent Percy J. Foxworth (right) was killed during the operation. (FBI)

Most of the South American governments willingly helped in the FBI's counterintelligence project. Leaders in these nations had been deeply concerned about the open displays of Nazi support and rumors that Adolf Hitler eventually would try to take over their countries and turn them into German colonies. But a few countries—Argentina in particular—were hostile, and police and government officials made the FBI's undercover work especially difficult and dangerous.

In Argentina, agents frequently were shadowed, and their native informants caught by police told of agonizing tortures inflicted on them.

In Buenos Aires Harbor, the FBI kept a creaking old motor launch carefully hidden in a secluded alcove. On occasion at night, a native informant being pursued by the police would steal through the shadows to the craft, whose skipper was an Argentinian. The fugitive would scramble silently onto *Crandall's Navy*, as FBI men had dubbed the boat, after the agent who had conceived and implemented the escape idea.

Moments later, the craft would slip out of hiding and into the harbor. On its way to the open sea, the skipper sometimes had to dodge police harbor patrols. Eventually *Crandall's Navy* would reach the safety of Montevideo, Uruguay.

Meanwhile, William Byers, the FBI agent masquerading as a journalist, had attracted the attention of the Argentine police. At least once a week, he was tailed. On those occasions, he worked especially hard at being a reporter and scrupulously avoided any contact with his native informants.

Like many free-spirited and adventurous individuals, Byers had an impish streak in him and could not resist taunting the police who were trying to catch him in espionage activities. In his role as a journalist he would call on the city's chief of detectives, the man who was directing the effort to nail him. "I just happened to be passing by and hoped you would join me in a cup of coffee," he would tell the police official.

"It must have driven that guy nuts!" Byers later would tell an associate. "And the detectives who were tailing me, too. They didn't know that a well-placed friend in the police station was tipping off my innkeeper informant about which days I was to be shadowed."

One day, Byers's informants told him that two Germans suspected of being spies had driven by automobile to a nearby Argentine city. Byers set out to determine precisely who they were, where they had gone after reaching their destination, and on whom they had called. It was a difficult assignment—the Germans' names were not even known to him or his informants.

Byers promptly went to see his innkeeper friend and was told to return the following day. Byers went back. The man said to come back the next day. Now Byers felt that he was either being given the runaround or the innkeeper was finding that obtaining information about the two Germans was like seeking the proverbial needle in a haystack.

On the third day, the innkeeper handed Byers a typed sheet identifying the Germans by name and the license number of their car—even the serial number of its engine. Moreover, the report stated where the suspects had gone and a summary of their conversation while driving to the neighboring city. It was the most detailed report involving espionage that the FBI man had ever seen.

Byers had been wrong on one key factor, it developed. There had been three Germans in the car, not two.

Astonished by the comprehensive account, Byers asked his friend, "How did you get all this stuff?"

Replied the other without change of expression, "The third 'German' who drove the car was one of my men."

The information from the innkeeper's contact led to the unmasking of a German espionage ring that had been operating in the region with the indifference of the police. However, the flood of media articles "reporter" Byers generated in Argentina and the United States succeeded in putting the spy ring out of business.

Brazil, also a hotbed of Nazi espionage activity, severed diplomatic relations with Germany and Italy in early 1942. Working with Brazilian authorities, the undercover FBI agents swooped down on and put out of business the six clandestine radio stations that had been sending coded intelligence to Nazi stations at three locations in Europe.

However, the biggest Nazi fish of all in Brazil escaped the dragnet. The FBI could not even learn his name. It was known only that he directed a spy ring that operated a secret radio station known by the call letters CIT.

The mystery spy was Josef Jacob Johannes Starzincy, a German engineer and scientist, a wiry man who peered owlishly through thick glasses. He had arrived in Rio de Janeiro by ship in the spring of 1941, smuggling past customs a large bag holding a radio transmitter, four codebooks, and microphotographic instructions. Five weeks later, the clandestine radio station, CIT, began sending information to Germany.

In mid-December 1941 Starzincy traveled to Santos, Brazil, to install another secret transmitter and found that he needed a wavemeter. He went to a small shop to buy the item, but the merchant told him it was out of stock. However, he could order the part and forward it to the customer if he would leave his name and address. The stranger wrote on a piece of paper, "O. Mendes, Hotel Santos, Santos."

Brazilian security agents had warned merchants to be cautious in selling radio parts to strangers, so the shopkeeper called in the police and gave them the customer's name and address. There was no "O. Mendes" registered at the Santos Hotel.

A week later, however, a man identifying himself as O. Mendes called the store about the wavemeter he had ordered. The shopkeeper said he expected the delivery any day now, and he promptly notified the police, who, in turn, informed the FBI.

Based on sketchy information provided by O. Mendes in his last telephone call, the FBI, teaming with the police, pieced together information that began to point toward Niels Christian Christensen, a respected "Danish" engineer who operated a business firm in Rio de Janeiro.

Christensen was arrested and eventually admitted that he was not a Dane but a German and that his real name was Josef Jacob Johannes Starzincy. His home and bank safety deposit box produced a bonanza of spying data—codes, copies of messages, secret instructions, and the names of his subagents and informants.

Not until years later did the FBI break its silence about its scintillating success in wiping out the widespread Nazi espionage apparatus in South America. During the war, 887 German spies were identified, 389 of them were arrested by local authorities, and 105 were convicted. Twenty-four secret radio stations were located, and 30 radio transmitters were confiscated by local authorities after being detected by FBI agents.

The undercover triumph had been costly. Four FBI men, including Assistant Director Percy J. Foxworth, were killed in carrying out their missions, all in airplane crashes.[7]

"War of Nerves" against England

ADOLF HITLER was relaxing at a mountain retreat in southern Germany's Black Forest when he summoned his two principal military confidants, Generals Alfred Jodl and Wilhelm Keitel. Stiff and humorless, Keitel was chief of staff of the Oberkommando der Wehrmacht. Jodl's function was to translate the führer's decisions into precise military directives. Hitler had selected these two officers because they were known to be *Führertreu*—blindly loyal to the supreme commander. It was early July 1940.

Hitler told Keitel and Jodl that they were to begin preparations immediately for the invasion of the British Isles, with the operation to be launched by mid-October. A week later, Jodl and Keitel presented Hitler with an outline of an invasion plan code-named See Löwe (Sea Lion).

After making a few minor changes, the führer signed General Order Number 16 for distribution to Wehrmacht commanders:

> Since England, despite her hopeless military situation, still shows no sign of any willingness to come to terms, I have decided to prepare for, and if necessary carry out, an invasion of England.
>
> The aim of the operation will be to eliminate the English homeland as a base for carrying on the war with Germany.
>
> Preparations for the entire operation must be completed by mid-August 1940.
>
> —Supreme Commander of the Wehrmacht

Hitler's instructions called for Sea Lion to be launched as soon as the vaunted Luftwaffe wiped out the much smaller Royal Air Force.

Great Britain, a nation at bay, braced for the cross-Channel onslaught. England's defenses were woefully weak. "If they come," Prime Minister Winston Churchill gloomily told confidants, "we'll have to hit them over the heads with beer bottles, because we have few other weapons."

In the wake of the führer's order, Josef Goebbels, the Nazi propaganda genius, launched a war of nerves to confuse and frighten the British home front. The diminutive Goebbels was known behind his back in Germany as the Propaganda Dwarf.

Cunning and cerebral, Goebbels kicked off his war of nerves on August 12, two months before See Löwe, when a Luftwaffe plane flew low at night over southern England and dropped several containers by parachute onto an open pasture. As anticipated, the containers were discovered after daylight, and local police rushed to the scene. They found two-way radio sets, explosives, lists of addresses of prominent Englishmen—including Prime Minister Winston Churchill—and instructions to German spies on actions to be taken as soon as the invasion hit.

In succeeding nights, a similar scenario unfolded at other locales in England. These parachute drops were clever ploys to cause a plague of jitters on

Josef Paul Goebbels, the crafty Nazi minister of propaganda and enlightenment. (National Archives)

the home front by implying that there was a large and active Nazi spy apparatus in the islands waiting for the signal to strike. British authorities kept these episodes from the media, but the machinations achieved Goebbels's goal. Word of the parachute drops spread like wildfire by word of mouth.

Actually, British secret service agents had rounded up perhaps all of the spies shortly after the war began eleven months earlier. Now, among jittery Britons, the butcher, the baker, and the candlestick maker had become espionage suspects.

Goebbels used the radio to maximum advantage in his war of nerves. Broadcasting from Berlin, announcers who spoke fluent, unaccented English and falsely claimed that they were British citizens flooded the airwaves with advice to civilians. And strange advice it was, indeed. Confused British listeners were urged to keep straitjackets handy, as many persons would go stark, raving mad once the powerful Luftwaffe began all-out bombings of British cities. "Those who go insane will be highly dangerous," the ominous broadcast voice warned. "They may go on murder rampages."

Another authoritative "voice" was heard over Radio Berlin almost daily. It was identified as that of a prominent German physician who had once lived in England and who now was interested only in relieving the suffering that would take place during the impending "rain of German bombs." Actually a member of Goebbels's staff, the benevolent "doctor" provided helpful instructions on how to give first aid to those who would be "hideously burned or mutilated."

Goebbels knew that British civil defense officials had been warning the population to be on the lookout for German paratroopers who might try to spearhead the invasion by dressing as priests, nuns, or in other nonmilitary garb. So German broadcasters let England in on a secret. The *Fallschirmjäger* (paratroopers) were equipped with "fog tablets" developed by German scientists. Each soldier would turn into a small cloud after he leaped from an airplane.

The expression "secret weapon" customarily has a haunting ring to it, so Goebbels applied it in his broadcasts, being careful not to dilute its impact by using it too often. One of these "secret weapons," said a German announcer, would be unveiled when the invasion took place. The führer's scientists had developed enormous parachutes. Far larger than any yet known, these parachutes would be attached to dirigibles and allow them to remain hovering in the air over England for twelve hours and be indistinguishable from clouds.

The Berlin broadcasters warned the British that London was being considered as a target for an attack by another of the führer's secret weapons—air torpedoes. These new devices would destroy the sprawling capital, the announcers declared. These air torpedoes would be guided to specific targets with pinpoint accuracy by a wireless device operated from aircraft flying five miles from the target. Heading the "hit list," it was stated, was Buckingham Palace, the home of the king and queen.

Knowing that British generals remained mystified over how "impregnable" Fort Eban-Emael, near Liège, Belgium, had been captured by the Germans in less than an hour during Hitler's invasion of the West three months earlier, Goebbels decided to capitalize on the enemy's perplexity.

Hitler himself had conceived an ingenious scheme to seize the fort rapidly and at minimum cost. A force of some one hundred paratroopers, code-named Granite, had landed in gliders on a grassy expanse inside the thick walls of Eban-Emael. Confusion reigned among the eight hundred Belgian defenders, who capitulated in forty minutes.

It had been the first gliderborne assault in the history of warfare. Although it was a spectacular success, the führer had resisted an impulse to trumpet the achievement to the world. Instead, he had chosen to keep it secret so he might use gliders again in the future with equal success.

Now Goebbels's broadcasters disclosed to the British for the first time how Fort Eban-Emael had fallen so rapidly: it had been destroyed by the use of electronic rays, a revolutionary weapon that was currently being readied for the impending invasion of Great Britain.

On the night of August 1, British radar tracked a flight of Luftwaffe bombers that winged over southeastern England and continued toward London. It looked as though this was the beginning of the promised massive air assault on Great Britain. But not a bomb was dropped. Instead, the aircraft scattered hundreds of thousands of leaflets printed in English and headed: "A Last Appeal to Reason."

This caper to subvert Britain through psychological warfare proved to be a failure. A Dover dockworker read the leaflet and summed up the reaction of most of the British population: "Old Hitler has come to our rescue. With all the bloody rationing here, he's showered us with toilet paper!"[8]

The Führer's Concrete Crocodiles

IN THE SUMMER OF 1940, Adolf Hitler was spending most of his time and energy overseeing preparations for the impending invasion of England, Operation Sea Lion. He was astonished at the gargantuan effort required by the generals and admirals in his high command to solve logistical problems.

Usually cocksure of himself and his grasp of military strategy, the führer felt uncomfortable with an operation that largely would be seaborne. So when he was besieged at the Chancellery in Berlin by those with unorthodox schemes for getting the invaders across the English Channel, he often paid close attention.

Gottfried Feder, the Nazi minister of economics, proposed that the Channel be crossed by concrete submarine barges that would crawl along the seabed. Each unit would carry about ninety soldiers or two tanks or a few artillery pieces. "Think how terrified the British would be if they suddenly saw hundreds of concrete barges crawling onto their beaches," Feder stated enthusiastically.

Hitler was fascinated by the concept of crawling "concrete crocodiles" and ordered the Admiralstab (naval staff) to make a thorough study of their possible rapid construction and eventual deployment. The German admirals, under secret circumstances, went through the motions of carrying out the order, then quietly let the project die a natural death.[9]

Tuned in to the Luftwaffe

SHORTLY AFTER DAWN, thousands of German airmen began climbing into Junkers, Dorniers, Heinkels, Stukas, and Messerschmitts at airfields in France, Belgium, Norway, the Netherlands, and Denmark. Armed with photographs, sketches, and maps of their targets (obtained before the war in flights over England by the civilian airline Lufthansa), the Luftwaffe men were brimming with confidence. It was August 13, 1940, a day marking the launch of an all-out assault against the British Isles by a sky armada of unprecedented numbers and striking power.

All across southern England, Royal Air Force fighter pilots, alerted by radar, leaped into Spitfires and Hurricanes and soared up to meet the approaching Luftwaffe bomber streams. These fighter pilots were a breed apart—brash, scrappy, courageous. A few years earlier, many had been avowed pacifists. Some had signed the controversial Oxford Pledge, in which they swore that they would never fight "for King and Country." Now, with the survival of the British Empire at stake, they fought.

For the entire day, fierce, murderous clashes raged above the English Channel and southern England. As the days and nights wore on, German air attacks grew heavier in what Prime Minister Winston Churchill labeled the Battle of Britain. Nearly five hundred RAF planes were destroyed, and British pilots, fighting bitter air duels almost constantly, were near exhaustion. Hundreds of Luftwaffe planes were shot down, but the much larger German air force could more easily absorb its enormous losses in the duel of attrition.

While the vastly outnumbered RAF pilots were performing heroics almost hourly in the bitter skies over England, on the ground the secret technical wireless intelligence organization, known simply as Y Service, was playing a crucial role in helping to combat the Luftwaffe bomber streams. A key component of the Y Service was a unit of the Women's Auxiliary Air Force (WAAF), who listened to conversations between Luftwaffe pilots in the air and to those at their home bases.

An important member of this monitoring outfit was Lieutenant Aileen Clayton, who had joined the WAAF as an enlisted woman soon after the war broke out late in 1939. Because she spoke German fluently, Clayton had been promptly assigned to an RAF station along the southern coast of England and became a bona fide member of the Y Service.

At that time, the Y Service consisted of British women who had lived in Germany and were intimately conversant with German idiom and slang. Women with these qualifications were scarce, so their numbers were soon augmented by nationals of France, Poland, and Austria.

Assigned in six-hour shifts, Clayton and others in the unit sat with earphones clamped over their heads and strained relentlessly to pick up every word from Luftwaffe aircraft above England and across the Channel. Their tedious work was rendered even more difficult by atmospheric quirks, by the use of pilot slang with which they were not always familiar, and variations in German accents. However, the Y Service women persevered and, in many instances, were able to recognize the voices of individual German pilots and squadron commanders. When these familiar voices were absent for a period of time, Clayton and the others concluded that these pilots had been shot down and, perhaps, were dead.

On one occasion the Y Service picked out of the air references to "Little Screw" and "Parlor." For many weeks these two obvious code words baffled the British experts. But eventually, it was discovered that these two words referred to a technique by which Luftwaffe night fighters were directed to their targets — RAF bomber fleets. After diligent effort, British scientists came up with methods for jamming "Little Screw" and "Parlor."

As the war progressed, various techniques were tried to expand the range of the Y Service monitoring sets. One scheme would have done justice to Rube Goldberg, the famed American comic-strip author who created seemingly plausible yet absurd "inventions." In this instance, operators and their listening sets were put in gondolas suspended below observation balloons. The experiment resulted in the conclusion that swaying gondolas were among the most rapid means for making the women violently ill. So the operators returned to earth, and the intercepter sets in the gondolas were operated by remote control.

Teutonic efficiency often resulted in much valuable information being culled by Aileen Clayton and other Y Service wireless monitoring personnel. The Luftwaffe had divided all areas over which its aircraft operated into districts, each with a headquarters responsible for operations and the well-being of air crews in its region. Listening to the radio traffic as Luftwaffe bombers and fighters entered and left these districts, the Y Service thereby obtained crucial intelligence on the range of German radar and the range of various kinds of Luftwaffe airplanes.

During the savagery in the air of the Battle of Britain, Clayton and the other Y Service listeners worked seemingly endless hours that would eventually affect their health. Over a two-month period, Clayton and another WAAF officer often would be on duty for thirty-six of forty-eight hours — they were urgently needed to make immediate analysis of the value of intercepted German conversations so counteractions could be taken by the RAF.

After more than two months of fierce aerial combat during the Battle of Britain, the Y Service and wireless intercepts called Ultra picked up haunting intelligence: Reichsmarschall Hermann Goering, the Luftwaffe chief, had proclaimed Eagle Day for September 15, 1940. On that day the Germans would mount a mighty, final onslaught to wipe out the RAF. If Eagle Day was a success, Hitler would invade; if it failed, he would postpone the cross-Channel attack.

By midmorning of Eagle Day, the brilliant blue skies of southern England were laced with contrails as twenty-five squadrons of Spitfires and Hurricanes engaged the one thousand bombers and seven hundred fighters Goering had sent to administer the knockout blow. By late afternoon the British air knights had broken Goering's lance.

Two days later, Ultra intercepted and decoded a signal from the Oberkommando der Wehrmacht, relaying Hitler's decision to postpone the invasion.

The Battle of Britain had been one of the finest hours in British history, a feat accomplished by the courage of a small number of RAF pilots, the information provided by Ultra intercepts, and the tireless dedication and the skills of unheralded women who secretly monitored enemy conversations for the Y Service.[10]

Hosting a Boy Scout Official

EARLY IN OCTOBER 1940, while the Battle of Britain's outcome had remained in doubt, the Foreign Office in London received a strange request from the Spanish government, whose *el caudillo* (leader), Generalissimo Francisco Franco, was a crony of Adolf Hitler's, even though Spain was officially neutral. Could a Spaniard who was highly active with youth movements in Spain come to England to study the wartime activities of the British Boy Scouts? Yes, indeed, come right ahead, replied the Foreign Office.

Although a war was raging, the British rolled out the red carpet for the Spaniard. Several Boy Scout officials met him at the airport, then escorted him to a suite reserved for him at the posh Athenaeum Court Hotel. His gracious hosts provided him with expensive whiskey and whatever else he might want. Jolly good fellows, these Englishmen.

Actually, the Boy Scout officials were MI-6 men, and the Athenaeum suite had earlier in the day been converted into an intricate maze of concealed microphones and tapped wires. British intelligence had known the Spaniard well and knew that everything he saw and heard in England would reach Berlin within twenty-four hours after his return to Spain.

Most of Britain's limited number of antiaircraft guns were protecting the coasts or the air approaches to the capital. There were only about four heavy ack-ack batteries in all of sprawling London, a target of the Luftwaffe bombing blitz. One of these batteries had quickly been moved into the park across from the Athenaeum. Orders had been given to the puzzled ack-ack gun crews: Fire continuously through every air raid alert, even if there are no Luftwaffe planes in range.

German bombers continued to pound London each night, and the antiaircraft guns in the park barked constantly. The racket was terrific, and the sleepless Spaniard across the street must have thought London was honeycombed with ack-ack guns. His hosts permitted the Spaniard to inspect the gun battery, where one of its officers (actually a secret service agent) was careless enough to let slip the altitude these weapons could reach (he gave a figure thousands of feet higher than these antiquated weapons could attain).

Next, the British escorts took the Spaniard to Windsor to inspect the activities of a large group of Boy Scouts there. By coincidence (it wasn't), one of the few fully equipped regiments in the British Isles and possibly half the tanks the army possessed were drawn up in parade formation outside Windsor Castle. The Spaniard's hosts mentioned casually that these tough-looking men constituted but a small force that could be spared from defense of the islands to act as a ceremonial bodyguard for the king and queen. The incredulous look on the Spaniard's face told his escorts that he had swallowed the hoax.

A day later, the Spaniard was taken to a Channel port to see more Boy Scouts. By now he must have been sick of Boy Scouts. His hosts were. As the little group drove onto the docks, they viewed a harbor jam-packed with Royal Navy vessels of all types. With knowing grins, the escorts hinted to the Spaniard that the Home Fleet was much larger than Britain's enemies realized and that what they were seeing in the harbor was typical of the naval force that protected each major port. The visitor's eyes bulged.

Within an hour after the Spaniard's departure, the harbor was almost devoid of ships. During the hours of darkness, the navy units had congregated in this one port. Now they rushed back to their regular assignments all along the southern coast of England.

Later, in Madrid, double agents working for British intelligence managed to copy the eyewitness report the "Boy Scout official" had sent to Berlin. It was a stunning document. Great Britain obviously was an armed camp, and the British, crafty fellows, had been portraying the islands as being weakly defended to entice Hitler into an invasion that would meet with bloody disaster.[11]

"We Came to Blow Up America!"

BY LATE 1940 Adolf Hitler's masters of skulduggery had fielded in the United States a formidable army of spies, saboteurs, propagandists, couriers, go-betweens, stringers, straphangers, sleepers, and Peeping Toms. The nerve center for Nazi espionage operations in the United States was the German embassy, on Massachusetts Avenue in Washington. Inside that dreary old brick building, Dr. Hans Thomsen, the chargé d'affaires and a zealous Nazi, had concentrated the most conspiratorial den of spies to be found in any Third Reich embassy in the world. A hotbed of intrigue.

Most of the supporting cast for the horde of hard-core Nazi agents were homegrown Americans, a motley crowd of small-time operators who were motivated by love for Hitler's New Germany or for U.S. greenbacks—mainly greenbacks. Most were willing stockholders in the Nazi espionage corporation; others were dopes or dupes.

Thomsen was deeply involved in masterminding a keep-America-neutral campaign because his boss, ambitious Foreign Minister Joachim von Ribbentrop, had been designated by Hitler to direct the pacification operation—at least until the führer's war against England had been settled.

Ribbentrop's grand strategy was to pound the United States with a deluge of keep-out-of England's-war propaganda and for saboteurs to refrain from committing acts of violence that might arouse the sleeping giant and draw her into the shooting war.

Thomsen, an energetic and resourceful man, was making great strides in achieving his designated objective of keeping America neutral. Behind the scenes, the cagey chargé d'affaires sought out U.S. newspaper correspondents and promised each a monthly "bonus" of $350 ($3,500 in 1997) to publish "the right kind" of newspaper and magazine articles. Because the United States was neutral, several of the reporters assured themselves, there would be no harm in beating the drums for the country remaining out of the European war.

Once these "favorable" articles were published and read by a gullible public, Thomsen had thousands of reprints made and mailed to all editors and editorial writers in the United States.

In light of the heavy wave of keep-out-of-other-nations'-quarrels sentiment that was sweeping the United States, Thomsen became highly agitated when he picked up rumblings over the Nazi grapevine that professional saboteurs were going to infiltrate the United States.

On January 25, 1941, Thomsen fired off a cable to Ribbentrop: "Dire consequences to our [pacification] plans could result if any attempt is made to carry out sabotage operations in the United States at this time."

Four weeks later, on February 20, a husky man walked into the German embassy, identified himself as Walter von Hausberger, and said he had been sent to the United States by the Abwehr to carry out sabotage on a massive scale. With him was a self-styled "master saboteur" who called himself Julius Georg Bergmann.

"We came to blow up America!" they declared confidently.

Dr. Thomsen was horrified to be sheltering a pair of boom-and-bang desperadoes who might well blow to smithereens the Nazi grand design for coercing the United States into remaining officially neutral. He cabled Berlin, protesting the presence of the two saboteurs on his doorstep.

Came a reply from the Foreign Ministry: A check had been made with the Abwehr, which reported the two men had been dispatched to the United States, but only to act as "observers." Hausberger and Bergmann had received strict orders not to conduct any action remotely resembling sabotage.

Actually, the two saboteurs had been sent to the United States a year earlier, and had been involved in drawing up a master plan for launching a series of sabotage plots against the United States. Through homegrown spies in the United States, a list of key targets had been drawn up, a detailed compilation that included power plants, factories, railroads, water works, telephone exchanges, government buildings, and military facilities.

Nazi agents in the United States also obtained descriptions and maps of all major cities by asking for free street charts at gasoline stations. One ambi-

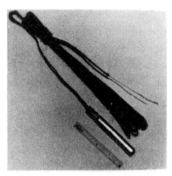

Electric blasting cap with copper wires.

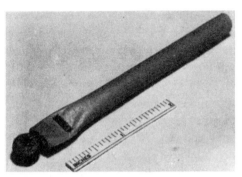

Safety fuse lighter for the ignition of standard safety fuse.

Electric match with screw cap removed— used in conjunction with timing mechanism and battery.

Capsule containing sulphuric acid encased in rubber tubing for protection.

Tools and instruments of destruction taken from Nazi saboteurs in the United States by the FBI. (FBI)

tious spy obtained the blueprints of New York City's water supply system. Another furnished details and maps of strategic spots in the U.S. railroad system, such as the Horseshoe Curve of the Pennsylvania Railroad near Altoona and the Hell Gate Bridge over the Harlem River in New York City. Yet another agent provided maps and blueprints of water-filtration plants and reservoirs for Los Angeles.

Reports for sabotage purposes were diversified—and often highly innovative. An enterprising Nazi operative suggested that German saboteurs sneak into the United States by aircraft, and he provided a map showing the locations of more than fifty Long Island golf courses that could be used for landing fields.

Far from being a benign "observer," Walter von Hausberger had long been an ardent boom-and-bang operative. Since arriving in the United States early in 1939, he had recruited homegrown saboteurs at the Packard, Ford, Chrysler, and Hudson automobile plants in Detroit; at the Harrison Gas Works in New Jersey; in the New York Liquidometer Factory; and at the four Brewster aircraft factories.

Julius Bergmann, the other "observer" whom the nervous Dr. Thomsen found himself harboring, was a hardened old pro in the espionage and sabotage arenas. Bergmann was an alias. His true name was Georg Busch, a onetime music publisher who had been a Hitler fanatic since early 1933.

Busch, too, had come to the United States in January 1939. His first act was to rent a modest home in suburban New York City and begin collecting a large cache of explosives, caps, and fuses. His plan was to blow up ships in New York Harbor. Taking along a pair of American toughs he had recruited, Busch conducted several reconnaissance missions along the waterfront, where many vessels were tied up.

Busch was astonished over the total lack of security. For more than an hour, the three men paced up and down the docks; they never saw a single policeman or other law officer. Looking for places to hide bombs, the three saboteurs boarded, without being challenged, the *Effingham* and the *Independence Hall*, wandering around the big freighters for more than thirty minutes.

Elated over the enormous boom-and-bang potential in New York Harbor, Busch excitedly told Abwehr controllers in Hamburg that he could "easily blow as many as ten vessels sky high." All he needed was money to recruit helpers and pay other expenses.

But by this time, no money was forthcoming. Fearful that ships being blown up in New York Harbor might tilt the American public and Congress toward active involvement in the war in Europe, Joachim von Ribbentrop went to Hitler, who promptly squashed sending any funds to saboteurs in the United States—at least for the present time—so that Dr. Thomsen could continue producing results in his slick pacification campaign.

While Walter von Hausberger and Georg Busch (alias Julius Bergmann) were collecting explosives and waiting for the signal to launch their widespread sabotage campaign, a major development that would stymie their plans took place in the United States. In early September 1939, only days after Hitler's powerful war machine plunged into Poland to trigger World War II, President Roosevelt instructed J. Edgar Hoover's Federal Bureau of Investigation to take charge of all investigative work in matters involving espionage, sabotage, and subversive activities.

Overnight, the spies' paradise that had been the United States vanished. As though a huge wand had been waved, scores of Nazi agents scurried for cover. Some didn't make it there. Among those seized by Hoover's G-men were Hausberger and Busch.

Consistent with the tenor of the times in the United States, spying and other acts of espionage were not considered major crimes. So Hausberger and Busch were released on relatively modest bonds (paid for secretly by the Abwehr) to await trial. When it was time for court action to begin, the two Nazi agents had disappeared, never to surface again in the United States.[12]

The Bogus Traitor of Flekkefjord

Twenty-three-year-old, blond, blue-eyed Gunvald Tomstad had been a highly popular figure in the southern Norwegian coastal town of Flekkefjord before Adolf Hitler sent his legions to take over peaceful Norway on April 9, 1940. Nine months later, when Tomstad joined the Nasjonal Samling (NS), the Norwegian Nazi Party founded by the notorious collaborator Vidkun Quisling, he became the most hated and reviled man in southern Norway.

Friends since boyhood looked the other way when Tomstad approached. Tacks were spread on the road in front of his farmhouse to puncture his motorcycle tires. One morning he found his beloved horse dead—its throat slit. When his cycle was parked in Flekkefjord, its tires were slashed. A small girl fell off her tricycle on the sidewalk, and when Tomstad tried to help her get up, she spit in his face. Numerous plots were hatched by patriots to murder the turncoat.

Tomstad's mother also was ostracized. Friends of decades ignored her. When she shopped, clerks told her the store was out of the items she wanted. On walking into church, parishioners looked the other way. At social functions she attended, there were whispers of "slut" and "whore."

At first, Mother Tomstad had refused to believe that her son had become a traitor—it hurt too much. It was no solace when a true old friend told her, "Gunvald can't be right in the head!" For weeks she stood up for her son, in the street, in people's houses, in doorways. "He never gave any hint about Nazi sympathies," she said repeatedly.

Her defense of her son became less convincing, because there were too many good, trustworthy people who believed his actions. But she could not bring herself to ask her son himself, for she was afraid of what the answer might be.

Mother Tomstad became even more disillusioned with her son's beliefs when she would leave her home in Flekkefjord and visit him at his ninety-acre farm at Helle, six miles away. On the walls of his living room were two huge photographs, one of Adolf Hitler, the other of Vidkun Quisling. And she was appalled at the stream of German officers, Gestapo agents, and homegrown Quislings who came to visit Gunvald.

Then one day, she entered the farmhouse and saw Gunvald wearing his gray NS uniform with its Nazi armband. She could not believe her eyes. In her anguish she began telling people, "I no longer have a son!" Yet she continued to agonize how Gunvald could have changed so utterly and so rapidly. What motives could her son, who had always been so proud of his ideas, have had for becoming a traitor to his country?

Knowing that his mother had publicly disowned him caused Gunvald to suffer excruciating inner torment. Yet he could not reveal to her that he was a staunch patriot and had been and was playing a highly dangerous role, one that required enormous courage and resourcefulness.

Political poster boosting notorious German collaborator Vidkun Quisling and his Nasjonal Samling party. (Author's collection)

Tomstad's transformation into a counterfeit Nazi fanatic had its origin soon after the Wehrmacht had overrun Norway. He became a leader in organizing an underground network of spies extending along the southern coast from Oslo on the east to the major port of Stavanger, some two hundred miles to the southwest.

During the early winter of 1940–41, the Flekkefjord network gained momentum, as did other resistance groups throughout Norway. Their clandestine fight intensified after German Reichskommissar Heinrich Terboven proclaimed that the Norwegian people's beloved King Haakon was no longer recognized as the nation's leader and that the despised Vidkun Quisling would replace him.

At this point the young patriots running the underground network hatched a scheme to penetrate German officialdom in the region in a way that would not cause the Gestapo or the Quislings (as the puppet leader's followers were called) to become suspicious. If the plan were to be implemented, one of the resistants would have to bear a burden of gargantuan proportions, one heavier, perhaps, than a human could withstand. Gunvald Tomstad was asked to shoulder the load—to become an outspoken, zealous Nazi.

Tomstad accepted the proposal. He was to go openly into the German camp and wage a secret, solitary struggle to bluff the Germans and get from them the details of what they had discovered about the Norwegian underground and warn those patriots in danger of imminent arrest.

Overnight, Gunvald Tomstad became Judas Tomstad. He who had always been anxious should people not like him, who could not stand arguments and was always the first to hold out his hand and offer to make up, and who loved his mother and other relatives, now had to act the role of a despicable traitor.

Only a handful of leaders in the Flekkefjord underground would know of Gunvald's masquerade. In his dual life he would continue as a leader in the underground.

One evening in February 1941, Tor Njaa, who ran the largest grocery store in Flekkefjord, called on Gunvald Tomstad at the Helle farm and said he had a surprise. His grocery store served as the network's "post office." Opening a large knapsack, Njaa pulled out a shiny new radio transceiver that had been smuggled to the grocery from a British undercover office in Stockholm, some 250 miles to the southeast, in neutral Sweden. Under Major Malcolm Munthe, the Stockholm operation arranged regular traffic of men, arms, ammunition, and communications equipment into neighboring Norway.

Gunvald was delighted at the sight of the transceiver. Now he would have the opportunity to play an active part in the war against Nazi Germany. As a wireless enthusiast since boyhood, sending and receiving messages from his farm would be a simple matter—unless he were discovered by German investigators and executed. The transceiver was hidden in the farmhouse attic.

The grocer Njaa took an American knife with a green handle from his pocket and told Gunvald to study it. "If a man comes to your farm and produces an identical knife, that man will be the 'owner' of the transceiver, and you are to take instructions from him," Njaa explained solemnly.

A short time before Njaa had left the priceless transceiver to be hidden on the Helle farm, Odd Starheim, who had escaped from German-occupied Norway to Aberdeen, Scotland, in a twenty-one-foot motorboat aptly named *Viking*, boarded a British submarine, and on New Year's Eve 1940 he slipped ashore from a rubber dinghy in a remote fjord on the southwestern coast of Norway. Starheim had been sent back with orders to contact a resistance group in the Kristiansand region.

A few days later, a stranger showed up at the Helle farm and introduced himself as Ola Svendsen. He and Tomstad eyed one another suspiciously. Norway was rife with spies and Nazi stooges. Tomstad waited tensely for the other man to produce the knife with a green handle. Svendsen made no move to do so. After a series of questions in which each man assessed the other, the newcomer pulled out the knife. Both men laughed and shook hands.

Norwegian Army Lieutenant Odd Starheim, alias Ola Svendsen, went to the transceiver, tapped out a predesignated call sign, and received an answer. Contact with London had been established.

Tomstad's transceiver was crucial, one on which everything with the underground network depended. No matter how efficient were the local agents in gaining intelligence, none of the information was of any value unless it could be transmitted rapidly and accurately to London, where the Allies could use it for either immediate action or in future plans.

Flekkefjord was ideally located for spying on German ships because of the nearby location of Kristiansand, Norway's third largest port, which the Kriegsmarine was using as a naval base. All ships going to or coming from Kristiansand hugged the shoreline to obtain the protection of the Germans' coastal batteries and air-raid system. Hardly a vessel sailed along that part of the coast without London being informed of its size, type, and course within a few hours.

At Kristiansand were two Norwegians who had earned the trust of the occupiers there. One was Viggo Axelssen, a ship's chandler, whom most Norwegians regarded as an easygoing chap who gave no thought about the progress of the war. Many had begun to regard him with contempt, however, because he catered to the German officers and even attended some social parties given by members of the Gestapo.

Axelssen had an almost unrestricted harbor pass. As a known friend of the Gestapo, the German harbormaster did not mind that the jovial Norwegian popped in and out of his offices. Quays, ships, and the sea had been Axelssen's life, so he helped the German naval guards check the outgoing and incoming ships. Good old Viggo!

The second Norwegian at the naval base who had earned the confidence of the Germans was Johannes Seland, a young journalist and secretary of the National Relief Fund, a phony organization. Although both Seland and Viggo Axelssen were regarded by the Germans as harmless, even quite helpful at times, they were key members of the underground with the special assignment of rooting out secrets in Kristiansand.

Meanwhile, Gunvald Tomstad was adroitly juggling his dual roles — Nazi fanatic and Norwegian patriot. Each day he made it a point to visit the Norwegian Nazi Party headquarters in Flekkefjord; then he would go back to his farm and radio to London bits and pieces of intelligence that had flowed into grocer Njaa's "post office" from all over southern Norway.

It was too risky for Njaa, a well-known figure, to personally carry the information to the Helle farm. What reason would a grocer have for making an almost daily trip away from his place of business? That problem was solved when young, pert Sofie Rorvig, who worked in the dairy in Flekkefjord and was Tomstad's fiancée, volunteered to be the courier. She held no illusions concerning her hideous fate should she be detected by the Gestapo with the incriminating bundle of intelligence bits.

One day in early May 1941, *Hauptsführer* (SS Captain) Rudolf Kerner, the head of the Sicherheitsdienst (SD) at Kristiansand, called in the counterfeit Nazi zealot, Gunvald Tomstad, to discuss an urgent matter. Kerner said his men had told him that their electronic direction finders had detected a clandestine transceiver, no doubt operated by Norwegian "terrorists." It was located in the Flekkefjord region. But the D-Fers, as they were called, could not pinpoint the site. Could Tomstad find the illegal transceiver?

The Norwegian assured the SD leader that he would do his best. Tomstad would, in essence, be investigating his own underground activities.

At Kristiansand, in the meantime, Viggo Axelssen, finding excuses to roam the mountainous countryside, spotted the powerful German battleship *Bismarck* and the cruiser *Prinz Eugen* holed up and camouflaged in a Norwegian fjord. This information was rushed to Gunvald Tomstad at the Helle farm, and within the hour it reached the British Admiralty, which had lost track of these warships.

Just past 7:00 A.M. on May 20, 1941, London received a transmission from the Helle farm: "Battleship, probably German, has passed Kristiansand heading west escorted three destroyers." The Admiralty was electrified. No doubt the *Bismarck*, the pride of the Kriegsmarine and a deadly threat to Britain's crucial shipping lanes, was breaking out for a rampage through the North Atlantic.

On the morning of May 24, the *Bismarck* and the *Prinz Eugen* were intercepted by a British Royal Navy flotilla that included the battleship *Prince of Wales*, the old battle cruiser *Hood*, and the cruisers *Suffolk* and *Norfolk*. A heavy firefight erupted. The old dreadnought *Hood*—the pride of the British fleet—was struck by a *Bismarck* salvo and exploded. Only three of the fifteen hundred men aboard survived.

A short time later, the *Prince of Wales*, one of the most modern of British warships, was struck by shells below the waterline, forcing the captain to break off the action. But the *Bismarck*, too, had been badly damaged by a British salvo. However, the mighty German ship, trailing oil, continued into the Atlantic with the *Suffolk* and the *Norfolk* shadowing her at a safe distance. Thus began a seventeen-hundred-mile chase, perhaps the most dramatic event of its kind in naval history.

At about ten o'clock that evening the *Bismarck* was struck by a torpedo from an aircraft launched from the carrier *Victorious*, and her speed and performance were further reduced. Through Ultra intercepts the British Admiralty concluded that the wounded ship was bound for Brest, at the western tip of the Britanny Peninsula in France.

Now the Admiralty sensed a kill. Two Swordfish torpedo-carrying aircraft from the carrier *Ark Royal* attacked the *Bismarck*, dooming her. More torpedoes and shells riddled the ship. At 10:40 A.M. on May 27, west of the French Atlantic coast, the *Bismarck*, a flaming and smoking mass of steel, turned over and sank. Two thousand men in her crew went to a watery grave. Only one hundred ten others were fished alive from the ocean.

The sinking of the pride of the German Navy triggered a surge of elation, not only in the Admiralty but also throughout the British home front. Many Royal Navy men involved were rightfully hailed as heroes. Yet the *Bismarck* may have escaped detection and been free to maraud the Atlantic and sink countless Allied merchant ships had it not been for the small groups of Norwegian resistance fighters in the Flekkefjord region.

In the wake of the global publicity about the *Bismarck*'s sinking, Gunvald Tomstad, the most hated man in southern Norway, had to put on a virtuoso acting performance when he walked into the Flekkefjord headquarters of the

Norwegian Nazi Party. Masking the elation that surged through him, he had to project an aura of personal devastation. Tomstad survived the war and became a national hero when his true role was made known.[13]

A One-Man Cloak-and-Dagger Agency

A THICK BLANKET OF SNOW covered Washington on the bleak morning of December 1, 1940, when William J. "Wild Bill" Donovan, a Wall Street lawyer, was ushered into the Oval Office of the White House after an urgent summons from Franklin D. Roosevelt. The president asked the stocky, gray-haired Donovan to be his "eyes and ears," to travel to the Mediterranean and Europe to "impress on everyone the resolution of the American government and the people to see the British through and provide all possible assistance to countries that have resisted Nazi aggression."

It would be the strangest of missions—supposedly wrapped in a tight cocoon of secrecy, and at the same time employing contrived leaks to the media to put psychological pressure on German and Italian spies, diplomats, and policymakers.

As colonel of New York's "Fighting 69th" Infantry Regiment in World War I, Donovan had received the Congressional Medal of Honor, the Distinguished Service Cross, three Purple Hearts, and other combat decorations. Now, eager for adventure and a chance to serve his country, he promptly accepted the challenge outlined by Roosevelt.

In his forthcoming mission, Wild Bill would be a one-man cloak-and-dagger agency. Secure in the belief that two wide oceans protected the nation, Americans were obsessed with minding their own business. Therefore the United States was the only major nation that had no secret service to ferret out the intentions of hostile powers. Nor did the United States have a military intelligence worthy of the name. Consequently Roosevelt, in reaching crucial decisions affecting the security—even the existence—of the nation had to "fly blind."

During the next few days Donovan dashed about Washington like a man possessed, calling on the leading lights in the Roosevelt administration in preparation for his espionage/diplomatic mission. Secretary of War Henry L. Stimson, who was regarded as having one of Washington's keenest minds, wrote in his diary:

"Colonel Bill Donovan came in this morning to tell me about the mission which he is going on. . . . His description of it made my mouth water. He is going over to take a look around and see what is *really* up."

Among those in Washington who took note of Donovan's forthcoming venture was Dr. Hans Thomsen, chargé d'affaires in the German embassy, an ugly brick building on Massachusetts Avenue. An ambitious, dyed-in-the-wool Nazi, Thomsen had converted the embassy into a hotbed of intrigue, a base for

William J. "Wild Bill" Donovan
was sent on a global espionage trip.
(U.S. Army)

extracting U.S. secrets from the high and the mighty in Washington, New York, and elsewhere. Only days after Bill Donovan had met with Roosevelt, German intelligence in Berlin knew of the impending mission.

Meanwhile, army and navy intelligence officers in Washington discussed ideas for Donovan's cover. Some thought he should travel abroad in a navy plane; others held that he should go incognito on regularly scheduled civilian airlines. Finally it was decided that he would travel under an assumed name on occasion and under his real name at other times.

It was nearing noon on December 6 when a taxi careened up to the pier in Baltimore where the *Bermuda Clipper*, the large, amphibious airplane that carried passengers to the Caribbean island, was preparing to lift off. Out of the yellow-colored vehicle stepped a middle-aged, well-dressed man who was listed as Donald Williams on the *Bermuda Clipper's* passenger list. A few reporters present spotted the WJD initials imprinted on his briefcase and recognized him.

Donovan masked his surprise over being accosted by reporters. Although it was widely known in Washington that he was departing on a crucial mission for the president, the actual overseas destinations, the true purpose of the trip, and the date and place of departure were kept secret. Now Donovan reflected on who had leaked word to the journalists that he was leaving from Baltimore. President Roosevelt?

A day after Donovan arrived in Bermuda, he climbed into the *Atlantic Clipper* for a flight to Lisbon, Portugal. On board were five U.S. Army officers in civilian clothes who gave no indication that they even knew Roosevelt's emissary. They had carefully avoided media cameras, for they, too, were on a secret mission within a secret mission.

Major General George V. Strong, chief of the undermanned and underfunded Army intelligence, had sent the five officers to help support Donovan in his mission. Or so Wild Bill had been told. Actually, they were to make a separate study and report on British military installations and troops. Army leaders feared that Donovan, on his return, would strongly recommend to Roosevelt that more military aid be given to the British.

Lieutenant Colonel Vernon S. Pritchard, head of the army delegation, had been instructed to bring back a highly unfavorable account of the British so as to coerce President Roosevelt into giving priority to building up the U.S. armed forces before trying to arm the British, who were already in good shape—or so the secret report was to indicate.

On December 17, the flying boat lifted off from the Bahamas with Donovan and the plainclothes intelligence officers aboard. It landed in Lisbon, from where Donovan was flown in a Royal Air Force plane to Poole, England. There he caught a train for London, where he took over a comfortable suite in Claridge's, the city's most fashionable hotel. The five army officers vanished, and presumably went about their appointed assignment of inspecting British forces.

A day later, Donovan dined at 10 Downing Street, the prime minister's residence, with Winston Churchill. The prime, as he was known to the Americans, stressed with typical eloquence that the United States and Great Britain must join hands to defeat Adolf Hitler. Donovan, relaying the instructions given him by Roosevelt, replied that the two countries must help one another during "this crisis in history."

During his stay in England, Donovan was a whirling dervish, intently probing the military situation and the entire political, social, psychological, and economic areas to try to predict if Britain could hold out against the powerful German Wehrmacht across the English Channel.

While Donovan was madly racing around the British Isles, Britain's supersecret XX Committee (Double Cross Committee) hatched a scheme to feed Berlin faulty information on the purpose of the legendary American's visit. Soon after war had broken out in Europe, the XX Committee had been created to subtly mislead and confuse Adolf Hitler and his generals.

A key ingredient of the XX Committee's deception system was German spies captured in Great Britain. Instead of being hanged, buried, and forgotten, the spies were "turned"—that is, put to work sending false intelligence to their former masters in the Third Reich.

Now one of the turned Germans was given a script, and with XX Committee men at his elbow, he was ordered to radio it to the Abwehr in Hamburg, where it was thought he was still roaming England freely. The message stated that the "notorious American spy and militarist," Colonel Donovan, had come to London to try to persuade Winston Churchill to avoid total destruction of England by seeking peace terms with Adolf Hitler. Hopefully, this message would slow any plans the führer had to invade England in the belief that Churchill would soon be begging for peace.

Just past two o'clock in the morning of December 26, Donovan was a passenger aboard a British flying boat that soared aloft from the dark waters of the English Channel and flew southward to Gibraltar, Britain's rock fortress in the mouth of the Mediterranean Sea. The limestone mass is connected with the Spanish mainland by a low, sandy isthmus a mile and a half long.

Spain was officially neutral in the war, but Generalissimo Francisco Franco, the country's dictator, was far less neutral toward Nazi Germany than he was toward the Western Allies. Consequently, hordes of German spies roamed Spain with impunity. No doubt one or more Nazi agents had taken up positions at the far end of the isthmus to peer through high-powered field glasses and watch the arrival of Bill Donovan.

After a whirlwind twenty-four hours of inspecting the defenses of Gibraltar, Donovan climbed on a Royal Air Force bomber and flew eastward to Malta, a British crown colony in the Mediterranean, where he was greeted that night by the most recent of the 125 heavy bombings the small island had endured.

On January 17, 1941, while heavy fighting was raging in the Libyan desert of North Africa between British and Italian forces, Donovan arrived in Cairo, Egypt, headquarters of the British Middle East Command. He promptly insisted that he be driven into the desert to see the fighting up close—and he refused to take no for an answer. Trekking in a jeep across the desert at night, Donovan knew that, on the trackless wasteland, no one could tell for certain where he was. So he was aware that at any moment, a roving enemy column could gain heroic stature by bagging President Roosevelt's "master spy."

After ten days of conferences and inspections in and around Cairo, Donovan flew to Athens, Greece. There he held a series of discussions with Premier John Metaxas and General Alexander Papagos, commander of the Greek Army. Although Greek soldiers were fighting Italian troops in the Balkans, Adolf Hitler had not yet invaded Greece, but was threatening to do so.

Soon after his arrival, Donovan was tipped off by Greek intelligence that Admiral Wilhelm Canaris, the cagey chief of the German Abwehr, knew that the American was in Athens and had sent a team of secret agents to tail him. Rather than being concerned about his personal safety during his jaunts around Athens, Donovan took glee in spotting Canaris's shadows, then taking evasive action to lose them.

After three days in Athens, Donovan boarded a night train for Sofia, Bulgaria. He noticed that his Abwehr tails were still with him, but he resisted an urge to wave a greeting to them. Arriving at his destination the next day, Donovan went directly to the U.S. legation, where George H. Earle III, a former governor of Pennsylvania, was to be his host.

Burly, ruggedly handsome, and in his early forties, Earle had been a diplomat in Austria in 1934 when he sent Washington reports that the new German leader, Adolf Hitler, was planning to rearm the Third Reich and that his intentions were to conquer Europe. Bureaucrats in the State Department in Washington scoffed at the warning. They frowned on Earle as a man with an inflated ego hankering for notoriety, a congenital troublemaker, and a disgrace to diplomatic drawing rooms.

After being assigned as an envoy to the court of Czar Boris III in Sofia a few years later, Earle, a free spirit, triggered one incident after another because of his strident anti-Hitler views. Once he found a German spy poking around in his quarters and handled the situation in a most undiplomatic manner— beating the intruder until he confessed his mission was to obtain derogatory information on the outspoken anti-Nazi Earle.

Two months later, Earle provoked a brawl with German agents in a Sofia nightclub. A few Nazis in the place asked the orchestra to play "Horst Wessel Lied," a sort of Hitler-era national anthem. Seated at a table, Earle seethed. When the rendition concluded, he rushed to the bandstand and demanded that the musicians play "Tipperary," a nostalgic British ballad dating back to World War I.

With the strains of "Tipperary" wafting through the crowded nightclub, an empty whiskey bottle was flung from the direction of the table occupied by the Nazi agents and crashed to the floor near George Earle and his three male companions, two American and one British. A brawl erupted. Fists flew. Furniture was used in supporting roles. The nightclub was largely wrecked. Afterward, Earle proclaimed his side victorious.

Now Wild Bill Donovan and George Earle, a pair of swashbuckling adventurers, talked for hours about Czar Boris and the situation in Bulgaria, which Adolf Hitler was threatening to take over. The next day Donovan held a lengthy discussion with the czar and came away convinced that the Bulgarian ruler planned to stand up to any threat by Hitler.

While Donovan had been talking with Boris, Earle was entertaining his Hungarian girlfriend back at the legation. She was a beautiful, curvaceous dancer—and a spy for the German Abwehr, a fact the diplomat had long known. When Donovan returned, Earle, eager to hear a rundown on Donovan's talk with the czar, sent her upstairs.

Before leaving for the palace to meet Boris, Donovan had left his briefcase in his room. In the container were top-secret papers that detailed U.S. and British plans to pour weapons and ammunition into Bulgaria and military actions to be taken in the event Germany invaded the country. While the two Americans were talking downstairs, the Hungarian beauty slipped into Donovan's room, picked up his briefcase, and rushed with it to her Abwehr contact in Sofia.

When Donovan went to his room, he discovered that the briefcase was missing. Clearly, it had been stolen. Wild Bill was not unduly concerned about his loss, however. The briefcase had been a plant, one designed to entice Earle's girlfriend to pilfer it. The "top-secret" documents were phony, having been created in London by the devious minds of the XX Committee to mislead German intelligence.

To add credence to the scheme, Earle telephoned a high Hungarian police official, one he knew was secretly working for the Nazis. In a slightly excited tone, he asked the Hungarian's help in recovering the briefcase, explaining that it held Donovan's passport, some personal papers, and a small amount of money. No mention was made of the "top-secret" papers.

A few days later, Ultra, the secret British cryptanalysis center at Bletchley Park forty miles north of London, learned that Adolf Hitler had swallowed the bait. From the decoding of German wireless messages, Ultra discovered that the Oberkommando der Wehrmacht had radioed the contents of the phony documents to army commanders and to top German diplomats.

A week after the stolen briefcase incident, Wild Bill Donovan was seated in the Oval Office of the White House, titillating President Roosevelt with a lengthy briefing on his travels abroad.[14]

Part Three

Conflict Spreads to the Pacific

One Briton's Revenge

FOR NEARLY SIXTEEN MONTHS since war erupted in September 1939, German Field Marshal Hermann Goering's vaunted Luftwaffe had been bombing cities in Great Britain with thousands of tons of explosives in an all-out effort to bring the beleaguered island to its knees. Scores of cities had been destroyed, thousands of citizens were killed or wounded. There was little the British could do to retaliate against Adolf Hitler's Third Reich.

There was one British soldier, however, who was determined to gain at least a measure of revenge. Major Grant Taylor was a free spirit and adventurer whose deeds and courage in two wars had made him something of a legendary figure in the British Army.

After fighting in France and being decorated for valor in World War I, Taylor left for the United States. Rumors reached old friends back in England during the next two decades that Taylor variously was a hit man for the Mafia, an undercover agent for the Federal Bureau of Investigation (FBI), and a bodyguard for the infamous gangster Al "Scarface" Capone. From 1937 to 1938 there were reports that Taylor had organized schools devoted to "silent killing" techniques for Generalissimo Chiang Kai-shek's Chinese Army that was fighting the invading Japanese Army.

After the outbreak of war in Europe in September 1939, Grant Taylor hurried back to England, was commissioned in the army, and set up a "killer school" for British commandos and for British spies who were to be parachuted into Nazi-occupied countries. He taught how an armed man in a sudden confrontation with six armed men in a small area (such as a room) could kill all six foes in six seconds or less—one shot for each, in the correct sequence, taking the most alert or dangerous man first, using the elements of surprise and speed. It was said that Taylor once had actually achieved that task—in three seconds.

Now, in January 1941, Major Taylor hatched a bold scheme to put his quick-kill techniques into action. Through Ultra, the British supersecret apparatus that unbuttoned (decoded) German wireless messages, and from underground contacts across the Channel, the swashbuckler learned that a group of Luftwaffe pilots who had been bombing London met each Friday night at a certain restaurant in a small town along the Channel coast to dine, drink, make merry, and spin tales of their aerial deeds. Taylor decided to invite himself to their party.

Armed with a .45 Colt automatic on his hip, another pistol in a shoulder holster, and a dagger strapped to his leg, Taylor crossed the Channel at night in a launch provided by the British secret service. Reaching the targeted town, the craft muffled its engines, slipped into the black harbor, and tied up at a deserted dock.

Disguised as a French fisherman, Taylor, noiseless as a jungle cat, leaped onto the dock and paused to listen for any telltale signs of imminent danger. The only sound was the gentle lapping of the surf against the dock. Presumably the German occupiers were so certain that the town was safe from any British interlopers that no sentries were posted along the shoreline.

Then Taylor began stealing through the streets toward the restaurant where the German bomber pilots gathered. He had secured its precise location from agents along the Channel coast before departing on the mission.

Arriving at his destination, the major paused briefly and checked his weapons. Blackout curtains covered the windows, but he could hear raucous singing and boisterous talk from within. No doubt the German bomber pilots' party was in full swing. "Enjoy yourselves, you bastards," Taylor reflected, "for you won't be able to sing much longer!"

Clutching tightly to his pistols, one in each hand, Major Taylor threw open the front door, spotted his adversaries across the room, and squeezed off several bursts. He was right on target. A couple of the startled Germans reached for their pistols, but it was too late. All six pilots crumpled to the floor and died.

Taylor raced back to the dock, leaped into the waiting launch, and by sunrise was back in England.

Typically, Major Taylor regarded his one-man rampage as only another day at the office, so to speak. Within seventy-two hours, however, word was received from clandestine sources that the Briton had not only gunned down six crack Luftwaffe pilots, but also his action had infected German soldiers along a wide stretch of the Channel coast with a severe case of the jitters.

In the weeks ahead, underground sources across the Channel reported that the German pilots continued to gather each Friday night, but not at the same restaurant. As a security measure, the party was held at a different place in various towns in the region, mainly ones several miles inland. Moreover, two German soldiers armed with automatic weapons were posted outside the restaurant where the gathering was taking place.[1]

Spies inside a U.S. Embassy

IN EARLY 1941, seventeen months after war had erupted in Europe, the Abwehr's wily Admiral Wilhelm Canaris had a spy in the U.S. embassy in Berlin. She was a middle-aged typist in a special department the embassy had set up to represent Great Britain and care for British prisoners of war.

Frau Frick (not her real name) had an office on the second floor of the building. Outside her office was a passageway where members of the embassy staff often stopped to chitchat or talk business. Frick was in an ideal spot to eavesdrop, and she picked up some important information on occasion.

On February 4, two officers on the staff of the U.S. military attaché, Colonel Bernard R. Payton, were overheard talking about a German experiment with a new type of greatly improved smoke screen that could hide large ground targets—airfields, port facilities, railway yards, even major portions of Berlin.

Frick could not be seen taking notes, of course. But she had a prodigious memory, and could later repeat almost verbatim discussions to which she was privy. On this occasion she hurried to her Abwehr contact and advised him that U.S. officers, wearing civilian clothes, were making visits to the locales where the smoke screen was being tested. Her information resulted in greatly tightened security at these test sites, and the American snoopers were no longer able to get close to them.

Frick was also able to identify for the Abwehr the specific assignments of various staff members whose titles were seemingly modest ones. One American was listed as a "Dr. Spencer," and his ostensible job was as a field service clerk in the British prisoner of war section. After returning from a trip to a PW camp in northern Germany, he filed a detailed report on a shipyard in Stettin that was building U-boats, she reported to her Abwehr controller.

Another embassy staffer was a man named "Howard," who worked in the embassy's wireless room as a simple operator. However, Frick informed the Abwehr, he actually held a Ph.D. in meteorology, and his true function was to collect weather information over Germany and radio it to the United States. There the data were instantly shuttled on to the Royal Air Force in England, where they were used in planning night bombing raids over the Third Reich.

Armed with Frick's intelligence, the Abwehr took a number of steps that reduced Howard's weather reporting to insignificance.

Elsewhere in Berlin, the Sicherheitsdienst (SD), the intelligence and security branch of the SS, was receiving copies of Frick's reports from inside the U.S. embassy. Although much of this information was overheard gossip and thirdhand intelligence, Frick had managed to come up with an occasional coup. So the SD, through the chief of its U.S. desk, Sturmbannführer (SS Major) Eric Carstenn, plotted to inject its own undercover agents in the American embassy.

Perhaps Carstenn had been nudged into taking the action by his boss, Obergruppenführer (SS General) Reinhard Heydrich, who was, in essence, the deputy chief of Reichsführer Heinrich Himmler's burgeoning SS empire. A tall, blond, hawk-nosed man, thirty-nine-year-old Heydrich was a bitter foe of Admiral Canaris of the Abwehr. Both men aspired to take charge of all German intelligence organizations once they were consolidated. So Heydrich no doubt was eager not only to match Canaris's penetration of the U.S. embassy in Berlin but also to exceed the Abwehr's espionage accomplishments there.

Carstenn scoffed at Frau Frick's "intelligence trivia," and he told his staff that he planned to extract high-level policy information, from which he could deduce what course the neutral United States would be taking in its dealings with the Third Reich.

Through his contacts in Berlin, Carstenn located a young man who seemed to be a logical choice to be planted inside the U.S. embassy. He was an American, spoke German fluently, had excellent credentials, and, above all, was secretly pro-Nazi. Moreover, he held a job he could drop without attracting undue notice.

As Carstenn directed, the man applied for a job at the U.S. embassy and was promptly hired with only a cursory check of his background. When asked for his preference, he was assigned to the political section, into which confidential or secret reports flowed almost continually from around the world.

Almost from day one, the American began paying dividends. On a daily basis he delivered to his SD contact a copy of the *Radio Bulletin*, a compilation of information the State Department in Washington was sending to embassies abroad. Much of the material was restricted.

This enterprising agent was only scratching the surface. In short order he was turning over to Carstenn copies of many of the secret dispatches Leland Morris, the chargé d'affaires, was transmitting to Washington. Much of Morris's communications dealt with the German war effort and also intelligence obtained by members of the embassy staff.

Carstenn also attacked the U.S. embassy on the social battlefront. At this stage of the war Berlin society was still clinging to its normal activities. American diplomats were invited to many of these glittering parties and dinners. By pretending to be critical of Adolf Hitler and the Nazi regime, many of these Berlin social lions and lionesses were able to extract valuable information from the Americans, whose tongues were often loosened by champagne and wine.

One middle-aged dowager feigned being a great secret admirer of President Roosevelt. Of course, she could not come out in the open and admit it, she whispered to a white-haired American diplomat. He could not resist impressing the vivacious woman, one of Carstenn's agents, so he recited at length the details of a conversation he had had with Roosevelt a few weeks earlier in which the president confided that the United States was going to do all it could to supply besieged Great Britain with weapons, ships, and airplanes.[2]

The "Evangelists" of New York Harbor

IN APRIL 1941, the Manhattan waterfront, Brooklyn, and the port cities of New Jersey were hotbeds of Nazi intrigue. Dingy saloons and flophouses catering to merchant seaman from all over the world were honeycombed with German spies and sympathizers. One of the most notorious of these places was the Highway Tavern in New Jersey. Another was the Old Hamburg in Manhattan, and yet another was Schmidt's Bar in Bayonne, New Jersey.

A bartender at Schmidt's was a Nazi agent, and he regularly plied seamen with drinks on the house, being a bighearted fellow. Then he listened avidly as their tongues loosened and they swapped tales of their adventures, including sailing dates from New York.

A favorite ploy of Nazi waterfront agents and informants was to take down the names of American merchant seamen and their home addresses. Then, after the dupe had gone to sea, his wife would receive a telephone call from a friendly individual who would ask: "Is Joe there?" The unsuspecting wife would believe that the caller was a friend of her husband, and she would tell the voice on the line everything she knew about the movements of her spouse's ship. On occasion, because of that seemingly innocent telephone call from a presumed friend, the husband would never return, his ship having been intercepted and sunk by an *Unterseeboot* (U-boat, or submarine).

From his headquarters in Lorient, France, Grossadmiral Karl Doenitz, commander of the U-boat fleet, tactically directed the operation to blockade America's Atlantic ports and cut the crucial shipping lanes to beleaguered Great Britain, especially those extending from New York. As reports flowed in from harbor spies in the United States, the U-boat chief, like a chessmaster adroitly moving pawns, shifted his underwater wolves into position to intercept ships streaming out of New York and other Atlantic ports.

Many of Doenitz's reports were coming from Nazi agents who were thick in New York Harbor branches of the Salvation Army and the seamen's missions. Hoboken, New Jersey, had a German seamen's mission. It was clean, well lighted, and provided wholesome meals. However, many German merchant marine sailers became irritated at its pastor, the Reverend Hermann Brückner, who clearly was anti-Nazi and often spoke out against the evils of Hitlerism.

None of the German patrons knew that the Reverend Brückner was actually a clever Abwehr agent. His function was not only to pick up shipping information but also to discourage foreign merchant seamen from working on ships taking war materials to Great Britain.

Brückner would send his "evangelists" into waterfront taverns and flophouses to urge the sinners—most of whom were drunk—to repent. One of these messengers of God, who went by the name Richard Warnecke, was especially zealous in redeeming the souls of the wayward seamen who had fled from their Nazi-occupied countries—Belgium, the Netherlands, Denmark, France, Greece, Yugoslavia, and Norway.

After praying over those targeted to have their souls saved, Warnecke would get quite solicitous regarding their physical redemption as well. "Why risk your lives at sea when you can return to your homeland and get good-paying jobs that

Bustling New York Harbor was a hotbed of Nazi spies. (Author's collection)

are safe?" the "evangelist" would ask. "Even though your country is occupied by German troops, when the war is over you will be alive and free."

The idea of this machination was to cause a slowdown in merchant sailing schedules because ships could not recruit full crews on a timely basis.

Warnecke told the sailors from Nazi-occupied countries that he had a method for sending them home through South America, and that their tickets would be paid for by the generous humanitarian Reverend Hermann Brückner.

Funds were never a problem for Brückner. A Nazi paymaster, long imbedded in a legitimate job in Manhattan, regularly called on the pastor and gave him hefty amounts of money to continue his task of saving the souls of merchant seamen. The paymaster received the U.S. currency from Abwehr agents posing as stewards on the German ocean liner *Bremen*.

Warnecke's evangelistic net hauled in a good-sized catch of dupes. Only later would the victims learn how cunningly they had been conned. When the men reached neutral Spain or Portugal, both of which were infested with Nazi agents, they were collared and forced to work on German or Italian merchant ships. If a shanghaied sailor balked, a threat to loved ones in his German-occupied homeland was sufficient to bring him into line.

Untold numbers of Warnecke's "converts" were destined to die when their German or Italian merchant vessels were sunk by American or British guns, bombs, or torpedoes.[3]

Confrontation at a Montana Airport

A MONTH AFTER Adolf Hitler had launched the invasion of Russia, Harry Hopkins, President Franklin Roosevelt's closest civilian confidant, flew into Moscow on a highly secretive mission. It was late July 1941.

Wearing a gray homburg hat and business suit, Hopkins bore a letter from Roosevelt to Iosif Vissarionovich Dzhugashvili, better known to the world as Josef Stalin, the Soviet dictator.

The letter read in part:

> Mr. Hopkins is in Moscow at my request for discussion with you on the vitally important question of how we can most expeditiously and effectively make available the assistance which the United States can render to your country in its magnificent resistance to the treacherous aggression by Hitlerite Germany.

It had been a dramatic shift in attitude by the United States, which had looked on the Soviet Union as a hostile nation since a year earlier, when Stalin and Adolf Hitler had signed a pact in which both nations pledged solemnly not to attack one another.

A day after arriving in Moscow, fifty-year-old Harry Hopkins, an Iowa native and son of a harnessmaker, was meeting face-to-face with Stalin behind the high, forbidding walls of the Kremlin, the seat of power in the Soviet Union. While the U.S. envoy was explaining why Roosevelt had sent him, the five-foot-four Stalin remained inscrutable. British prime minister Winston Churchill, after a visit to Moscow, had described the Soviet leader as having "all the charm of a cobra and is just as deadly."

When Hopkins finally paused for breath, Stalin bluntly demanded that the United States declare war on Nazi Germany. Hopkins evaded a direct reply but said that President Roosevelt, who had repeatedly assured American mothers that their sons would not be sent into "foreign wars," would supply the hard-pressed Red Army with a flood of tanks, airplanes, artillery pieces, trucks, jeeps, and other military accoutrements.

Earlier in the year, at Roosevelt's insistence, Congress had passed the so-called Lend-Lease Act, which authorized the president to sell or lease military material to any anti-Nazi nation in return for any kind of direct or indirect payment "which the president deems satisfactory." In reality, the United States never expected to be paid back. Never before had a president been granted such gargantuan discretionary authority.

Large sea convoys began carrying war materials to the Soviet Union. Josef Stalin took advantage of the golden era of lend-lease to flood Washington with hundreds of Soviet technical experts and government officials. Many of these individuals were spies or other undercover agents. They went on an orgy of intelligence-gathering and, as unofficial allies of the United States, few, if any, doors were closed to them.

The official U.S. policy was to give the Soviet "friends" whatever they needed in the way of goods, blueprints, and technical data. If any more information was needed, the Soviets could visit the U.S. Government Printing Office and, for twenty-five cents, collect data that agents of other nations would have immense difficulty obtaining—and then at exorbitant cost.

Incredibly, most of the U.S. Army's and Navy's training, doctrine, and weapons manuals were offered for sale. Other sources of valuable information for the Soviet agents were the document rooms of the Senate and House in the Capitol. Although the U.S. War Department had begun tightening information available to the media, military secrets still broke into print. Foreign operatives could obtain these data by spending three cents for a newspaper.

Soviet espionage was not limited to Washington. In the months ahead, Russians came into the United States on false passports and set up spy networks around the nation. They recruited gullible or greedy Americans, and infiltrated all sectors of the nation's economic, government, and military life.

In Great Falls, Montana, first point of an air route to Fairbanks, Alaska, and then to Siberia in the eastern Soviet Union, Major George R. Jordan was contact officer between the United States and the Soviet Purchasing Commission, which was actually a front for espionage activities. Jordan took his job seriously, and before each airplane lifted off for Alaska, he inspected the baggage of all Russians on board. This procedure greatly angered the commission members, who complained loudly that their luggage had diplomatic immunity.

There were thinly veiled threats that Soviet pressure would be exerted on Washington to have him transferred, but the major remained undaunted and continued to closely examine outgoing Soviet suitcases, bags, and trunks.

After displaying hostility toward Jordan for several months, the Russians, much to Jordan's surprise, cordially invited him to be their guest at a chicken dinner in downtown Great Falls. The major was suspicious, aware that the Russians had always been tight with their money. On a few occasions when he had found himself eating with them at the airport's officers' club, they always sat silently and stone-faced until he picked up their checks.

Because of the mistrust he felt, Jordan instructed the duty officer at the control tower to telephone him at the restaurant if an airplane landed. Then he left for the dinner. It was a lengthy affair. Much vodka was consumed, although Jordan did not drink. The Russians suggested toasts to Stalin, Roosevelt, Churchill, and numerous other Soviet and U.S. public figures.

While the toasting was still in progress, a waiter slipped into the room and told Jordan he had a telephone call. It was from the control tower officer, who said an aircraft had just landed. Explaining to his hosts that there was an urgent matter to which he had to attend, the major left the restaurant.

Jordan jeeped to the airport and went immediately to where the newly arrived plane was sitting. He boarded it and went to the luggage compartment, where two armed Soviet soldiers were standing over several suitcases. With menacing looks, they tried to bar his way. When the major began pulling out the luggage, the guards began screaming about "diplomatic immunity."

Ignoring their protests, Jordan began examining the suitcases, which were made of cheap leather with white ropes tied around them. His suspicions intensified when he saw the blobs of red sealing wax over the knots. Someone didn't intend for these bags to be opened until they reached Moscow, it seemed clear to him.

Jordan had brought along two of his own armed soldiers, and they stood over him as he ripped the cords off the suitcases. In one container were a few score of highway maps, the kind that could at that time be acquired free at almost any gasoline station. On the maps had been marked what Jordan believed to be the precise location of major U.S. industrial plants.

There were other maps—military maps. Scissored out had been the spaces where the words "top secret" would have been printed.

So far Jordan had seen nothing that would warrant his confiscating the suitcases and their contents—at least not without igniting a major rumpus in Washington and more demands by the Soviets that he be ousted from his job. However, he continued looking. In another bag he found printed materials that came from Oak Ridge, Tennessee, and included such words as "Manhattan Engineer District, uranium 92, neutrons, protons, fission, cyclotron."

All of this wording was just so much gibberish to Jordan, who, like nearly all Americans, had no way of knowing that the Manhattan Engineering District was the cover name for a mammoth project to build an atomic bomb, and that the other strange words dealt with that procedure.

There was also a copy of a memo from the White House signed "H. H." It said: "Had a hell of a time getting these away from Groves." Again, Jordan had no way of knowing that Groves was Major General Leslie R. Groves, director of the supersecret A-bomb project, whose headquarters was in Washington.

By now Jordan realized that the Soviets had invited him to dine so he would be absent when these materials arrived. Although highly suspicious, none of the materials seemed to involve espionage. Certainly Jordan could not have made a big fuss over some common road maps or something called the Manhattan Engineer District, which, he conjectured, must have been involved in public works projects in and around New York City, perhaps keeping the harbor open for ship convoys.

As for "Groves," he may have been some officious lieutenant who had been obstinate in parting with some routine materials a low-level White House staffer had been seeking.

Soon the airplane lifted off for Alaska, carrying with it the suitcases of espionage materials.[4]

Clandestine Payoffs in Mexico

COMMANDER TSUNEZO WACHI, the assistant Japanese naval attaché in Mexico City, was a busy man. In addition to his customary diplomatic duties, he was the chief of "L," Japan's largest overseas espionage network. His specific mission was to intercept messages of the U.S. Fleet in the Atlantic. By September 1941 he had broken the simple American naval code and was transmitting lengthy, detailed, and accurate reports to Tokyo on all ship movements in the Atlantic.

The Spanish-speaking nation of some 26 million people was fertile ground for Wachi's clandestine operations. Under General Lázaro Cárdenas, who held the official title of president, Mexico was involved in bitter disputes with the United States, Great Britain, and the Netherlands after Mexico had expropriated (i.e., stolen) the rich oil fields belonging to companies of those three nations in 1938. Because of the animosity displayed by the Mexican government toward the United States, Britain, and the Netherlands, Mexican counterintelligence services looked the other way at Japanese espionage activities.

As a sideline, Commander Wachi was buying mercury. This silver-white liquid element was produced in the form of mercury fulminate, a chemical mixture of alcohol, nitric acid, and mercury. Highly explosive, it was used chiefly for the percussion caps on shells and cartridges. Mercury was in extremely short supply in Japan.

Wachi, a smooth and clever operative, had already acquired an enormous amount of mercury—two thousand nine-pound bottles—by means of fattening the pocketbook of a Mexican general. Then Wachi began preparations for sneaking this heavy shipment out of the country. The large bottles were secreted in drums, with bronze and other metal scrap piled on top to hide the mercury.

In late September the large drums were being loaded onto a Japanese ship when some mercury spilled out. Not only did the Japanese spy want to keep the shipment secret, but also the Mexican government had the element on its embargo list, meaning it was not to leave the country.

Wachi's illegal machination could well blow up into a major scandal: a Japanese officer breaking Mexican law and trying to ship a huge amount of mercury to strengthen Japan's already formidable military juggernaut. However, in the event of just such a contingency, he had smuggled in a large number of $1,000 bills, a preferred currency of Mexican big shots on the take.

Wachi immediately called on his main contact in Mexico City, a wealthy and influential banker, who made a few quick telephone calls. Then the banker told the spy that the potentially blockbuster story could be suppressed, and he gave the Japanese spy a list of Mexican officials to be paid off. Heading the list was $100,000 for President Lázaro Cárdenas (a sum equivalent to $1 million in 1998).

Wachi eagerly paid the blackmail "fees." He was on the brink of a major espionage coup, so this was no time for him to receive a rash of media publicity and be called back to Japan in disgrace for botching the mercury shipment (which eventually reached Japan).

An American major, disgruntled after being booted out of the U.S. Army for some indiscretion, was already on Wachi's payroll, at $2,000 per month. Using the code name Sutton, the cashiered officer had been providing the Japanese spy with detailed reports on shipping in the Panama Canal. From his own decoded intercepts, Wachi knew that Sutton's intelligence was highly accurate.

When war would break out between Japan and the United States, Wachi planned to send Sutton to Washington, where he still had numerous friends in high places from whom high-grade intelligence might be extracted. In late November 1941, with war in the Pacific seeming to be a certainty, Sutton left for Washington, where he began frequenting an old haunt, the Army-Navy Club on Farragut Square, a popular watering hole for military officers.[5]

Urgent: Hide the Suez Canal

LIEUTENANT JASPER MASKELYNE, a renowned illusionist and magician in peacetime who had gained fame performing his legerdemain throughout Europe, had a frustrating experience before being accepted into the British Army. After the outbreak of war on September 1, 1939, he had been convinced that he could adapt the techniques of stage magic to the battlefield. But each time Maskelyne had tried to join up, army enlistment officers explained politely that Great Britain's need was for young fighting men, not thirty-eight-year-old magicians.

In mid-1940 a family friend had secured an appointment for Maskelyne with white-haired Professor Frederick Lindemann, the scientific adviser to Prime Minister Winston Churchill. Lindemann was crusty, opinionated, contemptuous of younger scientists, and interested only in facts, not illusions or sleight-of-hand techniques. So he sat back in his chair and listened skeptically as Maskelyne made his sales pitch.

"There are no limits to the effects I can create on the battlefield," Maskelyne exclaimed. "I can create cannon where they don't exist and make ghost ships sail the seas. I can put an entire army in the field and make airplanes invisible."

Lindemann was fascinated, although he was not certain if he was being confronted by a genius or a crackpot selling snake oil. However, Britain was being threatened by an invasion of Adolf Hitler's seemingly invincible war juggernaut, which had just conquered most of Western Europe in an amazingly short time. So perhaps a dose of magic might help, Lindemann finally concluded. There was certainly nothing to lose by trying a radically different approach to the concepts of warfare. A few weeks later, Jasper Maskelyne received a commission in the British Army.

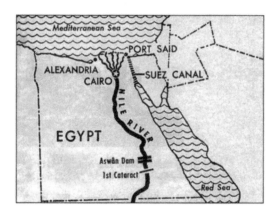

Location of the Suez Canal.

While the magician was in a training camp in England learning with which hand to salute, in far-off Tripoli, Libya, German General Erwin Rommel arrived in a Luftwaffe airplane on February 12, 1941. Rommel, a Hitler favorite, had been sent by the führer to rescue the floundering Italian Army, which was in danger of being kicked out of North Africa.

Two months earlier, British General Archibald Wavell and his reinforced army in Egypt had launched a full-blooded offensive against Marshal Rudolfo Graziani's numerically superior Italian Army. Soon the Italians were in full retreat, and Wavell's "Desert Rats," as his men would proudly call themselves, advanced 650 miles across the scorched landscape of Libya. By February 7, 1941, the Desert Rats, at a cost of 500 dead and 1,200 wounded, had taken 130,000 prisoners, 400 tanks, and 1,300 guns.

Adolf Hitler expected monumental things from Erwin Rommel, who had brought along the bronzed young warriors of the Afrika Korps to reinforce the Italian troops he would command. Rommel's goal was to drive the British all the way back across Libya and into Egypt, then cross the Suez Canal and seize the vast oil fields of the Middle East, on which Great Britain depended for much of her fuel.

Shortly after dawn on March 24, 1941, Erwin Rommel struck. His panzers destroyed the British 2nd Armoured Division, captured the port of Benghazi, overran the Indian Motor Brigade, trapped the Australian 9th Division in the port of Tobruk, and sent the remainder of the British Army reeling in disarray eastward all the way back to the Egyptian border. Now the triumphant Rommel awaited the order from Hitler to charge into Egypt and seize the Suez Canal.

In the meantime, the celebrated illusionist Lieutenant Jasper Maskelyne had arrived in Cairo and was assigned to the Camouflage Section of British headquarters in the Middle East. He was suffering from renewed pangs of frustration: the army brass didn't know exactly how to employ him.

Then, in early September 1941, Major Geoffrey Barkas, a movie set designer before the war, called on Maskelyne. The two men had known each other for years, both having been in show business. Barkas was chief of the Camouflage Section.

In a purposely casual tone, Barkas said that the brass had an urgent mission for the magician: hide the Suez Canal. Going along with what he thought was a joke, Maskelyne replied, "Hide it? Hell, I was hoping for some difficult task!"

"It's no joke," Barkas assured the illusionist. "They want something done to protect it from Luftwaffe bombers. It can't be done, of course, but you've got to do it!"

Running in a north–south direction for more than one hundred miles, the Suez Canal links the Mediterranean and Red Seas. The narrow waterway's presence was vital to the British because it reduced by a few thousand miles the shipping distance between London and ports in the Middle East. The canal was only about sixty-five yards wide and some forty feet deep at most points. If Luftwaffe bombings were to block the vital lifeline, British sea convoys would have to take the much longer, far more hazardous route around the Cape of Good Hope, at the southern tip of the African continent.

Already the Luftwaffe had tried to drop mines in the canal. To make it more difficult for the Luftwaffe to temporarily block the relatively narrow canal by sinking a ship in transit, minesweepers patrolled the passageway constantly, and antitorpedo nets were stretched a short distance underwater. However, the British high command in Cairo wanted to increase the canal's security, so it had tapped Lieutenant Maskelyne to weave his magic.

Delighted to have the daunting challenge, Maskelyne and another member of what had come to be known as the Magic Gang flew to the canal to inspect its defenses, which consisted of a few old antiaircraft guns dug in at what were considered the most vulnerable points.

Maskelyne's companion was totally pessimistic and urged Maskelyne to drop the project. But the magician returned to Cairo convinced he could make the Suez Canal vanish. He was confident that the same optical principles he had applied on countless stages across Europe for so many years would also work in this instance.

Maskelyne worked tirelessly and in great secrecy for many days and nights, conjuring up one black magic trick after the other, always having to discard them when they proved to be impractical. He became discouraged, then depressed. No illusion problem had ever licked him; now this one threatened to do so.

Then, just as he was on the brink of admitting to the British brass that he could not do the job, Maskelyne was suddenly struck by a solution to the monumental problem. During his long stage career he had used sudden puffs of smoke and flame to obscure a disappearance, or to exchange objects, or to draw the audience's attention to a specific part of the stage. No one, he knew, could

British warship passing through the Suez Canal. (National Archives)

ever resist the temptation to cast his eyes at an unexpected burst of flame or smoke puff.

Now he would apply that same principle to hoodwink Luftwaffe bombardiers when they approached the Suez Canal at night. The solution to his problem could be found in the searchlights at the antiaircraft gun batteries he had seen at critical points while touring the waterway. If enough searchlights were installed along the canal, Maskelyne concluded, a curtain of bright illumination could be created. German airmen trying to see through that intense veil of light would find it impossible to pick out the canal in their bombsights.

When the magician ran his scheme past his compatriots, they were pessimistic. Could he acquire enough new searchlights? Probably not, but the luminosity of those obtained could be intensified. Would the machination work in the daylight? No doubt it would, as anyone who has been temporarily blinded by a photographer's flashbulb in outdoor brightness could know.

As anticipated, there was an acute shortage of high-intensity searchlights in North Africa. Undaunted, Maskelyne and the Magic Gang set about researching means to magnify the power of each beacon they managed to scrounge. After much trial and error, they finally settled on a Rube Goldberg technique for magnifying the light's intensity. It consisted of twenty-four small tin reflectors welded to a curved steel band that fit around the searchlight lens. This adaptation divided a single searchlight into twenty-four individual beams. Each one was capable of covering roughly the same area of the sky as the original, projecting each of these twenty-four beams nine miles into the heavens.

Still, Maskelyne was not satisfied with the modification. He decided that the device could be improved if the twenty-four reflectors could be made to spin swiftly, thereby creating a dazzling cartwheel of light whirling through the sky. Working with an electrician from the Royal Engineers, the magician perfected the second modification.

Until now, Maskelyne's dazzling-light working model was merely a theory. Could it produce the desired effect against pilots and bombardiers? A demonstration was set for the night of September 21. The working model was set up in the dark desert outside Cairo, and Maskelyne lifted off as a passenger on a Royal Air Force transport plane.

When nearing the locale of the experimental searchlight, the pilot radioed the ground to ignite the beam. Off in the distance the magician in the aircraft could spot twenty-four exceptionally bright fingers reaching far up into the black sky. As the aircraft drew nearer, the white slivers began rotating madly and turned the night into day. Dazzling iridescence flooded the pilot's compartment and the cabin. The glare seemed to rip through eyelids, making it impossible for those on board to act rationally.

Suddenly the pilot lost control and the aircraft began spinning crazily downward. With bright specks dancing before his eyes, he tried to read the altimeter. It registered four hundred feet. Just before the plane would crash, the pilot managed to right it. All of those on board resumed breathing.

In the weeks ahead, a chain of twenty-one searchlights with the adaptations covered the entire length of the Suez Canal. The Luftwaffe flew numerous missions in an attempt to penetrate the dazzling curtain of light. All failed. The canal remained securely "hidden."[6]

A Covert Cruise in the Pacific

NAVY CAPTAIN MITSUO FUCHIDO, who was regarded as one of the most brilliant young officers in the Imperial Japanese Navy, and about one hundred other carrier-based pilots were called together in Tokyo, sworn to secrecy under pain of death, and had a blockbuster dropped on them. Fuchido would lead an attack on the U.S. Pacific Fleet anchored at Pearl Harbor, Hawaii. It was October 4, 1941.

There remained a major need to conduct a reconnaissance of the route the invasion fleet would take between Japan and Pearl Harbor. Obviously, a carrier or a battleship could not be sent on the mission; rather, the information would have to be obtained by covert means.

Toward the end of October, the Japanese ocean liner *Taiyo-maru* sailed from Yokohama for a carefree cruise to Hawaii. Among those in the crew were

Navy Commander Toshihide Maejima, a submarine expert who was masquerading as a ship doctor, and Suguru Suzuki, the youngest lieutenant commander in the navy and an aviation authority, who was disguised as the assistant purser. Suzuki was the son of a general and the nephew of a famous admiral.

How well Maejima and Suzuki carried out their covert missions could determine the success or failure of an impending attack against the U.S. Fleet at Pearl Harbor. The ship was jammed with genuine Japanese tourists, few if any of whom realized that the *Taiyo-maru*'s skipper had been sworn to secrecy, then ordered to alter his customary course for the cruise. The ship would sail far to the north, in the direction of the Aleutian Islands off the western tip of Alaska, then cut sharply southward to Honolulu—the precise course the Japanese fleet would soon follow to avoid detection.

Suzuki's secret task was to study sea and weather conditions on the trip to Honolulu. All through the long cruise, he took copious notes, eventually filling ten looseleaf notebooks. He checked the roll of the big ship. Could a scout seaplane be launched in those seas? It could be, he determined.

Suzuki regularly checked the wind velocity and the atmospheric pressure. Would there be any special refueling problems? Indeed there would be. Most encouraging, the young officer noted, was the fact that he had been scanning the horizon almost constantly but had not spotted a single ship.

Meanwhile on the *Taiyo-maru*, one American couple had grown uneasy, knowing that tension had been high between Japan and the United States in recent weeks. Day after day passed without an announcement of the ship's position, an unusual omittance on an ocean liner. And why was it so chilly and windy when the temperature heading toward Honolulu should have been growing warmer each day? Most alarming of all was when the two Americans tried to send a radiogram to friends in Honolulu to tell of their impending arrival and were told that no messages were being sent.

At about dawn on November 1, the *Taiyo-maru* was nearing the mouth of Pearl Harbor, a narrow passage that only a single ship could slip through. Minutes later, a launch carrying a contingent of U.S. marines edged up to the liner, and the servicemen hurried to the bridge and the engine room.

Lieutenant Commander Suzuki, the "assistant purser," was standing on the bridge watching the marines come aboard and take up predesignated positions. He presumed, quite accurately, that they were to prevent any attempt to sink the ship in the entrance and bottle up the U.S. Fleet in the harbor.

Soon a group of port officials and U.S. Navy officers routinely boarded the *Taiyo-maru* to pilot it into Honolulu. Smiling and typically affable, Suzuki asked how deep the water was at the harbor entrance. The Americans gave him the answer. Were there any mines? he asked. "No," was the reply.

Suzuki, a jolly good fellow, invited three of the U.S. Navy officers to be his guests at the ship's bar as the harbor pilot steered the vessel toward its berth. In casual conversation, the host learned from the three Americans that there was a steel net across the mouth of the harbor that opened and closed automatically. Suzuki was also curious about the whirling gadget on the mast of a nearby British warship. "Oh, that's something called radar," one American responded.

Plans for the secret snooping mission called for Suzuki and Commander Maejima to go ashore to gain firsthand intelligence. But a note was brought aboard from the Japanese consul general in Honolulu advising the two undercover agents that it would be prudent for them to remain on board. So Suzuki dashed off a long list of questions to be taken back to the consul general, whose spies were to provide the answers.

On the *Taiyo-maru*, Suzuki busied himself taking countless pictures of Pearl Harbor, the ships in it, and adjacent Hickam Field, a U.S. Army Air Corps base. All the while, Japanese agents were slipping onto the liner, bringing replies to Suzuki's written questions.

When the ship was preparing to depart for Japan on November 5, four days after its arrival, Suzuki had in his possession a wealth of high-grade intelligence. He knew the thickness of the concrete roofs of the hangers at Hickam Field, and the armor and gun caliber of the U.S. warships in Pearl Harbor. He also had scores of pictures of the harbor taken from vantage points on the surrounding hills by agents masquerading as Japanese consulate staffers.

At the nearby John Roberts civilian airport, one Japanese agent paid four dollars and climbed into the open cockpit of a private airplane, which lifted off for a fifteen-minute bird's-eye view of Pearl Harbor. All the while he took scores of photographs, paying special attention to the moored U.S. battleships. This precious film was also smuggled to Suzuki on the *Taiyo-maru*.

Indicative of Suzuki's importance, the ship's skipper inquired of him if it would be all right to hoist anchor and set sail for Japan. Approval was given. Just then a Japanese agent scrambled aboard with one final intelligence nugget: precisely drawn maps of the Pearl Harbor region, with the mooring of each warship plotted.

In Japan, the carrier *Akagi*, with Captain Mitsuo Fuchido and his pilots on board, sailed near dusk on November 17. One by one, so as not to present any connection, the thirty-two capital ships in the Pearl Harbor task force slipped out of several harbors and soon were swallowed up by the night.

To cover the mass sailings, the Japanese employed a unique deception plan to thwart U.S. wireless listening posts in the western Pacific. At the great naval base at Kure, Japan, the customary extensive radio traffic crackled, a ploy designed to give the impression that the Japanese fleet was still at home. The regular carrier operator had remained behind to give these radio signals their usual "touch," his touch or "swing" being as distinctive as his handwriting.

So realistic was this machination that a Japanese admiral, not privy to the ruse, telephoned the officer in charge of the Kure base and bawled him out for the flagrant breaking of radio silence.

Meanwhile, on November 19, Lieutenant Commander Suzuki, who had just observed his thirty-third birthday, arrived back in Japan from his covert mission to Hawaii. Four days later, he was aboard the aircraft carrier *Akagi* and conducted an extensive briefing for a group of naval officers that included Vice Admiral Chuichi Nagumo, commander of the invasion task force, and Captain Mitsuo Fuchido, who would lead the air strike.[7]

Four Frogmen against Two Battleships

SHORTLY AFTER DARK on the frigid evening of December 3, 1941, the Italian submarine *Scire* slipped out of the harbor at La Spezia, Italy, amid great secrecy. The underwater vessel was supposed to be going on a routine training cruise. Actually, it was bound on a mission that promised to be either a historical achievement or a resounding disaster.

On board the *Scire* were six Italian frogmen, whose covert mission was to blow up and sink two of the British Royal Navy's most powerful battleships, the *Queen Elizabeth* and the *Valiant*, which were anchored in the harbor at Alexandria, Egypt, three thousand miles from La Spezia.

Admiral Andrew B. "ABC" Cunningham, the able commander of the British Mediterranean fleet, felt confident that the two mighty battleships were immune to enemy attack by sea. The port was well protected and vigilantly guarded.

Five miles in front of the harbor entrance were several circular minefields with remote-controlled detonation as deep as nine yards. Directly in front of the harbor were the cables of an automatic alarm system. Mother Nature also helped protect the port by having formed a natural barrier with many sandbars around the entrance, forcing approaching ships to follow a narrow, specific channel.

Moreover, the huge harbor was separated from the open Mediterranean Sea by a breakwater several miles long to the west, and another, slightly shorter breakwater to the east. The gap between these two breakwaters was only about two hundred yards. This entrance was sealed off at night by three sturdy antisubmarine nets. At regular intervals, small British launches patrolling the gap dropped depth charges along the net at irregular intervals.

Fortified towers along the breakwaters were manned by guards. At night the harbor was illuminated for several miles out to sea by many searchlights. As a final precaution, antisubmarine nets were placed around the *Queen Elizabeth* and the *Valiant*, and sentries on the two battleships were constantly on watch.

Now, in the darkness a few miles out of La Spezia, the *Scire* rendezvoused with a ferryboat that transferred three strange-looking objects, each about fifteen

Two Italian frogmen rode this torpedo into Alexandria Harbor. (Author's collection)

feet long and two feet in diameter, to specially built watertight containers attached to the hull of the submarine. These objects were secret Italian inventions: torpedoes that two men could propel while sitting astride each one.

Powered by an almost silent engine, the torpedo could travel at about three miles per hour and had a range of some ten miles. It could travel on the surface or dive to a maximum of about ninety feet. The front section held a warhead that could be detached by releasing an airscrew, and then it could be attached to the hull of a targeted ship by means of a rope pulled through a ring either at its head or on the hull of a hostile vessel. The back of one torpedo seat contained crucial equipment: steel cutters, magnetic clamps to fix the warhead to a hull, and a compressed-air net-lifter.

On board the *Scire* were six torpedo-riders, who called their vehicles *maiali* (pigs). They had been training for this audacious mission for several months. Technicians in the Italian Navy had built a precise model of Alexandria Harbor, noting all the details from the frogmen's perspective, especially the intricate defenses.

Three torpedoes with two frogmen riding each were to invade Alexandria Harbor. Leading the assault would be twenty-seven-year-old Lieutenant-Captain Luigi Durand de la Penne. He and his companion, Leading Seaman Emilio Bianchi, were to tackle the *Valiant*. Captain Antonio Marceglia and Leading Seaman Spartaco Schergat were to attack the *Queen Elizabeth*, and Captain Vincenzo Martellotta and Sergeant Mario Marino would target an aircraft carrier.

After a fifteen-day trip in rough, wintry seas, the *Scire* reached its destination and surfaced to the height of its conning tower after nightfall. Alexandria Harbor was fewer than two miles away. Meanwhile, a second Italian submarine had reached a point off the town of Rosetta, at the mouth of the Nile River, which empties into the Mediterranean a short distance east of Alexandria. This second underwater craft was to wait and pick up the six frogmen, who were to find a fishing boat and row to the submarine.

Just past 8:00 P.M. the frogmen on the *Scire* donned diving suits, over which they put a breathing device known as the Davis apparatus. Ironically this special piece of equipment had been patented in England. The submarine surfaced and the six frogmen climbed out through the turret hatch onto the

Italian submarine Scire *before departing from La Spezia on a long mission. Torpedo tubes are on deck. (National Archives)*

slippery deck, laboriously took the torpedoes from their containers, and pushed the torpedoes into the water. After the six frogmen climbed astride their vehicles, the *Scire* hurried out to sea.

Navigating the torpedoes proved to be much simpler than expected. Although the British had shown enormous ingenuity in creating a harbor thought to be impregnable, a towering lighthouse onshore swept the region with its powerful beam. Lieutenant-Captain de la Penne, the leader of the intruders, used the beacon to guide the torpedoes toward shore. The frogmen could discern the silhouettes of guards on the breakwaters.

At the narrow entrance to the harbor between the two breakwaters, the frogmen encountered their first major obstacles: three rows of steel netting just below the surface. Diving to search for an opening, they discovered that explosives were hanging from the nets. Use of their compressed-air net-cutters was ruled out: the tools might touch off the explosives.

Meanwhile, as if to accommodate the Italians' needs for concealment once they had reached the barriers, the lighthouse beam shut off. After the three torpedoes and their riders had surfaced, the brilliant beacon suddenly burst forth again, focusing on the entrance.

De la Penne and his men thought they had been detected. But the light was shining to permit a British ship jammed with troops and its three destroyer escorts to enter the port, after the barriers had been opened. The six frogmen on their mounts simply followed, and in minutes they were inside the harbor— unnoticed.

Now the frogmen parted. De la Penne and Seaman Emilio Bianchi headed for the *Valiant*, while the other two torpedoes steered in the direction of their targets. Soon the dark outline of the *Valiant* could be seen, and De la Penne cautiously steered his torpedo along the hull of the big ship at a depth of ten to twelve feet.

After the torpedo reached the middle of the ship, near-disaster struck. A steel cable wound itself around the propeller, and the "pig" sank to the bed of the harbor. Glancing around, De la Penne saw that his partner had vanished. De la Penne was crestfallen. Months of preparation and effort appeared to have been in vain. However, he managed to drag the heavy torpedo through the thick mud, and got it right under the *Valiant*. He set the fuse on the explosive-laden warhead, then lapsed into unconsciousness from the exertion.

Miraculously, De la Penne floated to the surface and regained his senses sufficiently to climb onto one of the nearby buoys to which the battleship was attached. Clinging to the buoy was his missing partner, Seaman Bianchi, who was told the mission had succeeded because the fuses had been set.

A short time later, British sentries spotted the two frogmen and took them onto the *Valiant*. There De la Penne was grilled vigorously by a British officer holding a pistol in one hand. He demanded to know what the two frogmen's mission had been. The Italian shrugged. "Never mind," replied the Briton. "We know why you are here." Then the two men were confined in the ammunition storage area below which De la Penne had attached the warhead timed to explode before long.

In the meantime, Captain Antonio Marceglia and Seaman Spartaco Schergat had steered their torpedoes to the *Queen Elizabeth*, lying three hundred yards from the *Valiant*. The "pig" dove beneath the surface, slipped under the steel net surrounding the ship, and a heavy charge was planted directly under her hull. Surfacing close to the battleship, the two frogmen on the torpedo headed for a remote dock, having been told no one patrolled that locale. Near to shore, they sank their torpedo, which was equipped with a self-destruction device, after which they scrambled onto the dock and disappeared into the night.

Elsewhere in the harbor, the team of Captain Vincenzo Martellotta and Sergeant Mario Marino had spent hours traveling around in search of their aircraft-carrier target, which had sailed a day earlier. So they placed charges on the hull of the tanker *Sagona*. While they were trying to get back out of the harbor entrance while astride their torpedo on the surface, they were spotted by guards and taken prisoner.

Now explosives had been planted on three ships. The dark harbor was deathly still—a calm before the storm.

On the battleship *Valiant*, Luigi de la Penne glanced at his watch. It was fifteen minutes before 6:00 A.M. The charge was timed to explode in twenty minutes. He asked to see the ship's skipper, Captain Charles Morgan, and was taken to him. There was no hope to halt the blast now, the Italian told the British officer, and suggested that he might want to save his crew.

Again De la Penne was asked where he had placed the charge. He refused to give the information. Then the frogman was taken back to the ammunition storage room from which his crewman, Bianchi, had been removed. Now he was alone—and waiting to be blown to smithereens.

De la Penne waited through the final agonizing minutes. His heart thumped furiously, and perspiration covered his face. He could save himself by telling where he had planted the charge, but he refused to do so. Then, *Booommmm!* The mighty explosion rocked the *Valiant.* An undetermined period of time later, De la Penne regained consciousness and again found himself floating in the water. The ship had split apart and settled on the shallow bottom of the harbor.

The frogmen leader struggled aboard the half-submerged battleship and came face-to-face with Captain Charles Morgan, the ship's skipper. The two foes merely stood and stared at one another.

A short time later, just as the sun was peeking over the eastern horizon, another gigantic blast erupted—the *Queen Elizabeth* was torn asunder and she, too, settled on the harbor bed.

Meanwhile, a third explosion ripped off the stern of the *Sagona* and badly damaged the destroyer *Jervis Bay*, which was lying beside the tanker, taking on fuel.

Off the Nile River's mouth, the Italian submarine that was to pick up the six frogmen waited in vain. All of the torpedo-riders had been captured. They had wreaked so much damage on the Royal Navy's Mediterranean fleet that not until four months later, in March 1942, did British Prime Minister Winston Churchill advise Parliament of the fate of the *Valiant* and the *Queen Elizabeth*.[8]

The Superspy at Pearl Harbor

RAIN WAS PELTING the island of Oahu, where seventy-five of every one hundred persons in the Hawaiian Islands lived. High above Pearl Harbor, the main anchorage of the U.S. Pacific Fleet, a Piper Cub was slowly circling. The pilot's passenger was twenty-nine-year-old Tadashi Morimura, a junior diplomat at the Japanese consulate in Honolulu, who was taking a sightseeing flight. It was the afternoon of December 5, 1941.

Actually, the name Tadashi Morimura was a cover. His real name was Takeo Yoshikawa, a slender, handsome man who appeared younger than his years. Although ostensibly a minor employee at the consulate, Yoshikawa was the ace Japanese spy in Hawaii. Since arriving on Oahu the previous March, he had provided Tokyo with an incredible wealth of high-grade intelligence, even though a missing finger made him readily identifiable.

A reserve ensign in naval intelligence, Yoshikawa had graduated from the Naval Academy at Etajima. Later he served as a code officer on a cruiser. In the

Master spy Takeo Yoshikawa stole
Pearl Harbor secrets. (U.S. Navy)

spring of 1940 he was asked to volunteer as a secret agent in Hawaii, an offer he eagerly accepted, although it meant he would be turned into a civilian, assume a cover name, and ostensibly be assigned to the consulate in Hawaii.

In preparation for his cloak-and-dagger assignment, Yoshikawa spent a year studying international law and the English language at Nippon University, and conducted heavy research on U.S. politics, economy, and the ships, aircraft, and equipment of the U.S. fleet.

Then, in the spring of 1941, Admiral Isokuru Yamamoto, commander of the Japanese Combined Fleet, was putting the finishing touches on Operation Z, code name for a massive sneak attack on Pearl Harbor and surrounding U.S. military airfields. Although the Japanese had a small group of spies planted on Oahu, the admiral wanted a naval intelligence expert to send back detailed and authentic information. Ensign Yoshikawa was chosen for that crucial assignment.

Although well schooled in naval lore, and bright and energetic, Yoshikawa had no training in espionage. Undaunted, as soon as he arrived in Honolulu, he began improvising his own techniques to pry intelligence from the enemy, unaware that he would become one of history's most productive spies.

Yoshikawa instinctively concluded that he would be stopped by guards if he tried to enter U.S. facilities. So during a grand tour he made of the main Hawaiian islands, followed by two automobile jaunts around Oahu, he wore loud aloha shirts like any carefree tourist and was accompanied by attractive young women from the Japanese consulate or a *geisha*. When guards saw the "tourist" was with a female, they waved the couple on past the entrances.

Twice each week, Yoshikawa took a six-hour leisurely drive around the island, and almost every day he would gaze at the Pearl Harbor area from a hill.

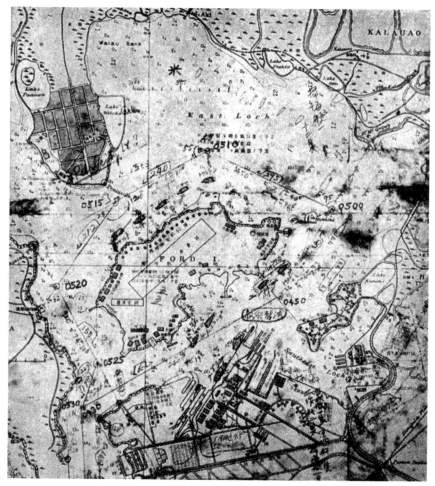

Chart used by Japanese pilots to locate targets at Pearl Harbor. (U.S. Navy)

But he wanted to get inside the fence, closer to where the American warships were anchored. Armed with a lunchbox and wearing coveralls, he tagged onto a group of laborers going to work and spent the entire day strolling around inside the fence without once being questioned. On another occasion he coerced a hostess in a private club for U.S. Navy and Army officers to hire him as a waiter at a big party. Toting a tray of drinks, he circulated among the guests, eavesdropping as much as possible on their conversations.

Two or three times each week the affable Yoshikawa, with a geisha on his arm in most instances, visited a snack bar and soda fountain run by an elderly Japanese alien on the pier at the end of the Pearl City peninsula. American sailors flocked to the place, and from them the spy learned many things: Was the fleet going out soon? Was it taking on new supplies?

On many nights the espionage agent spent time in Honolulu bars popular with U.S. servicemen. He and his female companion of the night, both congenial folks, bought the young Americans, who were usually strapped for money, all the drinks they desired. While being careful not to ask direct questions and possibly draw attention to himself, Yoshikawa was a good listener and picked up the service gossip, much of which would be valuable to Japanese intelligence.

One of Yoshikawa's favorite haunts was Shuncho-ro (Spring Tide Restaurant), a Japanese-style teahouse on Alewa Heights that commanded a superb view of Pearl Harbor and the nearby U.S. bomber base, Hickam Field. One time he feigned being too drunk to walk, so the friendly management tucked him into bed for the night in a room directly overlooking the harbor.

From that vantage point after daylight, Yoshikawa was awed by a spectacular sight: most of the U.S. fleet sailing out of the harbor. Without fear of being noticed or otherwise detected, he wrote copious notes on how long it took the armada to get out of Pearl Harbor, the kind of tactics utilized for that purpose, and the position each ship took in the armada.

Naval intelligence in Tokyo was especially delighted with that coup. If the U.S. fleet tried to sortie when the impending attack was launched, the Japanese admiral could adjust his schedule accordingly.

In early August, while tension was high between Tokyo and Washington, it was peacetime business as usual on Oahu. When the U.S. military announced that an "open house" would be held at Wheeler Field, a fighter base in the center of the island, and the public was invited, Yoshikawa and his geisha showed up. Although cameras were forbidden, the Japanese agent, who had a photographic memory, wrote up his observations in great detail as soon as he returned to the consulate in Honolulu.

A week later, Yoshikawa and a female companion took a taxi to Hickam Field. At the gate he told a bored sentry that he was supposed to meet a friend at the Officers' Club and was waved on through the gate. For nearly two hours the cab cruised around the large base without being stopped. Yoshikawa's "camera eyes" recorded countless details: the length of the two runways, the number and kind of aircraft, where the planes were parked when not in the air, and the pilots' quarters.

One day in early September, Yoshikawa received an urgent request from Tokyo: "Is there an antisubmarine net at the mouth of Pearl Harbor?" He did not know the answer. So clad in the usual aloha shirt and carrying a bamboo fishing pole, he strolled nonchalantly along a highway and then through some woods toward the mouth of the harbor. He hid in the brush until sunset.

When shadows began to creep, he began crawling on his hands and knees. Suddenly he almost bumped into two American sailors, who, for whatever their reason, were standing in the dark woods and talking. Yoshikawa froze until there was silence, then he quietly lowered himself into the waters of Pearl Harbor.

Swimming as silently as possible, he reached the channel entrance, then dived to try to find the net—if there was one. Five times he held his breath and went under, groping in the black water with his hands and feet. Nothing. Nearly exhausted, he swam back to shore. There was indeed a net, but he had been unable to find it.

On most nights Yoshikawa and his boss, Consul General Nagao Kita, met in a small room in the consulate after the staff had gone to bed. Both men were fearful that the FBI had bugged the consulate, so espionage conversations were not held. Instead, the two men, seated face-to-face, wrote messages, questions, and answers to one another. In the morning Kita would send a trusted courier in a chauffeur-driven limousine to one of the regular commercial cable offices, from where Yoshikawa's coded messages were sent to Tokyo.

Several hundred miles northwest of Pearl Harbor on December 5, the Japanese invasion fleet, which had sailed from the homeland eight days earlier, had safely passed the dangerous waters of Midway, a flyspeck island where the U.S. Army Air Corps had several reconnaissance planes based. Before turning southward for the final leg of the trek, every ship in the task force was fueled to capacity.

Just past noon, all crews in the fleet were summoned on deck. Emperor Hirohito's imperial war rescript was read, followed by a recorded exhortation from Admiral Yamamoto: "The fate of the Japanese Empire hangs on this one battle. Let every man jack do his best."

At the same time that thousands of Japanese sailors and airmen were lustily cheering Yamamoto's message, superspy Takeo Yoshikawa had completed his Piper Cub "sightseeing" flight over Pearl Harbor. Then he rushed back to the consulate to have an urgent report cabled to Tokyo:

> The following ships were in port on the morning of December fifth: Eight battleships, three light cruisers, sixteen destroyers . . . no carriers.

What the Japanese warlords in Tokyo did not know was that U.S. cryptologists had broken the J-19 code used by Consul General Nagao Kita and Foreign Minister Shigenori Togo for sending messages back and forth. Yoshikawa's blockbuster report had been intercepted and could have alerted U.S. forces throughout the Pacific that a Japanese attack on Pearl Harbor was imminent.

However, an enormous number of intercepts waiting to be decoded by U.S. intelligence created a logjam because of a shortage of cryptologists, lethargy, and interservice jealousies. So Yoshikawa's telltale intercept was placed in the "Hold" basket.

It was just past dawn on Sunday, December 7, and a brilliant sun, rising majestically over Tantalus Mountain, began drenching Pearl Harbor in its first warming rays. It was an uncommonly glorious and peaceful morning. Except for its handful of carriers, the U.S. Pacific Fleet was roosting drowsily.

*Italian propaganda piece depicts
powerful Japanese destroying
U.S. fleet at Pearl Harbor.
(National Archives)*

In Honolulu, secret agent Takeo Yoshikawa was eating breakfast at the Japanese consulate when he discerned a roaring noise that steadily grew louder. The windows started to rattle, and several pictures on the wall dropped to the floor. Dashing into the backyard, he squinted at the bright sky and spotted three aircraft overhead. A surge of elation gripped him: there were Japanese markings on the planes!

They've come! They've come! Yoshikawa told himself. Until that moment he had not known the date of the attack—or even if there actually would be an attack.

The spy clapped his hands, jumped up and down, and rushed to call to the consul general inside the consulate: "Mr. Kita! Come out! Come out! They're here!"

Kita, almost breathlessly, dashed into the yard. For long minutes the two men stood silently, holding hands and staring into the sky, which, by now, was awash with Japanese warplanes. Tears flooded their eyes. Finally Kita said simply, "Good job, Morimura!"

Yoshikawa had to remind him that his true name was not Morimura.[9]

An American Turncoat in Washington

A FEW DAYS before Christmas 1941, Washington was "invaded" by the British for the first time since the redcoats sacked and burned the U.S. capital 130 years earlier. Headed by sixty-seven-year-old Prime Minister Winston Churchill, the large delegation had come to meet with President Franklin Roosevelt and other top leaders to integrate Great Britain's war interests and operations with those of the United States.

About three weeks earlier, on learning that Adolf Hitler had declared war on the United States only two days after the Japanese attack on Pearl Harbor, Churchill's joy had been boundless. This had been the answer to his prayers. He regarded the United States as "a gigantic boiler—once the fire is lighted under it there is no limit to the power it can generate." No longer would Great Britain be standing alone against Germany's powerful war machine.

Now, at the first session of the two Allied leaders and their military chiefs at the White House, Churchill made an impassioned sales pitch. Knowing that the American people were especially furious at Japan over the Pearl Harbor treachery, Churchill hoped to sway the president and his military leaders into adopting a policy whereby Nazi Germany would be crushed first; then the full power of the U.S. and Great Britain would be hurled at the Japanese. The Germany-first strategy was adopted after only minimal wrangling.

Hardly had the crucial decision been reached in the series of conferences code-named Arcadia than it was picked up by Sutton, the code name for a former U.S. major who had been kicked out of the Army several months earlier and was on the Japanese clandestine payroll. In his espionage activities, Sutton had two factors working to his advantage: official Washington still had an unbelievably naive attitude toward security matters, and most of Sutton's friends in the army apparently were unaware that he had been cashiered from the service.

So it was a simple task for Sutton to pump what should have been top-secret information from chums with whom he socialized at the Army-Navy Club on Farragut Square. The spy sent this espionage bonanza to Tokyo through two channels. One was a German agent in Washington who transmitted reports to Berlin in code almost every night. Intelligence was also dispatched by ordinary air mail to the Japanese naval attaché in Buenos Aires, in neutral Argentina, after Sutton had written the messages in invisible ink.

No doubt Sutton's coup was received in Tokyo with great delight. It meant that the Japanese war juggernaut could maraud through much of the western Pacific without fear of massive reinforcements being sent to beleaguered U.S. outposts in the Philippines and on Guam and Wake Island.[10]

Part Four

The Turning Tide

The World's Richest Spymaster

NEIGHBORS IN THOMPSON, CONNECTICUT, had long looked on the wealthy Count Anastase Andreyevich Vonsiatsky-Vonsiatsky as an eccentric individual. Had he been poor, he would have been labeled a nut. He lived on a fabulous two-hundred-acre estate, where he painted swastikas on turtles and turned them loose to meander around the neighborhood.

Known as V-V to many, as "the count" to others, and "the millionaire" to some, his Nazi sympathies had long been evident by the time the United States went to war with Germany in early December 1941. A tall, husky man with a pleasant disposition, the count had often strolled around the community and told people that he would be leader of a government that would take over in the Soviet Union after the German Army conquered that nation and Josef Stalin was executed. He assured a number of residents that he would take them to Russia with him and appoint them to high posts in his government.

What the count's neighbors did not know was that the forty-eight-year-old, self-anointed nobleman was leader of a widespread Ukrainian underground apparatus whose goal was to overthrow the U.S. government and install a Nazi regime in its place. No doubt he was the world's richest spymaster.

As a teenager in the Ukraine, V-V had fought with the White Russian Army of Czar Nicholas II against Soviet Communist insurgents. After the Reds triumphed and the czar was executed in 1917, V-V fled to Paris, where he found a job as a chauffeur.

There his rugged good looks and engaging personality caught the eye of one of the richest women in the United States, Mrs. Marion Buckingham Ream Stephens, whose late husband, Norman F. Ream, had been a Chicago financier. The penniless young chauffeur and Mrs. Stephens, twenty-two years his senior, were married in Paris six months after they had first met. V-V promptly bestowed upon himself the phony title of count.

Two decades later, in 1939, the count first attracted the attention of the Federal Bureau of Investigation after he drove from his Connecticut mansion to New York City to put up bail for Fritz Kuhn, a former chemist with the Ford Motor Company and now leader of the German-American Bund, the Nazi organization in the United States. Kuhn had been thrown in jail for disorderly conduct and public drunkenness.

Count Anastase Andreyevich Vonsiatsky-Vonsiatsky, wearing the Nazi armband, at his desk in the war room on his Connecticut estate. (FBI)

Although neighbors regarded the count as a harmless screwball, the FBI considered him to be a dangerous, pro-Nazi radical, especially after the G-men learned from workers on the project that he had built on a hill within his estate a concrete bunker with walls two feet thick. Machine guns poked out of apertures along each wall, and a turret on top held a machine gun on a swivel.

Since 1939 the count had been building a clandestine military force, training its members on his rolling, pristine estate. Guarded by private detectives and howling bloodhounds, the acreage concealed an arsenal of rifles, machine guns, grenades, and explosives. V-V was especially proud of his goon squad of young Americans of Ukrainian heritage. They were boom-and-bang desperadoes, whom he personally trained as saboteurs and assassins.

Early in February 1942, after the United States had been at war for two months, the count climbed into his chauffeur-driven limousine and sped to Camden, New Jersey, across the river from Philadelphia. He was unaware that two G-men had been tailing him.

In Camden, V-V entered the home of Gerhard Wilhelm Kunze, who had replaced the discredited drunk and woman-chaser Fritz Kuhn as *Bundesführer* (leader) of the German-American Bund. The Feds knew all about Kunze; the FBI had been surveilling him for many months but did not have solid evidence to convict him for subversive activities.

As the G-men watched from their unmarked automobile parked along the Camden street a short distance away, another familiar figure swaggered up to the Kunze residence and was admitted. He was Kurt Molzahn, a Lutheran minister from Philadelphia. A former German Army officer and a Nazi firebrand, he had been receiving funds and his orders from Berlin through the German consulate in Philadelphia.

After nightfall the FBI agents, through binoculars, caught glimpses of the three Nazis bending over what apparently was a map of the United States and engaging in animated conversation. The sleuths concluded that something big was in the works.

Early the next morning the count took a train to Chicago. Riding along in an adjoining compartment were two G-men. Arriving in the city, the count took a taxi to the home of Dr. Otto Wilhumeit, a large, square-jawed man with a dueling scar on one cheek. "Scarface Otto," as he was known among domestic Nazis and their sympathizers, ran his midwestern espionage network from Haus Vaterland (Fatherland House), a popular saloon in Chicago.

Soon Wilhelm Kunze arrived at Wilhumeit's home, and an hour later, Dr. Wolfgang Ebell, a naturalized American who enjoyed a thriving medical practice in El Paso, Texas, joined the confab. When the covert conference broke up, the conspirators scattered around the United States. The FBI put tails on each of them.

Like a man possessed by demons, the count, traveling in luxury as befitting a man of his wealth, was dashing around the nation. His pattern was always the same, the FBI tails knew. After arriving at a shipyard or defense plant, he would make a call from a pay telephone outside, wait in his limousine, and a few minutes later, a worker from inside the facility would walk up. The chauffeur would get out and stroll around the vicinity as a lookout while the count and the employee (one of V-V's moles) would hold a brief discussion and envelopes would be exchanged.

For several weeks G-men followed the millionaire on his cross-country espionage tour. Helped by prior information obtained from FBI contacts, the sleuths were able to identify some thirty-five suspected moles in defense plants and shipyards. These moles would be dealt with later.

After the count returned to his Connecticut estate, the Philadelphia minister Kurt Molzahn paid him a visit. A few hours later Molzahn, lugging a large suitcase, departed in his automobile. FBI shadows were convinced that the suitcase held the U.S. defense secrets the count had collected during his long tour.

Instead of returning to Philadelphia, Molzahn drove to Chicago, where he handed over the piece of luggage to "Scarface Otto" Wilhumeit.

Meanwhile, Dr. Wolfgang Ebell had returned to his thriving medical practice in El Paso after the powwow of Nazi espionage leaders in Chicago a few weeks earlier. The seemingly always present Wilhelm Kunze now arrived in El Paso at about the same time that Wilhumeit was driving away from Chicago to take the precious suitcase to Ebell.

A day after receiving the piece of luggage from Wilhumeit, Ebell and Kunze drove across the bridge over the Río Grande into Mexico, going directly to a fishing village five miles south of Veracruz on the Gulf of Mexico. At the request of the G-men, Mexican police had taken over the surveillance. Soon the Mexican lawmen watched as Ebell and Kunze handed the suitcase to a pair of native fishermen, who had been bribed earlier by the Nazi spies.

The FBI agents in El Paso were convinced that it had been arranged for the two Mexican accomplices, who were eager for U.S. greenbacks and knew nothing about ideology, to rendezvous under cover of darkness with a German U-boat offshore. But the G-men were totally unconcerned. Due to an intricate counterespionage technique that had been in operation for more than two years, FBI contacts in each defense plant and shipyard visited by Vonsiatsky-Vonsiatsky had been given phony information that was cleverly allowed to fall into the hands of the count's moles. So it would be the bogus U.S. defense secrets that would find their way to the spymasters in Germany.

For months, FBI Director J. Edgar Hoover in Washington had been keeping in close touch with his men's surveillance of the count's espionage network, but the supersleuth bided his time until he was certain the Justice Department had a watertight case. Suddenly Hoover flashed the word to strike. In a series of deft actions, the G-men nabbed all five of the ringleaders.

The accused spies appeared before Federal Judge J. Joseph Smith in Hartford, Connecticut, in July 1942, and all of them, except for the Lutheran minister Kurt Molzahn, pleaded guilty. Molzahn was tried, convicted, and given a ten-year sentence. (Later, under circumstances that would remain a mystery, the clergyman was pardoned.)

Bundesführer Wilhelm Kunze was nailed with the stiffest sentence: fifteen years. Curiously, the espionage and sabotage network's mastermind and driving force, Count Anastase Andreyevich Vonsiatsky-Vonsiatsky, received the lightest sentence: five years. Possibly he had sold out his confederates in return for leniency.[1]

The Plot to Blow Up the Pan Am Clipper

IN APRIL 1942 Adolf Hitler stood on the threshold of victory over what British Prime Minister Winston Churchill called the Grand Alliance—the United States, Great Britain, and the Soviet Union. Through the ruthless and skillful employment of his powerful war machine, the führer had in two and a half years planted the swastika across an enormous swath of Europe and the Mediterranean.

At sea, Great Britain and the United States were suffering a calamity. German U-boats had been inflicting tremendous losses on Allied shipping in the

Atlantic, interdicting the supply lifeline between the two nations. German submarines were sending an average of five Allied merchant vessels to the bottom of the ocean every twenty-four hours.

Consequently the only relatively safe—and certainly the fastest—way for passengers to travel between the United States and Europe was on the Pan American Clipper, a large, amphibious airplane with a 130-foot wingspan that landed and took off from the Tagus River at Lisbon, the capital of neutral Portugal.

Since the outbreak of the war in Europe on September 1, 1939, Lisbon had been transformed from a serene, stately metropolis into a hubbub of feverish commerce, espionage, and international intrigue. German spies kept close watch on the Tagus River to determine the identity of those who came and went on the twenty-seat Clipper, which made three New York round trips weekly.

In Berlin, the Oberkommando der Wehrmacht apparently concluded that the Clipper flights provided means for boosting the American and British war effort, and at the same time were harming the Axis coalition (Germany, Italy, Japan, and their satellites). So at a staff conference in April, Field Marshal Wilhelm Keitel, who had been by Adolf Hitler's side since before the conflict erupted, ordered Admiral Wilhelm Canaris, chief of the Abwehr, to sabotage the New York-to-Lisbon flights by blowing up the Clipper.

Keitel was sort of a minister of the interior for the armed forces, an administrator at the highest level who did not, in the strictest sense of the meaning, intervene in field operations. He was a powerful figure in the Third Reich, and when he spoke, subordinates leaped to do his bidding.

As soon as the Berlin conference adjourned, diminutive, white-haired Admiral Canaris passed Keitel's order to his staff. Blowing up the Clipper should prove to be an easy task. There were already in excess of one hundred Abwehr agents in Lisbon, with perhaps another hundred elsewhere in Portugal.

No sooner had Canaris set the wheels in motion in the Clipper caper than he began scheming to thwart his own order, because the wily admiral was a key leader in the Schwarze Kapelle, which for two years had been conspiring to get rid of Adolf Hitler and his Nazi regime.

For self-preservation, Canaris had had to give the Clipper sabotage order, since he knew his every move was being carefully monitored by Brigadeführer (Brigadier General) Walther Schellenberg, the thirty-two-year-old chief of the Sicherheitsdienst (SD), the intelligence branch of the SS. Boyish, charming, ruthless, and highly ambitious, Schellenberg had a goal to one day become head of combined intelligence agencies, an objective that would require getting rid of Canaris by catching him in some malfeasance.

Following orders from Berlin, the Abwehr chief in Lisbon formed a three-man team of his most daring operatives, and the four men began drawing up a scheme to blow up the Clipper. The task appeared to be a simple one; there were no armed guards at the airplane's dock on the Tagus. All the saboteurs would have to do was to wait until the passengers and crew left the Clipper,

Wartime travelers disembark from a Pan Am Clipper in Lisbon. (Pan Am Airways)

then stroll toward the plane carrying suitcases loaded with explosives and blast-ing caps. Any onlookers would not be suspicious, because the three saboteurs resembled the passengers who got on and off the Clipper thrice weekly.

On the appointed day, everything went off as planned—like clockwork. A bomb with a timing device was placed in the Clipper's cargo hold, and the Abwehr agents casually walked away, got into an automobile, and drove off.

Meanwhile, Canaris had arrived in Lisbon, perhaps on routine business, perhaps to thwart the destruction of the Clipper. Whatever may have been the case, the admiral, after learning that the ticking bomb had been planted, con-jured up an excuse to have it removed. So two agents especially loyal to him crept into the Clipper under cover of darkness and retrieved the explosive.

A few hours later, the airplane lifted off from the Tagus and set a course for Port Washington, outside New York City. Passengers and crew would never know that an infernal device, timed to explode while the Clipper was high over the Atlantic, had been planted and then removed.[2]

Lady Luck Flies with the Führer

DURING THE SUMMER OF 1942 Karl-Friedrich Goerdeler, a former *Oberbürger-meister* (mayor) of Leipzig, Germany, called at the headquarters of Field Mar-shal Günther Hans von Kluge in a gloomy forest near Smolensk on the Russian

Front. Goerdeler traveled under a guise of great mystery and called himself Pfaff. He was dressed as an itinerant preacher and announced that he had come to save the souls of the *Feldgrau* (field gray, the average German soldier).

Actually, an appointment had been made for him to see Kluge, commander of Army Group Center and one of Adolf Hitler's favorite combat leaders. Known as "Clever Hans," Kluge was a nonsmoker and teetotaler with a reputation for bravery. Since 1938 he had adroitly avoided being drawn into a conspiracy by a tight little knot of prominent military officers, government officeholders, civil leaders, and clergymen to "eliminate" the Führer.

Two of the most active members of the anti-Hitler conspiracy, the Schwarze Kapelle, were members of Kluge's inner circle, forty-one-year-old General Henning von Tresckow, the chief of staff, and thirty-six-year-old Major Fabian von Schlabrendorff, an energetic and brilliant staff officer. For many months Tresckow and Schlabrendorff had been discussing plots to seize Hitler and have him tried for treason against the German people. Each time the führer visited the Eastern Front, the schemes were thwarted because the target was too closely guarded and always had gone to extraordinary means to conceal his movements.

Finally, the two officers decided that the only way their plans to eliminate Hitler could be realized was if their boss, Field Marshal von Kluge, with whom both were highly influential and on close terms, could be persuaded to join the conspiracy. Broaching the question to Kluge could result in their own executions, they realized. However, they arranged for Kluge to accept an appointment with Karl-Friedrich Goerdeler, who would try to recruit Kluge.

While Kluge and Goerdeler were strolling through the forest, the former oberbürgermeister explained that the conspirators, by circuitous means, had been in touch with Winston Churchill, and that neither the British nor the U.S. government was willing to make promises in advance as to the postwar treatment of the Third Reich.

Goerdeler explained that the conspirators would have to get rid of Hitler and his Nazi regime first and seek terms from Great Britain and the United States afterward. Josef Stalin, the Soviet Union dictator, was not even mentioned. German conspiracy leaders presumed that once peace had been made and a democratic government established in Berlin, the Western Allies would join the German Army in fighting the Soviets.

Knowing that his own life could be forfeited, Goerdeler asked the key question of Kluge: Would the field marshal put his office and stature behind the conspiracy? Kluge halted and stared at the other man. For long moments he made no reply. Then, no doubt to Goerdeler's great relief, Kluge said that ending the war was highly desirable, but he refused to take any action until Hitler was dead. Goerdeler rushed back to Berlin to inform conspiracy leaders that Kluge was willing to get aboard. Now it would be necessary only to wait for the opportune time to murder the führer.

That opportunity arrived about six months later, on February 2, 1943, when German Field Marshal Friedrich von Paulus's Sixth Army, including 24 generals and 90,000 ragged, frozen, and starving men, surrendered to the Red Army after being surrounded at Stalingrad. The momentous battle had claimed an additional 175,000 German dead and wounded.

Hearing of the disaster, one of the worst ever suffered by a modern army, Adolf Hitler flew into a rage and branded Field Marshal von Paulus an incompetent and fully responsible. The calamity infuriated many German generals—including Günther von Kluge. All knew full well that Hitler himself had been to blame for the Stalingrad catastrophe by repeatedly refusing Paulus's urgent requests to permit what remained of the Sixth Army to withdraw to new defensive positions before it was trapped.

Now Kluge was ready to act. At the instigation of his two confidants, General von Tresckow and Major von Schlabrendorff, he invited Hitler to visit his headquarters at Smolensk, and the führer agreed to come. Tresckow and Schlabrendorff had a simple plan: a bomb would be hidden in Hitler's private airplane and timed to explode while on the return flight from Smolensk.

Obtaining explosives and fuses, Tresckow and Schlabrendorff constructed the bomb. They inserted packages of explosives into a package that resembled two bottles of Cointreau, the only liqueur sold in square containers. A wrapping was fashioned so the fuse could be triggered from the outside without having to disturb the package. The bomb would be set running merely by depressing a small trigger, which would break a bottle of corrosive acid onto a wire holding back the detonating pin.

At noon on March 13, 1943, Adolf Hitler's Focke-Wulf-200 transport plane, escorted by a squadron of Me-109 fighters, roared above Smolensk, then swooped in for a landing at the headquarters airstrip. The führer, along with some thirty staff officers, his personal physician, and his private chef carrying special "unpoisoned" food supplies, stepped from the plane. Field Marshal von Kluge and General von Tresckow were on hand to greet the new arrival.

Hitler was driven to Kluge's headquarters, where the situation on the Russian Front was discussed for an hour. Then the führer was escorted to the dining room for lunch. Before the meal was served, Tresckow approached Colonel Heinz Brandt, a member of Hitler's personal staff, and asked him nonchalantly if he would take along a package containing two bottles of Cointreau for a friend, General Helmuth Stieff, in Berlin. Brandt cheerfully agreed.

After Hitler consumed the meal prepared by the cook he had brought along—the führer's doctor first had to taste the food in his sight—another hour's conversation was held with Kluge. Then Hitler and his entourage were driven to the airstrip for the return flight.

When Hitler was preparing to board the Focke-Wulf-200, Major Schlabrendorff energized the mechanism of the bomb, setting it to explode in thirty minutes, when the plane would be at eight thousand feet. Then he handed the package to Colonel Brandt, who placed it in the luggage compartment of the aircraft. Minutes later, the Focke-Wulf roared down the runway and lifted off. Schlabrendorff rushed back to headquarters and telephoned conspiracy leaders in Berlin that the führer's plane was in the air.

Late that afternoon, a teletype message was received at Kluge's office: Hitler and his entourage had arrived safely at his battle headquarters near Rastenburg, a complex of buildings in East Prussia. Flabbergasted, Schlabrendorff found an excuse to fly to Rastenburg immediately. There he was able to retrieve the bomb package before it was sent on to General Stieff in Berlin.

Schlabrendorff promptly left to return to Smolensk. As soon as he was alone, he opened the package and discovered, to his consternation, that Lady Luck had been flying with Hitler. The fuse had worked and the acid had started to seep onto the detonator wire. Before the striker was freed, however, the acid had frozen.

Only later would the conspirators learn that the führer's personal pilot had been approaching weather turbulence, and to spare Hitler any discomfort, he had taken the Focke-Wulf to a much higher altitude. This had caused the temperature to drop dramatically in the luggage compartment where Colonel Brandt had put the package, causing the acid to freeze.[3]

Rommel's Secret Informant

WINSTON CHURCHILL, angry and frustrated, was stalking back and forth in a large conference room at the headquarters of the British Eighth Army outside Cairo, Egypt. Waving a long cigar for emphasis, he growled to his assembled military commanders: "Rommel! Rommel! Rommel! What else matters but beating him?" It was mid-August 1942.

Churchill had flown to Cairo to give the British Army in the desert what he described as "the biggest shakeup in its modern history." The prime minister was shocked that during the first two weeks of June, Erwin Rommel had administered a crushing defeat to the British, destroying 130 of 325 tanks in one day alone; then inflicting 75,000 casualties on the British while driving them hundreds of miles eastward across the desert wastes of Libya to the hamlet of El Alamein, near the Egyptian border.

Compounding Churchill's astonishment was the fact that Rommel, at most, had commanded fewer than 100,000 men, of whom about half were Italians of varying degrees of fighting ability, while the British had in the theater some 750,000 men in uniform.

As promised, Churchill sacked his Middle East commander, General Claude Auchinleck, most of his key staff officers, and General Neil Ritchie, leader of the decimated Eighth Army. The new leader in the Middle East was

General Harold R. L. G. Alexander, while General Bernard L. Montgomery was made commander of the Eighth Army.

Rommel's monumental victories in North Africa had elevated him to legendary status on the home front in Germany. Adolf Hitler was exuberant, and promoted the officer now known as the Desert Fox to field marshal, the youngest in German history.

Before departing for London, Churchill told his new generals in what was virtually an order: "I don't want the Desert Fox chased into a hole—I want him killed!"

Other than for Rommel's acknowledged tactical skill, audacity, energy, and personal courage, what had been the secret of his scintillating battlefield successes over the British? That puzzling question had been debated at length by Churchill and his generals in Cairo. But no one at that conference had any way of knowing that a bold and clever Italian spy had been providing Rommel with a wealth of detailed information about the British army in North Africa, including its tactical plans.

Back in January 1941, before Rommel had arrived to take charge of German and Italian forces, the Italian was employed in the U.S. embassy in Rome. Hardworking, dedicated, intelligent, he was regarded as a prized employee. Actually he was an exceptionally cunning agent of SIM, the Italian secret service, which had falsified papers to get the embassy to hire him. His mission was to steal secret documents.

An expert in picking locks (it was said that he had served a term in an Italian prison when caught engaging in that practice in a bank before the war), the SIM operative saw his chance to score an intelligence bonanza when Colonel Norman E. Fiske, the military attaché, left Rome for a weekend in August. Rapidly picking open Fiske's safe, the Italian reached inside and pulled out the "Black Code," a secret cipher used by U.S. military attachés throughout the world and considered by Washington to be unbreakable.

Working swiftly, one ear tuned to the approach of embassy personnel, the SIM agent photographed the Black Code, then returned it to its place in the safe. Then the secret code was turned over to Cesare Amé, the SIM chief in Rome, who provided the Germans with a copy.

In Cairo, Colonel Frank Bonner Fellers, the military attaché at the U.S. embassy, had the covert mission of keeping the War Department in Washington informed of British military and diplomatic activities. He was liked and trusted by the British, so he had no trouble gaining everything he needed to know.

From early October 1941, when the United States was officially neutral, until August 1942, when America was at war with Germany and Italy, Fellers transmitted to Washington a daily report on British strength, reinforcements, equipment, morale, and plans throughout the Middle East and the Mediterranean. His reports included analyses of commanders' abilities, reputations, and tactical skills; the movements of warships and supply convoys; and the bases and serviceability of tank and air squadrons.

Field Marshal Erwin Rommel (second from right) with his commanders in North Africa. (National Archives)

Fellers had always been highly security-conscious. Each day he took his reports to the Egyptian Telegraph Office in Cairo and had them flashed to Washington in the presumably unbreakable Black Code. Each of these lengthy messages was taken down by Nazi agents who had penetrated the telegraph office, decoded, and passed on to Erwin Rommel. This intelligence had provided the German commander with the broadest and clearest picture of enemy forces and intentions available to any Axis general during the war.

In the wake of Rommel's continuing series of stunning victories in the desert of North Africa—he had seemed to anticipate every move by the numerically far superior enemy army—British security officers began a secret investigation of their wireless communications to determine if any codes had been compromised. Soon their suspicions focused on Colonel Fellers after a small raid on a German wireless post in the desert disclosed that the German and Italian cryptographic services were reading the Black Code.

Although Fellers, a highly capable and conscientious officer, had been the victim of the wily Italian spy's machination in the Rome embassy, he was crestfallen to learn that his wireless traffic was being read by Rommel. The U.S. cryptographic service in Washington quickly provided Fellers with a new code, which he began using.

However, the British used the unexpected turn of events as a means for passing deceptive information to Rommel. Fellers would use a new set of ciphers to send accurate intelligence to Washington. But he continued to transmit information using the penetrated Black Code—phony intelligence to mislead Rommel.

Fewer than three weeks after Fellers began sending fraudulent information in the Black Code, Rommel, on the night of August 30–31, 1942, launched an all-out offensive. Instead of gaining the anticipated thirty miles in the moonlight, his Afrika Korps was stopped cold. Part of the British victory had resulted from misleading intelligence funneled to Rommel from a turned spy in Cairo known as Kondor. Perhaps the phony and misleading messages sent in the Black Code by Colonel Fellers also had played a major role in Rommel's defeat.[4]

The Scientist Who Knew Too Much

THE NIGHT WAS STARLIT AND CALM over the English Channel. It was nearing midnight when the ghostly silhouettes of 252 Allied vessels, many filled with 6,051 handpicked assault troops, were taking up positions off Dieppe, an old pirate lair on what was known as the Iron Coast of France. Code-named Jubilee, the operation, an assault along a fifty-mile stretch of coast at and to both sides of Dieppe, was billed as a reconnaissance in force to test German defenses. It was August 18, 1942.

The soldiers were mostly Canadians but included detachments of British and French commandos along with fifty U.S. rangers. The invaders were to blow up docks, power stations, fuel dumps, and railheads; to destroy German coastal defenses; to shoot up the Saint-Aubin airfield a few miles inland; to bring back German invasion barges for study; to steal secret papers from a divisional headquarters; and to release French prisoners held in a Dieppe jail.

Known but to a handful of soldiers and a few key British commanders was a top-secret caper in which a scientist would be escorted by bodyguards through shot and shell to observe firsthand the operation of a Freya radar perched on a three-hundred-foot cliff just west of Dieppe. That perilous secret mission had been laid on at the urgent request of Winston Churchill by the director general of Signals and Radar, Air Vice Marshal Victor H. Tait. As the Germans had ceased using radio plotting, it was crucial to devise a means for forcing them to use their standby radio transmitter at the Freya site so the scientist could observe the transition.

This would necessitate cutting the German telephone lines leading into the radar station.

In the ongoing duel of wits with their German counterparts, British scientists were eager to learn details of the Freya, the German radar with the longest range. The accuracy and plotting precision of the Freya were not known. The "assault scientist" was supposed to gain that information for them.

In one of the troop transports off Dieppe was the scientist, Royal Air Force flight sergeant Jack M. Nissenthall, the twenty-four-year-old son of a Jewish

Allied aircraft cover the Canadian withdrawal from Dieppe. (Major Keith O'Kelly [Ret.])

tailor who had immigrated to England from Poland before the war. Nissenthall had volunteered for the mission.

Tough and well conditioned (he had taken the commando training course), Sergeant Nissenthall seemed ideal for the task. Despite his tender years, he had a lengthy background in radar, both before and after the outbreak of the war. Prior to his present mission he had been assigned to radar stations in Scotland and England, which provided one flaw in his makeup that caused British intelligence officers deep concern: he knew too many British radar secrets. If captured and forced to talk, Nissenthall could provide German scientists with technical information that would swing the radar duel advantage to Adolf Hitler's camp.

Such an eventuality was unthinkable. Radar could be crucial to victory — for one side or the other. The sergeant's capture, therefore, would have to be prevented, no matter how drastic the means.

Nissenthall would be going ashore with Captain Murray Osten's A Company of the Canadian South Saskatchewan Regiment. Prior to the Jubilee force's departure from England, Osten had been called in by the regimental commander, Lieutenant Colonel Charles C. Merritt, a Vancouver, British Columbia, attorney in peacetime. Merritt informed Osten that a "radar expert" was going in with A Company on a secret mission. Osten was to provide ten riflemen to "protect" the scientist at all times. "This fellow's not to be captured," Merritt said ominously. "Orders from above."

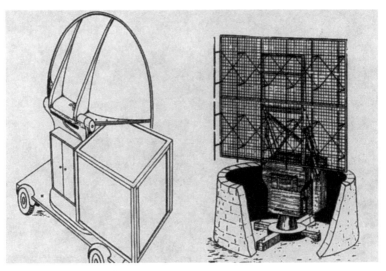

German radar: Wurzburg (left) and Freya. (Author's collection)

Captain Osten nodded his head. "I'll assign my best men to cover him," he said.

"I know that," Merritt replied. "But if he is wounded or about to be captured, you will have to deal with him. He knows too much to be taken prisoner. Is that clear?"

Osten was shocked. Indeed it was clear. If the man, a fellow soldier—The Scientist Who Knew Too Much—was about to fall into German hands, he was to be killed by his "bodyguards."

Now, a few miles off Dieppe just before dawn, ships lowered their landing craft, and the grim-faced soldiers scrambled down rope nets into the boats. After completing their various tasks onshore, members of the Jubilee force were to return to the ships in late afternoon and return to England.

As the rows of assault boats neared shore, the Channel was deathly quiet. Suddenly the tranquillity was shattered. Up and down the Dieppe coast brilliant white flares burst in the gray sky from German positions. Machine guns and antitank guns concealed in cliffside caves raked the invaders as they scrambled ashore.

Eighteen Churchill tanks crawled out of landing ships in Dieppe and bogged down on the shingle. Antitank guns fired into the helpless monsters, and within minutes most of the Churchills were twisted, burning pieces of junk, their crews dead or captured.

Just west of Dieppe, at Pourville, Captain Murray Osten and his company of South Saskatchewans had run into a buzz saw as they tried to scale the towering cliffs to seize the Freya radar station. Bitterly defending the station was the 23 Funkmess (Radar) Kompanie Luftgau Nachr, and Canadian dead and wounded were strewn around the approaches to the position.

While Nissenthall lay in a ditch with bullets hissing past like swarms of angry bees, he realized that the Canadians could not dislodge the dug-in and heavily armed Germans. Peeping over the rim of the ditch, the scientist noticed that the defenders were fighting from trenches in front of and to each side of the Freya building but that the rear appeared to be unguarded. He also spotted a telephone pole with eight wires leading up from Dieppe town, and Nissenthall knew that these lines led to a control center where approaching RAF squadrons were plotted on radar. If he could cut those wires, it would force the Germans to revert to radio plotting in the air battle raging above Dieppe.

Sergeant Nissenthall pulled wire cutters from his pack and began slithering over the bullet-swept terrain toward the unprotected rear of the Freya building. It was a hundred yards away, but he had to take a circuitous route to approach the structure from behind. He struggled forward, pouring sweat from the heat and tension. He finally reached his destination without being discovered and snipped the wires.

Slithering away, he reached a sunken road and dropped into it, then crawled back to Captain Osten's company. Panting heavily, Nissenthall slumped to the ground next to one of his bodyguards. Grinning, the man said, "Jack, I had you in my sights all the time." If the sergeant had been on the verge of capture while cutting the wires, the other man would have carried out orders and shot him.

At 11:00 A.M., according to plan, the remnants of the Jubilee force began withdrawing from the bloody coast. Nissenthall, along with the one survivor of his bodyguard team (the others had been killed or wounded), scrambled down to the smoke-covered shore. But there was no landing craft to evacuate them. Capture seemed imminent. The scientist eyed his "protector." Would his comrade really kill him as ordered?

Minutes later, a landing craft emerged on the horizon, and came closer to shore through the thick haze. The radar expert and his bodyguard swam out to it. A few hours later The Scientist Who Knew Too Much was back in England.

Militarily, Operation Jubilee had been an Allied disaster. Sixty percent of the assault force (3,625 men) were killed or captured. The Royal Air Force had 106 aircraft destroyed, and the Royal Navy lost 551 men plus a warship and 33 landing craft.

Jack Nissenthall's elation over being snatched from the jaws of death was tempered by deep depression. He had failed in his secret mission—inspecting the Freya. So he was startled to be greeted enthusiastically by Air Vice Marshal Victor Tait, who had sent him on the task. The RAF officer explained that British monitors at a listening station in southern England had picked up much valuable information on the Germans' Freya precision plotting, and

British scientists now knew for certain that the enemy would use radio transmission if his land lines failed.

This knowledge, Tait explained, would be invaluable in developing jamming techniques in the relentless radar duel of wits across the English Channel.[5]

The Dogs of Torigni

MORE THAN TWO YEARS after the Wehrmacht had conquered and occupied most of France, German commanders at Saint-Lô, a serene and picturesque town of eleven thousand people at the base of the Cherbourg Peninsula in Normandy, were growing steadily more angry and frustrated. There had been many night air raids against targets in the Saint-Lô region, antiaircraft guns had been shooting down British bombers, and crewmen had been seen parachuting to earth in the moonlight. Only a few of the Britons had been captured. Where were the rest of them? It seemed clear that the French underground had organized escape routes, the Germans were convinced. So the Gestapo was brought into the region to smash the clandestine apparatus.

Twelve miles from Saint-Lô, at Torigni, nine leaders of the local resistance gathered early each morning to discuss plans in the only place relatively immune from the prying eyes of the Gestapo—a back room in the ancient Catholic church. Among those present were Father Émile Gauraud, the village priest; Georges Lavelle, who operated a garage in Torigni; and thirty-seven-year-old Pierre Touchette, who was mentally impaired and who worked as a helper in Lavelle's business.

The Gestapo knew all three men and considered them to be harmless. Father Gauraud was dedicated to taking care of the spiritual needs of his flock. Lavelle was regarded by townsfolk as a Nazi collaborator who spent many late hours drinking and carousing with German soldiers in the local saloon. And Gestapo agents avoided getting close to the half-wit Touchette, who drooled and who slobbered on them.

Actually, Father Gauraud, diminutive and soft-spoken, was chief of the underground in the Saint-Lô region. Lavelle was his loyal and capable deputy. Only these two leaders knew that Touchette was neither a Frenchman nor an imbecile. He was a spy, a Canadian whose real name was George DuPre.

Back in 1940, DuPre had joined the Royal Canadian Air Force, but was told he was too old to learn to fly and was given a menial ground assignment. When his squadron reached England, he was eager to take an active role in the war. So when approached to become a spy and be dropped into German-occupied France, he leaped at the opportunity. Because he spoke French poorly, his British secret service controllers decided that he would masquerade as a man with the mind of an eight-year-old.

On many evenings the priest would climb onto his bicycle, pedal through the streets of Torigni, toss a friendly wave at any Gestapo agent he might pass, and ride into the countryside. Often he was on the way to help other resistance men recover containers of needed items parachuted from a British bomber.

Four times each week Father Gauraud pedaled to a barn four miles outside the village, where a radio transmitter was hidden under a large amount of loose hay. While other resistance men stood guard in the darkness nearby, the priest established contact with London.

As the Gestapo had suspected, the French resistance in the Saint-Lô area was helping downed British fliers. The Normandy escape routes began in villages farther inland, led to Torigni, and then continued to Saint-Lô. From there the evaders were escorted to the nearby English Channel coast, where they climbed into trawlers manned by legitimate French fishermen. Under a veil of night the trawlers went to sea and transferred their human cargo to speedy British launches.

Key ingredients in the escape network were the boys and girls utilized by the underground. They carried secret messages by bicycle to Saint-Lô and to other villages in the region, enjoying the "game" of outwitting the Germans. None of the youngsters knew the identity of *réseau* members, for the messages and instructions were left covertly at their homes by unknown persons.

The boys and girls were proud of their shiny bicycles, unaware that they were precise French models built in England and dropped by parachute to the resistance. These two-wheelers were different from legitimate models in that one handlebar unscrewed to reveal a space just large enough to hold a written message.

In early October 1942 a fifteen-year-old girl courier pedaled into Saint-Lô, and minutes later she lost control of her bicycle. It slid into a parked car, sending her sprawling onto the pavement. In an incredible stroke of bad luck, the automobile belonged to a Gestapo agent who had just started to enter it. Glancing downward, he saw that the impact had knocked loose half of the handlebar, and out of it protruded the incriminating secret message.

The girl was taken to Gestapo headquarters in Saint-Lô and forced to talk. Within two days, three other teenage girls involved in shuttling resistance messages were hauled in. All four of the youngsters were tortured hideously, but they did not reveal the names of the resistance leaders who had been spiriting downed British fliers out of France, for they did not know their identities.

A week later, a truck pulled into a field outside Saint-Lô, and the four girls were dragged out. Their hair was matted with dried blood, and their bodies were covered with cuts, bruises, and cigarette burns. Eyes had been blackened. Rough hands forced the girls toward an embankment. As the terrified, weeping couriers huddled together, they were riddled by machine-gun bullets and died moments later.

Father Gauraud, Georges Lavelle, and other underground leaders were devastated by news of the girls' deaths. But they pledged to continue helping

British fliers to escape. Pierre Touchette, who had been masquerading for two years as a mental incompetent, came up with an extremely novel solution to continue the crucial courier network.

Four Torigni teenage girls were recruited as couriers, and each was given a dog. They were told to live constantly with the pets, feed them, play with them, sleep with them, stroke them lovingly until girl and dog were inseparable. Meanwhile, craftsmen in the *réseau* fashioned round leather collars for the animals.

Soon the new couriers, trailed by their faithful dogs, were strolling casually along roads, paths through wooded areas, and across open pastures. Periodically the girls were stopped and searched by the Gestapo, whose agents were aware that teenagers had been used as couriers in the past. Nothing incriminating was ever found, and the girls were allowed to continue onward. All messages reached their destinations—concealed in the dogs' hollow collars.

During the two months following the resumption of the critical courier network between towns and villages, thirty-one British airmen were herded along the escape route and reached England safely.[6]

Conspiracy in Casablanca

AT HIS OFFICE in the U.S. legation in Tangier, Spanish Morocco, Lieutenant Colonel William A. Eddy of the Marine Corps was reading the decoded message from Washington. He felt a surge of excitement. President Franklin D. Roosevelt and British prime minister Winston Churchill had just put their stamps of approval on Operation Torch, an invasion of Northwest Africa. It was July 25, 1942.

Earlier in the year, Eddy had been recruited into the fledgling Office of Strategic Services (OSS) by its chief, William "Wild Bill" Donovan, who had asked Secretary of the Navy Frank Knox to send Eddy to Tangier as a naval attaché. Knox honored the request. Actually, Eddy was a spy.

Donovan had made an inspection trip throughout the vast Mediterranean region the previous year, and he had been convinced that North Africa would be a strategic battleground in the war with Nazi Germany and Italy. His vision had been vindicated.

Torch created a highly significant role for the OSS, which had been given the responsibility for secret and subversive activity. At the time, Donovan and his agency were under heavy attack from the traditional U.S. military intelligence establishment as "amateur meddlers."

"Our whole future may depend on the outcome of Torch and the accuracy of our intelligence estimates and clandestine actions," Donovan had told his staff in Washington.

Bill Eddy, who would spearhead the covert penetration of Northwest Africa in advance of the invasion, was shrewd, incisive, and energetic. Born in Syria, the son of missionaries, he spoke faultless Arabic and walked with a limp from a wound he had received in World War I, from which he emerged with a chestful of decorations.

Eddy was former chairman of the English Department at the American University in Cairo, and later he came to the United States to accept a post as president of Hobart College in New York State. After Bill Donovan tapped him to work for the OSS, he resigned at Hobart, telling the board of trustees that he had "fallen out of love with teaching." He could not tell them that he was going to become a spy for Uncle Sam.

Located on an inlet of the Strait of Gibraltar where the Atlantic Ocean joins with the Mediterranean Sea, Tangier was a hotbed of espionage and intrigue, the most critical intelligence cockpit in Northwest Africa. From his cosmopolitan perch Eddy had rapidly established a secret espionage network in Morocco, Tunisia, and Algeria. He had secret listening posts in several major cities, and each was given a code name. Tangier was Midway. All intelligence was sent to Midway, where it was given a field evaluation and then transmitted in code to Washington and London.

Midway's transmitter was located on the roof of the U.S. legation. But it had to be moved elsewhere after a diplomat's wife, who knew nothing about Eddy's true role, complained that a mysterious tapping noise on the roof was keeping her awake at night.

Eddy saw to it that weapons and ammunition were funneled to leaders of the French underground in Northwest Africa. From Gibraltar, the British rock fortress at the mouth of the Mediterranean Sea, U.S. rifles, tommy guns, pistols, ammunition, and explosives were carried by boat across the Strait of Gibraltar to the U.S. legation in Tangier. Under cover of darkness, the weapons and ammunition then were smuggled into Casablanca. There they were packed in cartons labeled "tea" and "sugar," loaded onto mules, and distributed to the underground leaders over a vast area.

In August Colonel Eddy was summoned to OSS headquarters in London, where a dinner party was given for Lieutenant General George S. Patton, Jr., who would lead a U.S. force ashore at Casablanca. Wearing his marine uniform decorated with five rows of World War I ribbons for valor, Eddy limped into the dining room. "I don't know who the hell he is," the irrepressible Patton remarked, "but the son of a bitch's been shot at a lot, hasn't he?"

For months, Colonel Eddy and his covert operatives had been keeping a close tab on the German Armistice Commission, which was living in splendor in Casablanca's plush Miramar Hotel. The Armistice Commission's task was to enforce the terms Adolf Hitler had imposed on the French in 1940 after the Wehrmacht conquered France in only six weeks. Based on the information he had received from his agents in Casablanca, Eddy hatched a scheme to deal with the German commission. On October 15 he rushed to London to present his proposal to U.S. Major General Mark W. Clark, chief planner for Torch.

Eddy was ushered into Clark's office, and after a brief exchange of niceties, he handed the general a sheet of paper stamped top-secret. The lanky, forty-seven-year-old Clark, who had been wounded as an infantry captain in World War I, began reading:

> I recommend that on D-Day, when the landing operations actually begin, I be authorized to arrange for the assassination of the members of the German Armistice Commission at Casablanca. About twenty of the German army and navy officers live in a hotel in Casablanca and the assignments have already been made for [their assassination] to men who have the demolition materials already in their hands.
>
> I might add that our principal secret agent in Casablanca is the father of a boy who was shot as a hostage [by the Germans] in Paris recently, and the father is impatiently awaiting permission to carry out this assignment.

Clark, a daring type who was regarded as one of the U.S. Army's brightest young officers, declared, "Okay. It looks good to me."

However, when Eddy's plot reached higher levels in the U.S. military command, it was squashed. Even though the targets were German military officers, Clark was told, measures such as these simply were unacceptable.

The rejection of the assassination scheme dramatized the greenness and naïveté of the U.S. Army. While the most brutal, no-holds-barred violence had been raging in Europe for nearly three years, the American leaders were trying to follow the Marquess of Queensbury rules of "fair play" used in athletic contests.

Disappointed but undaunted, Bill Eddy tried a new tack. A black African waiter, who spoke impeccable Oxford English and could quote Shakespeare at length, worked in an upscale Casablanca restaurant that was frequented by members of the German Armistice Commission. Just before Torch forces would come ashore, the waiter, who was one of Eddy's spies, would drop Mickey Finns into their drinks, thereby rendering them helpless at a time when they were needed most by their superiors in Berlin.

This latest scheme also was rejected by those in the upper echelons in London.

However, Eddy's agents kept a constant watch on the Armistice Commission. One report stated: "The Germans in Casablanca are getting nervous and now keep their effects ready packed and have been trained to clear from the hotel, complete with baggage within fifteen minutes."[7]

Outfoxing the Desert Fox

IN THE EARLY DAYS of August 1942 Field Marshal Erwin Rommel, who was credited by his legion of admirers with possessing *Fingerspitzengefühl* (intuition in the fingertips, or a sixth sense), was planning a sledgehammer blow against the British Eighth Army in Egypt along what was known as the El Alamein front. Typically, the Desert Fox would use secrecy and surprise.

Rommel's intelligence sources indicated—accurately—that the British defenses in the southern end of the line were thin. So it was there he would strike. During successive nights Rommel would shift his crack Afrika Korps from the northern to the southern sector. Then, when all of his units were in place, he would burst through the undermanned British defenses, head toward the northeast to the Mediterranean Sea, and trap the bulk of General Bernard Montgomery's army.

Under a cloak of darkness and with great stealth, the Afrika Korps began moving to the south, leaving dummy vehicles and artillery pieces behind so the maneuver would not be detected from the air or the ground. Strict radio silence was observed during the movement.

Rommel, however, radioed his battle plan to the Luftwaffe commander who would support the attack and to Berlin and Rome. Ultra intercepted and decoded the messages, which reached General Montgomery at about the same time as they arrived at their German recipients. Consequently, Montgomery, with speed and secrecy, moved the bulk of the British armor and some 350 artillery pieces to the south. There the units lay camouflaged, concealed, and dispersed.

While awaiting the German assault, Colonel Francis W. "Freddy" de Guingand, Montgomery's chief of staff, studied maps of what was called the Ragil depression, a vast indentation in the desert, through which Rommel might attack. De Guingand noticed from a German map captured earlier that Rommel actually had little knowledge of the terrain conditions to his front in the south. In many areas the sands were shifting, deep, and treacherous—a place where German panzers might well become bogged down.

Moreover, de Guingand was convinced that Luftwaffe reconnaissance planes could not detect this flaw in Rommel's terrain knowledge, because most sandy regions looked hard from the air. So the chief of staff told Montgomery that the way to inflict a major defeat on Rommel was to encourage him to attack—through the Ragil depression.

But how could the wily Desert Fox be coerced into launching a blow through the desired sector? De Guingand thought he had the answer: "turning" two captured German spies in Cairo to provide false information to Rommel. So along with British Colonel Dudley W. Clarke, who had helped conceive and was the leader of A-Force, a huge British deception organization in the Near East and the Mediterranean, de Guingand hatched a scheme to lure Rommel into a trap.

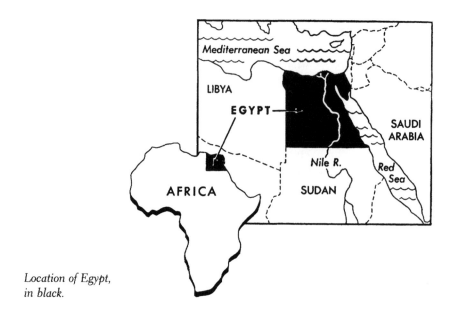

*Location of Egypt,
in black.*

The first component of this machination would be the Kondor Mission, the code name that had been given by German intelligence to two German spies and a network of subagents operating in Cairo. For many months the pair of agents, twenty-eight-year-old John Eppler and twenty-six-year-old Peter Monkaster, had been providing Rommel with detailed, high-grade intelligence that spelled out British battlefield plans.

Eppler, born of German parents in Alexandria, Egypt, grew up rich in nearby Cairo. Monkaster, tall and slim, had been an oil explorer and spent most of his life in East Africa. Both men spoke fluent English. Their papers, crafted by Abwehr experts in Berlin, identified Eppler as an Anglo-Egyptian businessman and Monkaster as an American oil-rig mechanic.

Departing separately from Berlin on a long, leapfrog route, both men slipped into Cairo in May 1942. Eppler had brought with him two American transceivers and a copy of *Rebecca,* for the Kondor Mission would send coded messages to Rommel based on the Daphne du Maurier novel. This cryptographic principle was impenetrable unless the person trying to solve it knew the system. Eppler based his cipher on the prearranged use of certain pages of *Rebecca* on certain days.

In Cairo the two men settled into a small house in a suburb, and Eppler began searching for subagents in the Egyptian population. Luck was with him. By accident he stumbled onto an intelligence bonanza that customarily evolves only in Hollywood spy movies. Its centerpiece was statuesque Hekmeth Fahmy, widely regarded as Egypt's foremost *danseuse du ventre*—belly dancer—who was the feature attraction at the popular Kit Kat Cabaret.

Eppler and the dancer rapidly became close friends, and she disclosed that she was a spy working against the British for the Muslim Brotherhood and for the Free Officers' Movement of the Egyptian Army. Furthermore, she revealed that her main source of important information was a man identified only as a "Major Smith," who was on the staff of British general headquarters in Cairo. Smith was her lover.

When Eppler convinced her that he was a German spy working for the famed Field Marshal Erwin Rommel, she agreed to cooperate in a clandestine scheme. When Major Smith visited the Nile houseboat on which she lived, he always brought along a bulging briefcase. While the belly dancer and the British officer were in bed in another room, Eppler and Monkaster pored over the contents of the briefcase, learning much about British troop strength, problems, dispositions, and battlefield intentions.

Using the *Rebecca* cipher, the Kondor agents reported to a German listening post in Athens, each time at about midnight, over the transmitter that had been hidden in a Cairo church of an Austrian priest.

Even spies need to seek occasional relaxation, so one night Eppler, dressed in the uniform of a British captain, went to a popular nightclub on the roof of the Metropolitan Hotel. There he picked up a bar girl, who said her name was Yvette, and bought her numerous rounds of expensive champagne, paying for it in British currency. She accompanied him back to his lodging and spent the night there.

Yvette was a spy for the Jewish Agency, which was working with MI-6, the British secret service. She reported to her controller her suspicions that Eppler was a German spy, pointing out that he had been using British pound notes, apparently believing that English currency was still the legal tender, as it had been when he was living in Cairo before the war. "He spoke with a Saarland accent," Yvette added.

British Major A. W. Sansom, the chief of field security in Cairo, was notified. He discovered that the "British captain" had paid for his drinks at the Metropolitan Hotel with pound notes and recovered some of the currency from the bartender. The money had been clever forgeries that were known to be of German origin.

On the afternoon of August 10, 1942, Sansom ringed the houseboat in which Eppler and Monkaster now lived with armed troops. Orders were passed to capture, not kill, the suspects. They were to be taken alive, even if they opened fire. At a given signal the troops closed in, barged onto the houseboat, and seized the two Germans after a physical struggle.

Later, the belly dancer Hekmeth Fahmy was also arrested. Her houseboat was searched, but all that was discovered were a few uniforms belonging to her boyfriend Major Smith. Facing the prospect of a firing squad, she talked freely about her relationship with Smith and how Eppler and Monkaster had read the contents of the Briton's briefcase.

By a stroke of luck, Major Sansom located one of the American transceivers. Eppler had pitched it overboard when the British soldiers stormed his houseboat, and he had opened the bilges, causing the vessel to scuttle itself. But the houseboat was raised, and under it, protruding from the mud, was the transceiver.

Although the mechanism was smashed, it was still set to the frequency for the Kondor Mission's last transmission to Athens. Although he now had the wavelength to the listening post in Greece, Sansom did not have the cipher. However, he and his colleagues suspected it was based on *Rebecca*, a copy of which was found in Eppler's room. Eppler and Monkaster, although facing execution, knew the importance of the cipher and refused to talk.

At this point, Winston Churchill happened to be in Cairo, and he asked to interrogate the spies. They continued to remain silent until he promised that their lives would be spared if they "cooperated." They changed their minds, and gave the secrets of the *Rebecca* cipher.

Now, with Field Marshal Rommel having secretly (or so he thought) shifted his Afrika Korps to the southern end of the El Alamein line, Colonel Dudley Clarke, the chief of the A-Force, began putting his agile, fertile mind to work to hoodwink the Desert Fox. Clarke began sending phony Kondor transmissions to Rommel through Athens. Allegedly quoting a high British source, Kondor reported that General Montgomery's defenses were especially weak in the south, and that if Rommel were to attack now, he might easily achieve a breakthrough. Actually, the British had most of their armor and a few hundred artillery pieces waiting to ambush the Afrika Korps when it struck.

Seventy-two hours later, the British impersonator of Kondor sent another message to Athens, giving a phony Eighth Army order of battle along the southern end of the line.

Now, to make certain Rommel grabbed the bait that was being dangled before his eyes, Colonel de Guingand hatched a unique machination. He had his cartographers make a map of the Ragil region that was painstakingly accurate—except it falsely showed the depression to be "hard going," thereby ideal for panzer operations.

Then the problem was how to play the map into Rommel's hands in such a way as not to arouse suspicions about its authenticity. "Major Smith," who had been under arrest and facing charges of the utmost gravity since the Kondor Mission had been unmasked, was chosen for the job. He was compelled to take a scout car into the desert near the German lines as though lost, a frequent occurrence by both adversaries in the barren terrain.

While the Germans were holding their fire, they heard a loud explosion, and the scout car leaped into the air, then settled into a wrecked heap. A German patrol was sent out and found the major's corpse—together with the doctored map he had on his person.

A suitcase radio transceiver (combination transmitter and receiver) of the type used by Kondor agents. (Jim Phillips)

The plot worked. Ultra disclosed that Rommel planned to send his panzers along the trails marked "hard going" on the false map. On August 24 he notified Berlin that he would launch his offensive under moonlight on the night of August 30–31. Montgomery, through Ultra, read the same message and put the Eighth Army on the alert.

On the eve of the crucial battle, Rommel wrote his wife, Lucie Maria: "There are such big things at stake. If our blow succeeds, it might go some way toward deciding the whole course of the war. If it fails, at least I hope to give the enemy a pretty thorough beating."

At 2:00 A.M. the German panzers roared toward British lines and began to get bogged down by the score in areas marked "hard going" on the fraudulent British map. As their crews got out to try to free the vehicles, swarms of Royal Air Force fighter planes, operating in the moonlight, swooped in to bomb and strafe them. Disaster continued to pile on disaster throughout the day. By night the bleak desert was littered with hundreds of burned German panzers, armored cars, half-tracks, and trucks.

After the carnage had continued for three days, Rommel ordered a general retreat. He had lost nearly five thousand men, fifty tanks, and seventy guns. Not a single objective had been obtained. The Desert Fox had been outfoxed.[8]

Smuggling Two Men
out of Morocco

EARLY IN SEPTEMBER 1942, Allied officers in London planning Operation Torch, the looming invasion of North Africa, put in an urgent request to David K. E. Bruce, the chief of the U.S. Office of Strategic Services for Europe. Two French navigators familiar with the waters in the Casablanca, French Morocco, region were desperately needed to guide in elements of the invasion fleet there.

Bruce, the forty-four-year-old multimillionaire son of a U.S. senator and married to steel baron Andrew Mellon's daughter, had surrounded himself with other bluebloods he had known, along with a bevy of intellectuals—Ivy League professors, attorneys, and scientists. Only a short time ago these Americans had been engaged in tranquil civilian pursuits. Now they found themselves executives in a dark and sinister "business," and they milled about in bewilderment and confusion at the OSS headquarters in fashionable Grosvenor Square.

Despite their lack of cloak-and-dagger experience, Bruce and his inner circle immediately plunged into the task of locating two French navigators. Fortunately, William Donovan, the gung-ho head of the OSS in Washington, had already established a network of his agents in Morocco and neighboring Algeria. So Bruce learned from those undercover agents that there were two anti-Nazi Frenchmen with the desired qualifications who were hiding out in Casablanca. They were Carl Victor Klopet and Jules Malavergne.

Klopet had lived in Casablanca for many years, and his work in the marine salvage business had given him intimate knowledge of the port facilities, beaches, and coastal defenses along the shoreline. Malavergne had been a ship's pilot on the Sebou River at Port Lyautey, sixty miles northeast of Casablanca. Invasion plans called for sending a U.S. destroyer charging up the Sebou to capture an important airfield inland.

OSS agents located Carl Klopet, cut a deal with him, provided him with phony documents, and helped him steal out of Morocco and make his way to London. There he was taken in tow by OSS agents and hidden in a safe house.

Forty-eight hours after Klopet had been found, two OSS agents approached a Casablanca house under cover of darkness and knocked softly on the door. Jules Malavergne responded and invited the two Americans inside. After a lengthy conversation during which the OSS men had to convince the leery Frenchman that they were genuine Americans and not Gestapo agents, Malavergne agreed to help guide in the invasion fleet.

As a security precaution, the Frenchman was given no specifics and was told only that his job would be critical to Allied success and the invasion would come "soon." The latter revelation could not be damaging if Malavergne were captured and forced to talk: It had been rumored in Casablanca for weeks that the Anglo-Americans were going to invade.

Now the Americans were confronted with the problem of smuggling the Frenchman out of Casablanca. There were police checkpoints throughout the sprawling city. So the OSS agents located a large trailer and concealed Malavergne behind several drums of gasoline. Then they covered him with a large Moroccan rug and a canvas tarp, which was fastened down tightly. The trailer was hooked up to a battered, huffing old Chevrolet the OSS men had been driving.

The Americans knew they had their work cut out for them and hoped that luck would be on their side. They would have to sneak their "cargo" past Casablanca police checkpoints, then French border guards in western Morocco, and finally frontier sentries in adjoining Spanish Morocco before they reached the port of Tangier, at the western end of the Mediterranean Sea.

As the car-trailer tandem chugged along over dark and bumpy roads, one OSS man would say to the other on occasion, "We'd better check Malavergne again." They would stop the Chevrolet, get out, and lift up one end of the tarp to see how the Frenchman was making out.

"Not dead yet!" Malavergne would reply. However, his eyes were blurred and his nose was running; fumes from the gasoline drums were seeping into his hiding place.

When the rolling tandem reached the western border of French Morocco, bored guards waved the travelers onward without as much as a second glance. The Americans' relief was short-lived. On the other side of the frontier, in Spanish Morocco, a guard insisted on inspecting the rig. The Americans felt their hearts beating faster. Spain, they knew, although officially neutral, was working hand in glove with Nazi Germany.

While the OSS agents stood by, the guard slowly circled the Chevrolet and its trailer. One American lifted a portion of the tarp at the back, just far enough so the Spaniard could see the gasoline drums that were concealing Malavergne. At the same time, the guard's dog began sniffing loudly and scratching vigorously at the front of the trailer where the Frenchman lay hidden.

Thinking quickly, the other American took from his lunch box a can of meat and opened it for the dog. Forgetting the business at hand—detecting persons hidden in vehicles—the animal began devouring the meat. Delighted over the generosity and the obvious love of animals of the two Americans, the Spaniard grinned broadly and motioned for them to get back into the Chevrolet; then he waved for them to continue their journey. A mile down the road, the OSS men and Malavergne resumed breathing.

From Tangier, Malavergne was flown to London, where he joined Carl Klopet in providing Torch planners with a wealth of information about ports, beaches, and coastal defenses, intelligence that would save countless American and British lives. The two Frenchmen were flown to Washington, D.C., then on to Norfolk, Virginia, where the Casablanca naval task force was forming.

When Operation Torch would near the North African beaches, the two Frenchmen would guide in the first destroyers.[9]

The Creeps and the Atomic Scientists

COLONEL LESLIE R. GROVES, at forty-six years of age one of the oldest officers in his rank in the U.S. Army, was in high good spirits. Twenty-four years after graduating fourth in his class at West Point, he was finally going to get the chance to prove what he could do on the battlefield. He had just been offered command of a combat regiment overseas after serving as the engineer in charge of military construction from a base in Washington.

Later that day, September 17, 1942, Groves was told that Secretary of War Henry L. Stimson had selected him for a crucial post and that President Roosevelt had approved the choice. The colonel, whose weight fluctuated between 250 and 300 pounds, asked: "Where?" In Washington, was the reply.

Groves was in shock. The general's stars he sought so eagerly seemed to have vanished. Soon he was advised that he would take charge of the faltering atomic bomb project code-named the Manhattan Engineer District. News that he was being promoted to brigadier general was only of slight comfort. This meant the end of his dream to lead troops in combat.

General Groves, the son of a Presbyterian minister who became an army chaplain, was gruff, outspoken, and regarded as arrogant by many who had known him. Lieutenant Colonel Kenneth D. Nichols, who had served with Groves in Nicaragua, described him as "the biggest son of a bitch I've ever met!"

Those were the precise traits President Roosevelt and Secretary Stimson had been seeking for a man to invigorate the torpid atomic bomb project. Even those who disliked Groves regarded him as a go-getter, a can-do type.

If Groves was overawed when he learned details of what would become the greatest single engineering project ever attempted, he gave no sign of it. Perhaps no one in the history of the world would be under such gargantuan pressure as would Groves. If successful, he could shorten the global war and save countless Allied—and enemy—lives. If Hitler won the clandestine race to build an atomic bomb, the führer would rule the world—including the United States.

Groves's debut with high-level policymakers came less than a week after he pinned on brigadier general's stars. He was present at a conference in Stimson's cavernous, ornate Washington office. Others in attendance included Army Chief of Staff George C. Marshall, two Nobel Prize–winning physicists who would play key roles in the atomic project, and Lieutenant General Brehon B. Somervell, the hard-nosed logistics genius who headed the global Army Service Forces and who had recommended Groves for the job.

After the conference had droned on for hours, Groves rose from his chair, glanced at his watch, and asked, "May I be excused? I've got to get out of here if you are through talking. I don't want to miss my train for Tennessee."

It was a gross breach of unwritten protocol. Officers at conferences attended by those senior to them do not get up and excuse themselves. Silence fell over the room. Groves departed.

At the small, sleepy town of Oak Ridge the next morning, Groves gave a green light for the construction of a uranium separation plant that would ultimately employ more than eighty thousand persons. Construction of this vast, vital complex had been delayed for many months by indecision and confusion. Then the new boss climbed on a train and returned to Washington.

A few hours after reaching the Pentagon, Groves ran into General Somervell, who broke out in a broad smile and said that Stimson had been impressed by Groves's abrupt exit. "You made me look like a million dollars!" Somervell exclaimed. "I'd told them that if you were put in charge, things would really start moving!"

Almost from the minute he took charge, Groves stressed secrecy. "Let silence be the rule," he declared. Toward that goal, he had working for him a swarm of agents known as Creeps. Groves had selected thirty-year-old Lieutenant Colonel John Lansdale, Jr., a Harvard Law School graduate, to be in charge of the Creeps.

Lansdale brought sophistication, a keen intellect, and enormous vitality to a job he himself considered to be "nasty" yet critical. At Oak Ridge and at a score of other places connected to the Manhattan Project, Lansdale and his assistant, Major William A. Consodine, launched history's greatest secrecy campaign under a motto created by General Groves: "Protect the Project."

Lansdale's clandestine corps of young men and women, the Creeps, were mostly lawyers trained in security by the War Department; others came from the army's Counterintelligence Corps (CIC) and the Military Police. For safety from spies and possible enemy bombers—or even long-range rockets known to be in the development stage in Germany—Groves had the project's operations dispersed: at Oak Ridge; at Hanford in Washington State; at Los Alamos in New Mexico; and elsewhere. Among the scientists at these places, mention of such terms as "atoms," "uranium," "heavy water," or "secret weapon" was strictly forbidden. When it was necessary to discuss a problem, atoms were called "tops" and the bomb was a "boat."

There could be no such thing as a misplaced document in the Manhattan Project, as it became popularly called. If it took a week or a month, the paper had to be found. Every carbon copy was listed in a register, given a code number, and carefully filed in a specific cabinet.

Each night after the scientists and staff had left for home, Creeps agents systematically entered offices to search for loose papers or unlocked desks.

On one occasion Colonel Lansdale donned civilian clothes; went to Berkeley, where supersecret experiments were being conducted at the University of California; and easily penetrated the laboratories. Introducing himself as a "research consultant" for Dr. James B. Conant, director of the Office of

Scientific Research and Development, Lansdale drew out several atomic scientists, was shown a new cyclotron, and was told related work was taking place at the University of Chicago.

After two days the scientists were assembled and Lansdale, wearing his military uniform, spoke to them about the secrets he had learned. "Suppose I had been a spy," he said. The scenario had the desired effect: security was tightened drastically.

In Washington, President Roosevelt received frequent written reports. But Secretary of War Henry Stimson took the documents to the Oval Office of the White House, watched the president read them, then took them away with him.

The scientists—hundreds of them—were the main headaches for the Creeps. Many were temperamental and had towering egos. They resented being tailed (hounded, they called it) by Lansdale's men. The Creeps expended tens of thousands of man-hours tapping telephones, secretly opening letters, and collecting details of extramarital affairs, alleged homosexual tendencies, drinking habits, and political affiliations.

Defenses against espionage were especially intense in Los Alamos, at the atomic laboratory in the remote New Mexico desert where six thousand scientists, technicians, and their wives and children lived within the high wire fences. Senior scientists, many of them Nobel Prize winners, were assigned bodyguards and fake names. Drivers' licenses were made out to numbers, not names. Mail came and went only to P.O. Box 1663, Santa Fe. Creeps sent counterspies into Santa Fe to visit bars and other gathering places to spread phony tales about the project. Agents were placed in Santa Fe hotels as room clerks.

Most scientists were discreet, but several "security scares" occurred. At a university lecture, one of them blurted out things that were top secret. Another left a briefcase with important information on a train. Six Creeps worked all night and finally found it—with the papers intact. But had enemy spies photographed the documents?

Many of the scientists loved to bedevil the Creeps by playing childish games. A physicist had managed to open the secret steel safe in the Los Alamos records office and placed a sheet of paper on top of the priceless atomic secrets it contained. Printed on the paper were the words: "Guess who?" Colonel John Lansdale was not amused.

One of the chief targets for surveillance by the Creeps was Dr. J. Robert Oppenheimer, the frail theoretical physicist whom General Groves had selected to be the scientific director of the Manhattan Project. For months Lansdale had been playing a cat-and mouse game with Oppenheimer because of the scientist's former association with an array of Communist groups, his financial contributions to far-left causes, and his friendship with Communist "fellow travelers."

Groves himself had questioned Oppenheimer and was convinced that the man he called his "closest, most indispensable collaborator" had earlier severed all connections with his Communist past. He had ordered the Creeps to cease surveilling his scientific director. Lansdale ignored the order and continued to watch.

Lansdale and his Creeps also focused on Oppenheimer's vivacious, hard-drinking wife, Katherine, whom Robert had met in 1939, when he was a professor and she a research fellow in biology at the University of California. Kitty, as she was known to friends, had a background steeped in Communist connections. Her second husband, a Dartmouth graduate and son of a wealthy investment banker, had been a Communist union organizer and died fighting with the Abraham Lincoln Brigade, a Communist outfit, during the Spanish Civil War. During this marriage, Kitty, whose IQ was 196, typed letters for the Communist Party while living on welfare in Youngstown, Ohio.

What especially concerned the Creeps from a security point of view was Kitty's candor and outspokenness. Sitting on the floor clutching a bottle of whiskey, she told a casual acquaintance that she had deliberately allowed herself to become pregnant by Oppenheimer during her third marriage so he would marry her. Her divorce and fourth wedding had taken place in Nevada on the same day, and a son was born a few weeks later. She nicknamed the baby "Pronto" for his alacrity.

If the hard-drinking Kitty told such intimate secrets to virtual strangers, Colonel Lansdale thought, could she keep her mouth shut about Oppenheimer's task? Or did she know the nature of his work? Her scientist husband told Lansdale she was in the dark about his Los Alamos function. Yet . . .

In Washington, meanwhile, Lieutenant Colonel Boris T. Pash, chief of the Counterintelligence Branch, Western Defense Command, suggested to Pentagon superiors that the Communist Party might be conniving to "divorce" Robert Oppenheimer officially but that the split would be only a smoke screen. "There is a possibility of him developing a scientific work, then turning it over to the [Communist] Party, perhaps through an intermediary," Pash stated. He recommended that Oppenheimer be "removed completely from the [Manhattan] Project and dismissed from employment by the U.S. Government."

General Groves had great respect for Pash and held him in high regard. Nevertheless, in this instance, he rejected bouncing Oppenheimer, trusting in his own judgment about men. Besides, the Manhattan Project boss exclaimed, he needed his scientific director.[10]

Part Five

Beginning of the End

The Spy Who Refused to Die

ON A MOONLIT NIGHT in March 1943, a Lysander airplane landed in a pasture outside the French city of Rouen. As was the practice, a secret agent, twenty-seven-year-old Philippe Liewer, scrambled out and onto the ground before the small aircraft halted. Liewer, who was using the *nom de guerre* Charles Staunton, had been a prominent French journalist.

Two years earlier, Staunton had organized some of the first underground cells in the South of France. He had been captured by the French secret police of Nazi puppet aging, senile Marshal Henri Pétain, but escaped with several others in a daring prison break.

Staunton, as bold as he was enterprising, made his way through Spain and eventually reached England, where he was recruited by the Secret Operations Executive (SOE), the cloak-and-dagger agency whose leader Prime Minister Winston Churchill had ordered tersely: "Set Europe ablaze!"

Staunton's orders were to establish an underground circuit, code-named Salesman, to cover the region of Rouen, a trading center and port on the Seine River about seventy miles northwest of Paris, and Le Havre, an English Channel port forty miles west of Rouen where the Germans had built pens for refitting their U-boats.

A few weeks after Staunton set up his Salesman circuit headquarters in Rouen, where the British had burned Joan of Arc at the stake in 1431, and established a radio link with London, Staunton was joined by twenty-year-old Robert Mortier (code-named Maloubier), who soon proved to be an innovative and daring operative. Mortier was put in charge of the crucial but risky business of coordinating and receiving arms, ammunition, and supplies being parachuted steadily into the region by British aircraft.

Late in 1943, nine months after Staunton had arrived in the Rouen region, he was picked up by a Lysander and flown to London for consultations and a brief respite from the constant tension. He left Bob Mortier in charge of the Rouen network.

Shortly past midnight just before Christmas, Mortier was on a motorcycle, with one of his men on the saddle behind him. They were rolling along in the direction of a pasture where supplies were to be parachuted. Soon the two resistance warriors were aware that a German field police car was chasing them.

Mortier slowed the cycle, and his companion leaped off and raced into the nearby woods.

When Mortier stopped, the Germans demanded to know what he was doing out so late at night. The French youth explained that he had been working until 11:00 P.M. and was on his way to see a sick friend in Grande Couronné, a few miles ahead. Suspicious, the policemen told Mortier that he would have to go to the field station at Oissel, where his identity would be checked. That development could be Mortier's death warrant, because he was on the Gestapo's black list as a "terrorist."

Perhaps to assure the Frenchman's compliance, one German mounted the passenger saddle and stuck his pistol in Bob's back. The other German followed in the car. When the group arrived at its destination in Oissel, Mortier knew he had a last chance to escape, and he bolted into a dark side street next to the police station.

There were loud shouts of *"Halten! Halten!"* and the sound of hobnailed boots running on the concrete. A fusillade of bullets hissed past the fleeing man; three of the pellets tore into him, two penetrating his lungs.

Although seriously wounded and bleeding extensively, Mortier managed to keep running. Gasping for breath, he dived into a ditch. He was convinced he was doomed. For whatever their reason, the two Germans ceased the chase.

When silence had descended over the dark town, Mortier dragged himself laboriously from the ditch and crawled to a nearby house. Weakly, for his strength was nearly gone, he scratched at the door. Moments later, a light came on inside, and the homeowner, who happened to belong to the underground, carried Bob inside and telephoned a doctor, who also was a member of the resistance.

This was a dangerous action. If the homeowner, his wife, and the physician were caught harboring a "wanted terrorist," they would be summarily executed.

After examining the ashen-faced Mortier, the doctor looked up and nodded his head sideways at the house's residents. Outside in the hall, he whispered to them that he doubted if the badly wounded man would survive the night.

Now the Good Samaritans were confronted with a vexing problem: What to do with the body? A death had to be reported to the authorities, the funeral arranged, and a grave acquired. Even if that procedure went undetected by the Gestapo, how would the Good Samaritans explain the three bullet holes in the would-be corpse?

After a lengthy and worried discussion, the homeowner and the doctor decided that they would arrange for disposing of the remains the same night. They would put Bob's body into two potato sacks—he was very tall—which would be stitched together, weighted with heavy rocks, and pitched into the Seine River. With luck, the corpse would never be found; if it one day floated to the surface, it would be so badly decomposed that the authorities would be unable to identify the remains.

The sacks were rapidly prepared. Then the waiting began. Bob, however, survived the night. Miraculous, exclaimed the doctor. But, he said, the situation was only temporary. The wounded man was certain to expire that day, and the burial procedure would be carried out after darkness again blanketed the region.

Mortier continued to cling to life for several days, and then, to the astonishment of the physician, he slowly began to improve. A day later he was able to sit up in bed, and then he began demanding a square meal, which he consumed. Gawking in amazement at Mortier, the physician raised his eyes upward and made the sign of the cross. It had been the Miracle of Oissel.

Ten days after he had been riddled with bullets, Mortier was able to join with his hosts in a small New Year's Eve celebration by drinking a toast that the year 1944 would see the liberation of France from the Nazi yoke.

Early in February, several members of the Salesman circuit drove Bob and Charles Staunton, who had been ordered to return to London, to a dark pasture some ten miles from Rouen. There the two men were picked up by a Lysander and flown to England, where the wounded man continued his incredible recovery, in a hospital.

On April 15 Staunton and his courier, a strikingly beautiful and highly intelligent young woman named Violette Szabo, landed in a Lysander near Paris. Since Staunton was thought to be well known by the Gestapo in Rouen, London had ordered Szabo to travel to that city and reconnoiter it while Charles remained in Paris.

Violette took the trip with forged papers identifying her as Corrine Leroy. Reaching Rouen, she was shocked. Some eighty members of the resistance had been arrested by the Gestapo, and the city was plastered with fairly good photographs of Bob Mortier and Charles Staunton, offering a large reward for the capture of the two "terrorists." Clearly, a French traitor had been at work.

On April 30 a Lysander picked up Staunton and Szabo near Chartres, just east of Paris, and returned them to London. There Staunton was like a caged tiger. He demanded to go back to France. Bob Mortier was clamoring to go along. But it would be suicide for the two wanted men to return to Rouen. So it was decided to send them to Limoges, some 225 miles southwest of Paris, to inject some order and discipline into a motley crew of some six hundred resistance men who were neither trained nor armed properly.

On the night of June 6–7, 1944—eighteen hours after Allied forces had stormed ashore in Normandy—Staunton, Mortier, and Violette Szabo parachuted near Limoges and set up a headquarters. Two days later they received word that advance elements of the crack 2nd SS Panzer Division, moving northward from the South of France to reinforce the German Army in Normandy, was only some twenty-five miles south of their location.

Jacques Dufour (code-named Anastasie), the leader of the local underground, and Violette headed southward in an automobile to locate the oncoming German armored unit. Rounding a curve, the vehicle was raked by automatic

Violette Szabo. Captured after gun battle and executed by Germans. (Author's collection)

Jacques Dufour. French resistance leader code-named Anastasie. (Author's collection)

weapons fire; they had bumped into the spearhead. Neither Dufour nor Violette was hit.

Scrambling out of the bullet-riddled automobile, they ran across a field. Violette fell and badly wrenched her ankle, which she had hurt in a parachute leap while training in England. Dufour carried her for about a hundred yards while the pursuing Germans sent bullets hissing past them. The young woman insisted that he put her down and save his own life. He hesitated, but finally complied and ran to a farm, where he was hidden under a pile of logs by a farmer.

Violette, in the meantime, had crawled into a cornfield and taken cover behind a cluster of trees. She was soon discovered, and several German soldiers opened fire on her. An expert with several firearms, as she had proven in training, she returned the fire with her Sten gun (an automatic weapon). When she ran out of ammunition, her adversaries captured her and took her to a prison in Limoges.

For nearly an hour, the Germans searched the farm where Dufour was hiding. At one point two of them sat briefly on the pile of logs that covered him. After the Germans had gone, Dufour rushed to see Charles Staunton and Bob Mortier and told them of Violette's capture. A rescue mission was quickly conceived.

Slipping into Limoges, Staunton and Mortier watched the prison for several days. They saw that twice each day, Violette, who had been badly beaten, was taken from the prison to the Gestapo office nearby, where her brutal interrogation continued. The underground leaders decided to seize Violette from her guards on one of these walks, and set the bold rescue mission for June 16, six days after she had become a prisoner.

A plan was conceived. Early on the day of the "kidnapping," Staunton and six resistance men, all heavily armed, were to steal into Limoges and take up positions near the prison gate. Then Mortier and four men were to drive up in an automobile while Violette was being led from the prison to the Gestapo headquarters and snatch her from her guards. After the woman had been driven away, Staunton and his comrades were to prevent a close pursuit by shooting it out with the Germans.

At sunrise on the day set for the desperate rescue operation, Violette was taken to Paris, where she was grilled by Standartenführer (SS Colonel) Hans Josef Kieffer, chief of the Sicherheitsdienst's counterintelligence service in France. Despite seemingly endless hours of shouts and demands, she refused to talk about her underground activities or to identify resistance leaders.

Eventually Violette was imprisoned at the Ravensbrück concentration camp. On January 26, 1945, with Allied armies closing in from the west and the east, she was removed from her dingy cell, taken to the yard behind the crematorium, and shot to death with a bullet through the head. Her remains were immediately cremated.[1]

Blowing Up a Locomotive Works

IN THE SPRING OF 1943 the Western Allies began implementing a program of 'round-the-clock bombing. Germany and its facilities in occupied France were pounded night and day. When the sun went down over Adolf Hitler's Festung Europa (Fortress Europe), Royal Air Force four-engined Lancasters and Stirlings rumbled overhead in the darkness. And when, through the swirling smoke, the sun rose, U.S. Liberators and Flying Fortresses began roaring through the aerial highways.

Despite the hundreds of thousands of tons of explosives showered on Germany and France from the air, the key locomotive works at Fives, an eastern suburb of the major city of Lille, France, escaped with only minor damage. This was because the Germans had concentrated their heaviest antiaircraft guns and searchlights on the approaches to Lille, which lies 130 miles north-northeast of Paris.

In early May, Michel Trotobas (code-named Sylvestre), the French underground chief in Lille, received an urgent request from his London contact. Could he and his agents conduct a direct action against Fives? Trotobas radioed back that he would try to sabotage the locomotive works. It would be a highly formidable and perilous mission, one requiring large quantities of high explosives, which were not available to the resistance in Lille.

A short time later the Royal Air Force began dropping containers loaded with explosives in the dark and grassy fields in the Lille region. A few resistance men were caught by the Germans while transporting the cargo into Lille. The captives paid with their lives. However, by late June, Trotobas and his men were ready to strike.

At about 9:00 P.M. Trotobas and twelve of his friends joined the large number of Frenchmen entering the Fives locomotive works for the third shift. Earlier, the underground leader had enlisted the aid of a foreman whose job was to screen the workers coming into the plant. The foreman never changed expression as the thirteen saboteurs, wearing work clothes and carrying lunch pails, strolled past nonchalantly. The pails were filled with explosives.

Again with the help of the foreman, who risked arrest, torture, and execution if his role became known to the Gestapo, the saboteurs worked feverishly for the next five hours, placing eighteen charges at key points they had already determined would cause the widest possible destruction.

Just before 2:00 A.M. the saboteurs, in a keenly coordinated operation, lit the fuses, allowing themselves only a few minutes to get out of the train sheds. When the intruders were about a hundred yards away, a clock in a nearby steeple began to strike two. Then: *booooom . . . boooom . . . boooom!* The explosions rocked the city and sent bits and pieces of wood, metal, and glass hurtling into the black sky. Moments later, the entire locomotive works was engulfed in roaring flames.

Despite the frantic efforts of the Germans to rush fire brigades to the scene, the blaze raged until the next afternoon. Hundreds, perhaps thousands, of Lille civilians had congregated to watch the carnage. Gazing at the brilliant blaze with them were the only Frenchmen who knew how the fire had started: Michel Trotobas and his twelve friends.

After enjoying his handiwork for hours, Trotobas returned to his safe house and radioed London: "Operation completed." Back came the reply: "Well done, please send photographs."

Meanwhile, Lille had turned into a madhouse. German soldiers and Gestapo agents were dashing about the city, arresting railroad workers and breaking down doors to take wives and children hostages. The German commander in Lille threatened to shoot every tenth man working at Fives unless the perpetrators of the "abominable terrorist outrage" were made known to him. The German security police whose job was to safeguard Fives were arrested and awaited court-martial.

Now Trotobas went about the job of taking the pictures of the carnage for London. Walking to Fives, he was delighted to get a daylight view of his activity: the entire works was a pile of twisted steel and smoking rubble. Pulling out

Fake German documents created by the British Special Operations Executive (SOE) for its agents. (Author's collection)

a forged document that identified him as a manager of the Société Nationale d'Assurance Industrielle, Trotobas showed it to a German officer and asked to be taken to the SS colonel who was in command at the scene.

Calmly, the underground chief explained to the colonel, who eyed him suspiciously, that his company would have to pay a huge amount in insurance claims, and that he had been sent to take photographs to enable his firm to assess damages. Most of these claims, the SS officer was told, would go to the SNCF (French national railways) to permit the facility to be rebuilt at the earliest possible time.

Knowing that higher-ups in Berlin were closely monitoring events at Fives because of its great importance to the German war effort, the colonel not only agreed to allow Trotobas to take pictures but also assigned several SS men to assist in the project. When the task was completed, Trotobas arranged to have the film taken to a mail drop in Normandy, from where it was picked up at night by a Lysander airplane and flown to London.

In the weeks ahead, the Germans, trying desperately to identify and arrest the "terrorists" who had pulled off the Fives caper, sent Trotobas two Frenchmen. They had been vouched for by trustworthy but gullible underground operatives but were actually in the pay of the Gestapo. Their assignment was to find the Fives perpetrators.

Within days Trotobas became highly suspicious of the two men. "Encouraged" to talk, they confessed and were shot. Their bullet-pierced bodies were dumped at night near the back entrance of Gestapo headquarters in Lille. Attached to the corpses were cards with a printed message: "Courtesy of the French resistance."

One of the participants in the Fives sabotage job had been a sturdily built young French engineer code-named Olivier. He was one of Trotobas's boldest operatives. Together they continued to carry out sabotage actions. Olivier had an Achilles heel, however, one about which Trotobas was unaware: the engineer could not resist boasting loudly in bars and elsewhere about his exploits.

On November 27, five months after the locomotive works had been blown up, the Gestapo charged into a house where Olivier was sleeping and dragged him away. Under torture, he admitted his involvement in the Fives sabotage and provided the address of Trotobas's safe house, hoping that the resistance chief would be away on a covert mission.

Rushing through the black streets, a Gestapo group reached Trotobas's house and began breaking down the front door. Trotobas, asleep upstairs, awakened, grabbed the pistol from beneath his pillow, and began firing at the Germans. He killed the leader of the raiding party. Moments later, a German bullet struck him in the head.

Michel Trotobas, code-named Sylvestre, twenty-seven years of age, died instantly.[2]

The Mystery Man of Algiers

WHILE FIGHTING was raging in North Africa in early 1943, a middle-aged civilian boarded a long-range transport plane outside London and the craft lifted off and set a course for Algiers, where the headquarters of General Dwight Eisenhower was located in the venerable St. George Hotel. The civilian's papers identified him as a British national named Mr. Hornsby, and he was flying to North Africa to develop recreational facilities for British soldiers.

Actually, Mr. Hornsby was a *nom de guerre*. He was Professor Solly Zuckerman, a scientist with a medical degree who was highly regarded in the intellectual community for his pioneering research on apes in captivity. It was an unlikely background for the unprecedented mission on which he had been sent. He was to create a plan that would permit the Anglo-Americans to capture the small but strategically important island of Pantelleria by bombing alone.

Located in the Mediterranean Sea some seventy miles southwest of Mazara del Vallo, Sicily, and about fifty-five miles east of Cape Mostefa, Tunisia, Pantelleria had been turned into a fortress by Italian dictator Benito Mussolini in the mid-1920s, and he declared it off-limits to foreigners in 1926. Consequently, Allied intelligence had gaps in its knowledge of the island's defenses.

Men of the Italian garrison at Pantelleria gather after surrender in front of a huge underground hangar. (National Archives)

Allied air reconnaissance disclosed that Pantelleria had more than a hundred gun emplacements, many hewn from solid rock, supplemented by pillboxes, machine gun posts, and other strong points. Hundreds of high, thick stone walls, which divided the arable land into fields, provided excellent defensive positions for the estimated ten thousand Italian troops defending the rocky, hilly five-by-eight-mile island.

Mussolini boasted, with a great deal of merit, that Pantelleria was impregnable. Allied planners feared that the Italian leader's description might be accurate. Yet General Eisenhower and his planners knew that the island had to be seized before the Anglo-Americans could invade Sicily in early July 1943.

No surprise assault against Sicily could be launched because of the German Freya radar stations on Pantelleria. Moreover, the warplanes on Pantelleria could threaten the Sicilian shipping lanes, and the small island was known to be a refueling point for German U-boats and motor torpedo boats operating in the central Mediterranean.

An Allied amphibious operation to capture Pantelleria could cost the Allies hundreds, perhaps thousands, of casualties. The island's coastline is irregular, with steep cliffs and an almost total absence of beaches. The only feasible landing area, in the harbor of the town of Porto di Pantelleria, was ill suited for an amphibious assault. Only shallow-draft vessels could be used there. Tricky offshore currents and high surf would further complicate the landing operation.

Despite the impressive defenses—Italian propagandists called Pantelleria the Gibraltar of the central Mediterranean—the garrison was a mishmash of men drawn from numerous elements of the armed forces. None had been in battle, and their morale was said to be low. In fact, they felt isolated and considered themselves to be expendable—that is, sacrificed—if need be.

Weighing all factors, General Eisenhower decided to conduct what would be a sort of laboratory experiment to determine the effect of concentrated bombing on a defended locale in an all-out effort to obtain the surrender of Pantelleria. Consequently he ordered his deputy, British Air Chief Marshal Arthur Tedder, to utilize all the medium and heavy Allied bombers in the Mediterranean. The saturation bombing scheme was code-named Corkscrew.

Solly Zuckerman's secret task in Algiers, therefore, was to create a scientific bombing plan to cause the Italian garrison to surrender without the need of an amphibious invasion. He was provided with every available detail of information culled from air reconnaissance photographs and other sources of intelligence about Pantelleria's highly formidable defenses. There were 109 guns of various calibers on the island, and these potentially destructive weapons would be Zuckerman's main focus.

Around the Algiers headquarters, Zuckerman was referred to as the "mystery man," one who was always intensely active in some unknown task and who had the cooperation of the highest brass. His work was wrapped in a cocoon of secrecy. Conjecture was boundless over what he was actually doing.

When the scientist finished his report, complete with graphs, charts, and illustrations, it ran to 283 pages. Zuckerman pointed out that to try to put bombs directly onto each big gun on Pantelleria would mean "a prolongation and magnification of effort out of all reason." The defenses could be neutralized and rendered ineffective by other causes: casualties and the disruption of communications along with the wiping out of range finders, predictors, searchlights, control posts, ammunition dumps, roads, barracks, shelters, and supplies of food and water.

"Bombs not only damage the ground and the material units which make up a gun battery, they also demoralize, and demoralization can play a big part in silencing a battery," Zuckerman emphasized.

No one knew if the scientific bombing campaign would work. So D-Day for the amphibious invasion of Pantelleria was set for June 11, 1943.

Meanwhile, U.S. and Royal Air Force planes followed Zuckerman's detailed formula and dropped 14,203 bombs on 16 of the Pantelleria batteries. Out of 80 guns bombed, 43 were damaged, 10 of which were beyond repair. As the "mystery man" had designated, all communications were destroyed, as were most ammunition dumps, bunkers, and other elaborate ingredients of a sophisticated artillery system.

Had robots been manning the guns, 47 percent of the pieces would still be able to fire. But, as Zuckerman had concluded as a result of earlier studies of the effect of bomb blasts, it was not necessary to score direct hits on the guns. It was not the guns, but the impact their blasts had on the batteries' support accessories and the Italian soldiers that resulted in the weapons falling silent.

After Pantelleria had been deluged with bombs, the commander of a British naval task force of five cruisers and eight destroyers demanded the island's surrender. Vice Admiral Gino Pavasi, in charge on Pantelleria, reported to Rome: "[Allied] bombers have plunged island into a hurricane of fire and smoke. . . . The situation is desperate, all possibilities of effective resistance have been exhausted."

At 10:00 A.M. on D-Day, the men of Major General W. E. Clutterbuck's British 1st Infantry Division climbed over the railings of troop transports eight miles offshore and into assault boats. As the invasion spearhead neared the landing beach at Porto di Pantelleria, the British soldiers were greeted by an amazing and reassuring sight: hundreds of white flags were waving across the island.

Follow-up troops went ashore, and eleven thousand dazed and bewildered Italian soldiers were rounded up. The only British casualty was a Tommie who had been bitten by an ill-tempered jackass.[3]

Top Secret: Parachuting Mules

A MERCILESS SUN, hanging like a huge ball of fire high in the cloudless sky, beat down on the desolate, rock-hard desert around Oujda, French Morocco, in North Africa. Bivouacked in long rows of pup tents in the region was the green but spirited U.S. 82nd Airborne Division, known as the All-Americans. Traveling in rickety old boxcars that had signs in French painted on them reading "40 Men or 8 Horses," the paratroopers and glidermen had just arrived after a tedious eight-day trek in stifling heat and blinding sandstorms from the port of Casablanca, far to the west. It was late May 1943.

Only Major General Matthew B. Ridgway, commander of the 82nd Airborne, two other generals in the outfit, and the three regimental colonels knew that the next Allied blow would be an invasion of Sicily. D-Day was set for July 10.

One day, Ridgway called in thirty-six-year-old Colonel James M. "Slim Jim" Gavin, leader of the 505th Parachute Infantry Regiment, which would leap behind U.S. beaches before the amphibious troops stormed ashore, and gave him a bizarre assignment. Someone in the high command had decided that mules would be most helpful in carrying supplies to the paratroopers on the rugged, mountainous island, Ridgway explained. So Gavin was told to conduct experiments on parachuting the sturdy, surefooted beasts into Sicily with his men.

Secrecy was crucial, Ridgway stressed. If German intelligence learned from native spies, of which there was no shortage in French Morocco, about the unique tests, it might be able to deduce that the next Allied target was Sicily.

Gavin turned over the mule-dropping venture to Major Mark J. Alexander, executive officer of the 2nd Battalion. Alexander also was warned that secrecy was vital.

Hundreds of mules were brought into Sicily by boat. (U.S. Army)

As was his custom, Alexander energetically plunged into the clandestine task. Along with two of his sergeants and a corporal, the major purchased a pair of mules from an Arab after considerable haggling over the price. The animals were fitted with huge, forty-eight-foot parachutes and taken to an airstrip out in the desert. Through herculean effort, the paratroopers managed to get the mules up a crude wooden ramp and into the hold of a C-47 transport plane, the type that carried paratroopers.

Once inside, the mules became highly uncooperative, showing no great enthusiasm for the experiment. The animals were blindfolded. The airplane lifted off, gained altitude, and circled some six hundred feet above the airstrip. Then the mules were shoved through the open cargo door.

The test was a disaster. Although their parachutes opened, both mules received broken legs on crashing into the ground and had to be destroyed. The project was promptly abandoned by higher headquarters.

It would be long after the 82nd Airborne bailed out over Sicily to spearhead the U.S. assault that Major Mark Alexander learned that the island already had more mules per square foot than nearly any other locale in the world. Nevertheless, when the American divisions came in by sea, they brought with them a few hundred of the long-eared animals, thereby increasing the mule population of Sicily.[4]

America's Fifteen Thousand Secret Snoopers

NEIGHBORS WERE FLABBERGASTED. That morning of June 27, 1943, two grim-faced special agents of the Federal Bureau of Investigation had knocked on the door of the residence at 123 Oxford Place, Staten Island, and hauled off the mild-mannered homeowner, Ernest F. Lehmitz. There must have been some drastic mistake, neighbors were convinced. Lehmitz was accused of being a spy for Nazi Germany on the payroll of the Abwehr.

Tall, lean, and stoop-shouldered, Ernie Lehmitz was regarded by his neighbors in the New York City suburb as a good ol' boy, kindhearted and a superpatriot. Fifty-six-year-old Ernie really took his volunteer civil defense air-raid warden's job seriously, they always said, for he would bawl out people for not masking lights. And Lehmitz tenderly nurtured the neighborhood's largest backyard "victory garden" in response to the government's request that citizens raise their own vegetables.

Lehmitz, however, was indeed a Nazi spy, one of the best. While visiting his native Germany in 1939, Lehmitz, a naturalized American citizen, had been recruited by the Abwehr and given an intensive course in espionage and sabotage at the academy in Hamburg. He returned to the United States on the liner *Siboney* in March 1941. For selling out his adopted country, Lehmitz received a paltry fifty dollars per week from the Abwehr.

Lehmitz bore no resemblance to Hollywood's stereotype of a spy, one dashing about with a bomb in one hand and a stolen military blueprint in the other. There had been no glamor in his life, no beautiful women accomplices. Only an ugly, nagging wife. He wore cheap, ill-fitting suits, old-fashioned rubbers on his feet when it rained, and his most daring vice was an occasional glass of beer in a tavern.

Lehmitz's espionage "beat" was the New York waterfront. His "cover" as a Civil Defense air-raid warden deflected any suspicion from him. He held a job as a handyman in a waterfront saloon frequented by merchant seamen, and he sent his reports to the Abwehr in Hamburg through a mail drop in Lisbon.

Only much later would Ernie Lehmitz learn that the unmasking of his role as a Nazi spy responsible for the deaths of countless merchant seamen, many of them Americans, resulted from the diligence of some of the fifteen thousand snoopers of the U.S. Office of Censorship who, for more than three years, opened other people's mail, eavesdropped on telephone conversations, inspected overseas cabled messages, and meddled with movies, reading matter, and radio programs.

When the chief of the Office of Censorship first went to work in late 1939, he had only a borrowed room and two employees in Washington. Eventually the agency expanded into ninety buildings throughout the United States and, with Canada and Great Britain, established the first global censorship network.

Most censors were experts in some field. There were decoders and translators, technical, legal, and financial experts. One Ivy League professor spoke nine languages and could identify ninety-five others. There were linguists who could read shorthand in three hundred languages.

A torrent of mail—some one million pieces—crossed the censors' desks every day. Work had to be accelerated at a frantic pace. Air mail could be delayed only twenty-four hours, surface mail not more than forty-eight. All mail was checked against a watch list—persons known to be or suspected of being enemy agents. The list fluctuated between seventy-five thousand and one hundred thousand names at any given time. Correspondence to and from the leaders of the United States and Allied governments was not to be opened—or so the rules stated.

The greatest worry of the censors was messages in secret codes and inks. Each letter was scanned for the strange use of numbers or symbols, for awkward expressions, for paper that looked dried-out or scratched. These suspicious letters were sent to the Technical Operations Division (TOD), a deliberately misleading name, in Washington, which tested for code, ciphers, and secret inks.

Every cable filed in the United States was inspected by censors. If the meaning was clearly understood and the censors were certain it was harmless, the cable was approved. Often censors would change one word in a questionable cable, a word that might be a code. A sailor cabling his girlfriend that he was sending her "a box of chocolates" might be changed to "a box of candy," just on the off-chance that "chocolates" was a code word.

On one occasion a censor altered "father is dead" to "father is deceased." Back to the cable-sender came an urgent question: "Is father dead or deceased?" A dead giveaway.

Among the most tedious tasks for censors was monitoring international telephone calls. Wearing headphones, the censor had a pencil in one hand and the other hand on a switch that could instantly cut off either of the talkers. Most of the cutoffs involved calls by high officials in Washington, including a general's aide in the War Department who telephoned London and started to give the names and departure date of five bigwigs in the Roosevelt administration who were flying to Europe. This would have been a juicy invitation to the Luftwaffe to intercept and shoot down the aircraft.

Wartime censorship was a double-edged sword: it kept valuable intelligence from the Germans, Italians, and Japanese, and it uncovered significant leads in tracking down Nazi spies burrowed into the fabric of the United States. One night, a censor at a station in Hamilton, Bermuda, plucked from the avalanche of newly arrived mail a typewritten, seemingly innocent letter being sent to an address in Lisbon in neutral Portugal. That particular address was on the watch list, for it was known to be an Abwehr blind. Given the heat treatment, invisible-ink writing was brought out in the letter:

> Eleven ships leaving for Russia Feb. 12, including steamer with airplane motors and 28 long-range guns. One steamer has deck-load airplanes. Boeing and Douglas airplane parts on steamer, and small munitions, searchlight, and telegraphic materials.

The letter was postmarked New York and signed "Fred Sloane." In the days ahead, the alert censors fished out other letters from "Sloane." All were rushed to the FBI at Foley Square in New York City, and a probe was launched to locate him. The only clue to "Sloane's" identity was a brief mention that he was an air-raid warden—of whom there were 98,276 in Greater New York.

In April 1943 Bermuda detected the thirteenth letter signed by "Fred Sloane." It contained an innocent reference to the "wonderful week I spent on the beach at Estoril."

Estoril! The name rang a bell with the FBI men continuing with the maddening ordeal of trying to identify the ace Nazi harbor spy. This could be a gigantic break. Estoril, the sleuths knew, was a popular resort outside Lisbon—and a clearinghouse for Nazi spies.

Armed with copies of "Fred Sloane's" signature, a team of G-men descended on the U.S. Customs office in New York City and began comparing "Sloane's" handwriting with those on tens of thousands of baggage declarations by individuals who had entered the United States from Portugal since 1941.

It was a gargantuan task. Day after day, night after night, for weeks, the bleary-eyed FBI agents waded through mountains of baggage declarations. Just after 9:00 P.M. on June 9, 1943, a weary G-man picked up the 5,192nd form he had inspected under a hand-held magnifying glass. He intensely compared the signature of "Fred Sloane" with that of one Ernest F. Lehmitz, then let out a loud war whoop. The handwriting matched perfectly.

For more than two weeks, G-men tailed Ernest Lehmitz from his home to the waterfront where he strolled about before going to his job at the saloon. Other FBI agents clad in seamen's clothing hung around the saloon, watching the suspect's every action, feigning drunkenness, and replying falsely to questions he asked on sailing dates of their nonexistent ships and the cargoes to be carried. Other sleuths, posing as insurance salesmen, meter readers, and deliverymen, were picking up incriminating evidence through discreet inquiries of Lehmitz's neighbors on Oxford Place.

At the New York City headquarters of the FBI after his arrest, Lehmitz was shown copies of his letters that had been intercepted by the alert censors in Bermuda and the mass of other evidence collected by G-men in his neighborhood and at the waterfront saloon. Lehmitz denied everything, then finally broke down and signed a confession. In September 1943 he was tried for wartime espionage in federal court in Brooklyn, found guilty, and sentenced to thirty years in prison.

A few months later, the Japanese, from nine thousand miles across the Pacific, launched the most bizarre attack of the war—a bomb-laden balloon barrage against the heavily timbered Northwest of the United States. Tens of thousands of acres of land in Oregon, Idaho, Washington State, and northern California were destroyed by roaring forest fires.

Made of paper stuck together with paste from potatoes, the balloons were thirty feet across, seventy feet high, and filled with hydrogen. They were released into the high-altitude winds of the jet stream across the Pacific. A unique mechanism caused the balloons to land in the United States Northwest and triggered incendiary devices.

Some balloons went astray. One bomb was found in a Detroit suburb; another fell on a street in Medford, Oregon. Near Bly, Oregon, a woman and five children on a picnic were killed when they apparently tampered with a fallen balloon loaded with bombs.

Japanese warlords in far-off Tokyo would have been delighted had they known how close one of their bombs had come to inflicting a calamity on the United States. A balloon loaded with explosives got tangled in power lines just outside a supersecret plant near Hanford, Washington, where fuel was being refined for a revolutionary device known as an atomic bomb. A short-circuit in the power for the nuclear reactor cooling pumps ensued, but backup devices restored power rapidly. Had the cooling system been off much longer, a reactor might have collapsed or exploded.

In Washington, D.C., President Franklin Roosevelt and other government leaders were concerned that Japan would gain an enormous propaganda bonanza if the world learned how devastating the balloon barrage had been. The Japanese warlords hoped the tactic would severely shake civilian morale and cause Uncle Sam to "lose face" throughout the vast Pacific and the Far East.

Consequently the Office of Censorship scored its most monumental triumph in suppression in support of the war effort. This intricate feat gained the crucial cooperation of newspapers, magazines, and radio stations, all of which remained silent as thousands of acres were consumed by fire each day in the Northwest.

As far back as 1936, Germany and Japan had signed an agreement whereby intelligence gathered by Nazi agents in the United States would be shared with Tokyo, and, in turn, Japanese undercover operatives in the Pacific would provide information that would be shuttled on to Berlin. Since the United States had gone to war, however, Director J. Edgar Hoover and his G-men had broken up the Nazi spy networks, arresting and convicting some eighty persons and causing a few hundred others to flee the United States or go deep into hiding.

So there were no foreign agents to advise Tokyo about the massive destruction resulting from the widespread blazes.

Meanwhile, the 555th Parachute Infantry Battalion, an all-black outfit at Camp Mackall in the Carolinas, was eager to take on Adolf Hitler's best troops. But that was not to be the destiny of the Triple Nickels, as they were known. Orders were received for the battalion to report to Pendleton Air Base in Oregon for a "highly classified mission." There the troopers were given a crash three-week course in forest-fire fighting by parachute, including demolition training, tree-climbing techniques, handling fire equipment, jumping into pocket-sized drop zones studded with rocks and tree stumps that could kill on impact, and surviving in heavily timbered and mountainous locales. Finally, the Triple Nickels learned the touchy business of defusing live explosives and incendiary devices.

Soon the entire battalion had qualified as parachute firefighters and gained the temporary nickname "Smoke Jumpers." In the weeks ahead the black paratroopers jumped into tiny clearings in dense, mountainous forests of the Pacific Northwest to bring under control roaring conflagrations. It was dangerous, exhausting, but vital work. However, the Triple Nickels, to a man, were deeply disappointed that they would never have a chance to tangle with the Germans or the Japanese.

No doubt the warlords in Japan were waiting eagerly each day for some news about the carnage caused by the bomb-laden balloon barrage. But nothing appeared in or was heard from the United States media. Although 334 bombs were found by the U.S. Forest Service and the Triple Nickels, secrecy was so airtight that the Japanese eventually concluded that the bombs were not even reaching the Pacific Northwest. After having launched 9,000 bomb-laden balloons, Tokyo abandoned the project.[5]

Coercing Surrender of the Italian Fleet

WHILE CLANDESTINE peace negotiations were going on behind the scenes between the Anglo-Americans and the Italians in early August 1943, Lieutenant Commander Stanley M. Barnes's U.S. PT-boat Squadron 15 was based at the port of Palermo, in northwest Sicily. None of the PT-boaters had any way of knowing that some of them would be involved in one of the most dramatic covert missions of the war.

Soon after its arrival in Palermo, Stan Barnes's squadron was joined by a bevy of OSS operatives under the command of navy Lieutenant John Shaheen, who had long been bursting with schemes for inflicting mayhem on the enemy.

While stationed in Washington a few months earlier, he had hatched a plot to blow up Tokyo Harbor with midget submarines. That idea had been scuttled because of insurmountable logistics problems.

Another member of the OSS contingent was navy Lieutenant Michael Burke, an All-American football star at the University of Pennsylvania and a close pal of Shaheen's. Before heading for the Mediterranean, Burke and Shaheen had decided they would kidnap rotund Reichsmarschall Hermann Goering, the number two official in the Third Reich and commander of the Luftwaffe.

The clandestine plan was to lure Goering aboard a seagoing luxury yacht of his good friend Axel Wenner-Gren, a Swedish industrialist, then seize the Nazi leader and make off with him. There was one major flaw in the scheme: feelers extended to Wenner-Gren disclosed a total lack of enthusiasm on his part to cooperate.

Also in the OSS contingent were John Ringling North, whose two uncles had founded the famous Ringling Brothers Circus; Joseph "Jumping Joe" Savoldi, a onetime football star at the University of Notre Dame and later a renowned professional wrestler; and swarthy-complexioned U.S. Navy Lieutenant Marco Ricci.

Soon the PT-boaters began to wonder about Ricci's bona fides. His receding hair and coarse skin accentuated the fact that he seemed to be far too old to be a junior officer in the U.S. Navy. The suspicions would prove to be well founded. Ricci was the identification given to him by OSS operatives in Washington. Actually, he was Marcello Girosi, an Italian who married into a wealthy New York family.

Girosi would be the crown jewel in a hush-hush operation code-named McGregor. It was an intricately planned and intricately timed venture, one that could shorten the war—or end in disaster for the participants. The mission's goal was to persuade Italian admirals in Rome to bring their fleet over to the Allies instead of their being seized by the Germans after King Victor defected.

One of the New Yorker's brothers was Admiral Massimo Girosi, a member of the Italian Navy's Supreme Command. Another brother, Cesare, was an Italian Navy captain. The role of the PT-boaters was to clandestinely land an agent ashore near Rome. He would carry a handwritten letter from Marcello Girosi (Lieutenant Ricci) to his brother Admiral Girosi, suggesting that the Italian Navy abandon Nazi Germany and come over to the Allies.

Only after the OSS contingent had reached the Mediterranean—they traveled individually and in pairs in assorted disguises and under phony orders—did Jumping Joe Savoldi learn of his role in the escapade. OSS security people in Washington had been suspicious that Marcello Girosi might be a double agent whose true loyalty was questionable. So Savoldi, who was built like a gorilla and was just as tough as one, was assigned to keep an eye constantly on Girosi.

"If he tries anything sneaky," the Italian-born Savoldi had been told, "take care of him." Savoldi, who had come to the United States when twelve years of age and spoke Italian fluently, was fully aware what was meant by those instructions.

The agent who would take the letter ashore was a young Italian called Tommy. He was expected to utilize his knowledge of the Rome region and his contacts there to get the written message in the hands of Admiral Girosi.

Commanding the PT boats that would be involved in McGregor was twenty-three-year-old Lieutenant Richard H. O'Brien, a U.S. Naval Academy graduate who had served on the aircraft carrier *Yorktown* until it was sunk by the Japanese in the Battle of Midway in June 1942. After surviving that ordeal, O'Brien had requested flight training, but he was assigned to the PT-boat service.

As soon as he was briefed on McGregor, O'Brien began an intensive training program near Palermo, teaching his men how to handle and paddle a rubber boat while waiting for a suitable dark-moon period to launch an operation.

At sundown on August 10, 1943, two PT boats sailed from Palermo and set a course high up on the Italian boot. Each of the speedy vessels carried drums of fuel on deck. Without this extra load the boats could not make the round trip. In one craft, in addition to the ten-man crew, were John Sheehan, Mike Burke, John Ringling North, and the Italian courier Tommy. Richard O'Brien, the flotilla commander, rode in the other boat.

Five hours later, O'Brien concluded that his navigator had hit the target right on the nose—a remote region on the Gulf of Gaeta, about sixty miles south of Rome. The moon had gone down; visibility was nearly zero. Cautiously, with the two Packard engines muffled, the two boats slipped into the gulf.

Tommy, the twenty-two-year-old courier, waited nervously on deck. Part of the inducement for him to accept this perilous task had been that Mike Burke promised to introduce him to his favorite Hollywood movie actress, Loretta Young, after the war.

The PT-boat crewmen also were tense. Stomachs knotted. Palms and foreheads perspired despite the sea breeze. No one had asked them if they wanted to go on a two-craft mission two hundred miles deep into enemy territory. It was like playing Russian roulette: no one knew if the coast at that point was free of German soldiers or saturated with them.

As the two boats were stealing toward shore, a string of some twenty-five lights was spotted ahead. Had the Germans been tipped off about McGregor? Slowly, the flotilla edged onward. Then it was discerned that the lights were actually flares, one or two of them on Italian fishing boats. Logic told O'Brien and the OSS men that the Germans might well be watching the fishermen.

The PT boats lay dead in the water while a muted discussion was held on what to do next. Then came another scare. Radar on O'Brien's craft picked up a German E-boat, the Kriegsmarine's equivalent to the PT boat, stealing out of

A portion of the Italian fleet, including a midget submarine (front), is tied up at Malta after Italy's armistice with the Allies. (U.S. Navy)

its base on the northern end of the gulf. However, the E-boat went to sea without spotting the two intruder craft.

A decision was reached that Tommy could not be put ashore on this night, at this place, without the quite real chance of discovery. So the PT boats idled out to sea, then opened throttles and barreled for Palermo.

Two days later, on August 12, the PT boats and their passengers left Palermo again. This time the distance was cut down greatly. The courier would be landed near the town of Tropea, 160 miles south of the Gulf of Gaeta and near the toe of the Italian boot. This was a potentially more dangerous landing point because the region held thousands of German soldiers who had been pulled out of nearby Sicily in recent days.

Stealing slowly through the blackness to a point only two hundred yards offshore, Mike Burke and John Shaheen silently lowered a rubber boat into the water. Tommy, the courier, and an agent being put ashore at the request of British intelligence climbed into the conveyance and began paddling ashore. Moments later the two spies were swallowed by the night.

After interminable minutes of tension-racked waiting, the PT-boaters and their OSS passengers glimpsed three quick flashes from Tommy's infrared light. The intruders were ashore. Creeping back out to sea, the torpedo boats picked up speed and were back in Palermo by dawn.

Fifteen days after Tommy had paddled ashore, Lieutenant Dick O'Brien took three PT boats on a long run to rendezvous with the courier. At midnight the craft stood two hundreds yards off the dark beach near Terracina, some fifty miles south of Rome. OSS operatives John Shaheen, Mike Burke, and John Ringling North were on the lead boat with O'Brien.

Anxiously, the men tried to pierce the blackness with their eyes, but there was no sign of Tommy. Perhaps he had lost his infrared signaling light. An hour passed. Then two hours. The waiting was almost unbearable.

As a last-gasp measure, O'Brien had his three boats sneak along the shoreline in the event Tommy had miscalculated the rendezvous point or was not able to reach it. Nothing.

Depressed and worried, O'Brien and the OSS men held a whispered conversation. It was decided that they would have to head for Palermo. It was 2:30 A.M. and they would have to put distance between them and Italy before daylight would expose them to Luftwaffe attacks.

On the ride home there was much discussion about Tommy's failure to show up. Had he been captured by the Gestapo? Did he, under torture, tell all about McGregor? If so, the Germans no doubt would promptly seize the Italian fleet at anchor in La Spezia and Genoa, far up the boot. Perhaps Tommy was a wily double agent and was back with his German controllers.

Three weeks later, the main body of the Italian fleet, which included six modern battleships, suddenly steamed out of the two harbors to go over to the Allies. On the following morning, when sailing southward along the coast of Sardinia, the armada was pounced on by Luftwaffe planes firing revolutionary wireless-controlled glider bombs. A direct hit was scored on the battleship *Roma*, which blew up with great loss of life. A second battleship was badly damaged but steamed onward.

Twenty-four hours later, this powerful and valuable fleet rested safely under the guns of fortress Malta, a British crown colony sixty miles south of Sicily.

Tommy, the missing Italian courier, apparently had succeeded in getting Marcello's letter to Admiral Girosi in Rome. Yet none of the PT-boaters and OSS men participating in McGregor would ever learn for certain what had become of Tommy.[6]

Deception Role for the Panjandrum

WHILE THE FULL WEIGHT of the shooting war between the Western Allies and the Germans was centered in the Mediterranean in August 1943, Winston Churchill and Franklin Roosevelt knew that before Adolf Hitler and his Nazi regime could be brought to their knees, powerful Anglo-American forces would have to be assembled in Great Britain. One day they would charge across the English Channel to engage the Wehrmacht in massive battles on the Continent.

Consequently, in preparation for that cataclysmic struggle, British Lieutenant General Frederick E. Morgan, an affable and capable officer, established a headquarters known as COSSAC (Chief of Staff, Allied Command) at

Panjandrum on the beach after test run. (National Archives)

Norfolk House in St. James Square in London. The forty-nine-year-old Morgan's mission was to develop plans for a cross-Channel invasion of northwestern Europe to be launched in the spring of 1944.

Morgan's task would be a formidable one, for Hitler had long been making preparations to smash any Allied assault crossing the Channel against his stolen empire. Back in March 1942 the führer had signed Directive 40, decreeing that a barrier known as the Atlantikwall, stretching from the snowy fjords of Norway to the Spanish frontier, be constructed with "fantastic speed."

Since that time, some one hundred thousand slave laborers had been toiling around the clock to build a chain of fifteen thousand concrete and steel bunkers immune to bombing and naval gunfire. As a matter of priority, the major ports were especially heavily fortified, with open beaches given the lowest precedence.

"If we can keep a major port out of the hands of the [Allies], we can defeat any attempt by them to gain a foothold," Hitler told his generals. Therefore he proclaimed several ports in France and the Low Countries—including Cherbourg in Normandy—to be "fortresses" and required their commanders to sign oaths swearing to defend the ports "to the last man and the last bullet," then utterly destroy the harbor facilities.

In London, General Morgan and his COSSAC staff quickly reached the same conclusion as had Hitler: a frontal assault on a heavily fortified German-held port would be suicidal. So an operational plan was drawn up whereby the Allies would go ashore on the open beaches of Normandy along the Bay of the

Seine. Then U.S. divisions on the right of the invasion sector would head northward and seize Cherbourg from the rear, where defenses would be far less formidable.

Although the Normandy invasion was still ten months away, the London Controlling Section (LCS) developed a scheme to reinforce in Hitler's mind his conviction that the Allies would make an amphibious frontal assault on a major port. The LCS was a supersecret bureau that had been established by Winston Churchill early in the war to concoct and coordinate stratagems to deceive Nazi Germany on true Allied intentions, thereby surprising the enemy and gaining an advantage on the battlefield.

Planning a key role in the deception scheme would be the Directorate of Miscellaneous Weapons Development (DMWD), a group of brainy, free-wheeling Royal Navy scientists whose specialty was conceiving offbeat machinations to inflict on the Germans. The chief and guiding spirit of the DMWD, whose members called themselves the Wheezers and Dodgers, was Lieutenant Commander Charles F. Goodeve. A Canadian in his late thirties, he had been a prosperous civilian scientific consultant before moving to England twelve years earlier.

Goodeve was given instructions for the DMWD to develop an apparatus that could blow a hole in a concrete wall five feet thick, permitting foot soldiers and tanks to charge through the opening. Although Goodeve may have surmised that the target would be the vaunted Atlantikwall, he was not told that fact.

After much noodling over the formidable problem, the brain trust of the Wheezers and Dodgers produced a prototype of a weird contraption christened the Panjandrum. All the work had been done in a closely guarded building in great secrecy. Only a limited number of persons with passes had been allowed to enter the structure.

The Panjandrum consisted of two enormous wheels, each ten feet in diameter, with a tread about a foot wide. These wheels were connected by a drumlike axle, which would hold a ton of high explosives. The monster would be propelled by as many as sixty slow-burning cordite rockets fitted around the circumference of each wheel.

The apparatus would be carried on a tank landing craft. When offshore, the ramp would be lowered, the rockets would be ignited, and the ponderous contraption would propel itself through the water and onto the beach. There it would pick up speed, to about fifty miles per hour, and hurtle into a sturdy concrete wall. On impact, the steel wheels were to collapse and a mechanical device would set off the dynamite, blasting a huge hole in the barrier.

In the darkness of September 2, 1943, amid great security precautions, the Panjandrum was taken from its shed and loaded onto a flatbed transport manned by soldiers. With an escort of motorcycle policemen, all sworn to secrecy, the vehicle headed for western England, where it would be given trials at COXE (Combined Operations Experimental Establishment) on the coast.

After daylight, a baffling situation emerged. All efforts by a special team to assure secrecy to the project had vanished. When the tarpaulin was removed and the Panjandrum rolled off the transport, hundreds of residents and vacationers gawked in astonishment at the strange apparatus. Only then did Commander Goodeve and his men start to realize that the Panjandrum project had been and was an intricate subterfuge to strengthen Hitler's belief that a major port would be assaulted by the Allies when they crossed the English Channel.

With all the hoopla and the large crowd of people, word was supposed to eventually reach German intelligence that a large number of Panjandrums were being built to assist in cracking open the thick, high walls in one or more ports.

Now the maiden trial of the Panjandrum was to begin. The explosives drum was filled with dry sand, and the apparatus was put aboard a landing craft that took up a position a few hundred yards offshore. The boat's ramp was lowered, and the rockets were ignited. Smothered in clouds of smoke and flame, the contraption edged down the ramp, plowed through the surf, charged onto the beach, and headed for the thick wall that was its target. Then the Panjandrum sputtered to a standstill, well short of the concrete barrier.

Several other trial runs also flopped. So the Wheezers and Dodgers returned to London, held countless discussions, and made numerous adjustments to the Panjandrum. They felt that the kinks had been worked out, so two new contraptions were built.

Returning to COXE, the Wheezers and Dodgers were ready for yet another test. Gathered on the dunes behind the beach was a galaxy of admirals, generals, and scientists, who had come to pass judgment on the Panjandrum. These observers were presumably unaware that the entire scenario was a subterfuge.

Down the ramp and through the water went the Panjandrum. When the smoking, belching apparatus reached the beach, it picked up enormous speed, perhaps eighty miles per hour. Then it went berserk, swerving and lurching violently. It swung in a great curve and raced toward the band of generals, admirals, and scientists, all of whom conducted a spontaneous strategic retreat, flinging themselves headlong into a mass of barbed wire.

Moments later the Panjandrum crashed onto its side, causing the rockets to explode madly, like a string of gigantic firecrackers. Soon the contraption was a blackened chunk of wreckage, but perhaps it had played a role in fooling the führer about Allied tactics when *der Grossinvasion* would hit.[7]

Bedeviling the Gestapo in Toulouse

WHEN FRANCE had surrendered to Nazi Germany in June 1940, French Army Captain Marcel Taillandier shed his uniform but refused to capitulate. Instead he made his way to Toulouse, an ancient city about 380 miles south of Paris. Confident that the Allies would one day return to liberate France, Taillandier went underground to carry on the war against the Germans.

Toulouse is the home of the University of Toulouse, founded in 1229. The tomb of St. Thomas Aquinas is in Toulouse, a city of some 250,000 persons. During the war years Toulouse was a hotbed of espionage and intrigue, infested with spies and secret agents.

Both the Abwehr and its intelligence rival, the Sicherheitsdienst (SD), were especially active in Toulouse, because it was a major link along an overland escape route for Allied airmen shot down in France, Belgium, and the Netherlands. A secret organization called MI-9, under British Brigadier Norman R. Crockett, had been responsible for organizing the underground railroad.

Crockett had realized that the Germans were guarding the English Channel coast so tightly that it would be impossible to smuggle the escapees directly across to Britain. Therefore the escape line extended from the Netherlands all the way to the Pyrenees Mountains on the French-Spanish border.

Captain Ian Garrow, tall, energetic, clever, who had escaped to Paris from the English Channel coast after his Scottish 51st (Highland) Division had been trapped and forced to surrender in May 1940, had arranged for a series of safe houses in the French capital. In these houses he collected Allied airmen from northern France, Belgium, and the Netherlands, and dispatched them with French underground escorts toward Toulouse.

Wearing ill-fitting, threadbare civilian clothing, the escapees traveled singly or in tiny groups by foot, bicycle, horse and cart, bus, train, and car. Along the way, French civilians risked their lives to shelter and feed the fugitives.

Earlier, MI-9 had arranged for an unlikely secret agent, Nubar Gulbenkian, to organize a standard procedure to smuggle the escapees from France over the Pyrenees into Spain. Gulbenkian was young, personable, wealthy, and an official in the legation of neutral Iran in London.

Following instructions by his MI-9 controller, Gulbenkian had slipped into France and made secret contact with a garage owner code-named Parker in the city of Perpignan on the French side of the border with Spain. Parker's real name was Michel Pareyre. Gulbenkian cut a deal with Parker in which the British treasury paid £40 for each Allied officer and £20 for what the British call "other ranks."

In the scheme worked out by Gulbenkian and Parker, the Frenchman hid the escapees in his garage after they arrived from a Toulouse stopover, then turned them over to guides Parker had recruited. It was risky business. The Gestapo knew of the escape line and patrolled the Pyrenees on the lookout for the Allied fugitives.

All of the guides knew the rugged, towering Pyrenees intimately, having either worked in them or hiked over them for recreation before the war. Once the escapees crossed the mountains, the Allied airmen were interned by neutral Spain, but most of them were released by diplomatic pressure and continued to England.

In Toulouse, meanwhile, the former French Army captain Marcel Taillandier spent the first three years of his underground activities stockpiling hidden arms and ammunition dumps around the region. These would be used for an uprising in Toulouse once the Americans and British invaded France.

Then a French traitor, for a few pieces of gold, tipped off the Gestapo about Taillandier and his secret arms dumps. Although the underground leader escaped the German dragnet that ensued, many of his men did not. They were tortured, then executed. All of the secret dumps were located and seized by the Gestapo.

Saddened and furious by the tragic turn of events, Taillandier decided to change his tactics. No more passive roles, such as building arms dumps. He vowed to commit mayhem on the Gestapo, the Abwehr, the Sicherheitsdienst, and the French traitors in their pay.

Within a few weeks Taillandier had established the nuclei of a resistance group he code-named Morhange. These underground warriors soon became celebrated for their bold attacks against the German counterintelligence groups. Morhange seemed to have its agents and informers everywhere in the Toulouse region. Because of their cruel and often inhumane actions, the Gestapo was a particular target of Morhange violence.

So effective had the Morhange become that the Abwehr and the Gestapo forgot their long-standing feud and joined hands to fight the fierce band of *résistants* who were wreaking mayhem in the Germans' ranks. No Gestapo agent knew when he would suddenly be shot down in the street, while eating in a restaurant, or leaving his place of lodging. Some of the Germans were overpowered, whisked away, and never seen again.

Meanwhile, Marcel Taillandier had performed an incredible exploit. Somehow he had ingratiated himself with the Gestapo and seemed to have joined its ranks as a traitor and informer. One of his first assignments was to identify a band of terrorists headed by an unscrupulous Frenchman going by the code name Ricardo.

Taillandier plunged into his assignment, but he didn't have to hunt very far. Actually, he himself was the wanted Ricardo, and the "terrorists" were his Morhange. In essence he was conducting a search for himself. Playing his collaboration role to the hilt, Taillandier reported regularly to his Gestapo contact on the fruits of his investigation. He provided many leads—all of them leading *away from* the Morhange.

All the while, the elusive Morhange continued to function. On one occasion its members kidnapped an Abwehr officer, spirited him off to a safe house, and forced him to disclose the names of the résistants under suspicion. That action resulted in those the Abwehr thought to be underground members to flee the region or go into hiding before they could be arrested.

In December 1943 a Morhange agent who had been planted in the Toulouse Gestapo headquarters got word to Taillandier that a Gestapo vehicle convoy was to travel to the Riviera city of Nice on New Year's Day 1944. The convoy would be carrying secret papers intended to assist the Gestapo along the Riviera to break up the French underground in southern France.

When the string of German vehicles was rounding a curve in a mountainous area fifty miles south of Toulouse, it was raked by heavy fusillades of rifle and automatic weapons fire from Taillandier and his band. All the Gestapo men were killed, as were their soldier escorts. Then the priceless records were carted away, and soon the underground along the Riviera was alerted and scores of those scheduled to be executed were able to go into hiding.

A few months later, Marcel Taillandier's luck ran out. In a fierce gun battle with several Gestapo agents, he was wounded, captured, and taken to a hospital. Soon four Gestapo agents entered the Frenchman's room and roughly hauled him from the building. He was never seen again.[8]

An X-Craft Calls on the *Tirpitz*

THROUGHOUT THE FIRST FIVE MONTHS OF 1943, what British Prime Minister Winston Churchill had labeled the Battle of the Atlantic reached unprecedented scale and violence. Allied navies, mainly British, sought to clear the vast ocean of the deadly menace of the German U-boat wolfpacks to secure the critical lanes through which large numbers of military men and war matériel from the United States flowed to Great Britain.

The brutal conflict also involved aircraft, radar, wireless, and cryptanalysis (decoding of messages). Neither side seemed to have been aware that the other was reading its secret cipher communications. Victory, it appeared, would go to the adversary who had the will and the stamina to sustain the ferocious conflict in the ocean.

The year began with more U-boats marauding the Atlantic than ever before. There were about 110, compared to 57 at the outbreak of the war. In only two months, January and February, the underwater wolfpacks sank 102 Allied ships, mainly cargo vessels, of 360,000 tons. In March the Allies suffered the greatest losses of any month in the war — 108 ships of 627,000 tons.

Slowly, almost imperceptibly, the turning point in the Battle of the Atlantic came in May, when the Germans lost 41 U-boats during the month and Allied shipping losses were down to 200,000 tons. These devastating losses could not be sustained, so Grossadmiral Karl Doenitz, commander of the U-boat fleet, withdrew all his wolfpacks to an area southwest of the Azores.

Doenitz, however, had not given up the savage struggle. Nor had Adolf Hitler, the supreme commander of the Wehrmacht. The führer approved mass production of a radically improved U-boat, the Mark XXI. This was an all-electric craft of 1,600 tons with triple the underwater speed of existing boats and a ventilating apparatus (called a snorkel) that enabled it to recharge batteries without surfacing. However, the first of the Mark XXI boats would not be operational until the end of 1944.

With the eradication of the U-boat imperilment, Allied generals focused their attention on the remaining threats to the vital Atlantic shipping lanes: the

A British X-craft. (Imperial War Museum)

three powerful surface warships anchored beside the towering black mountains along Alta Fjord in northern Norway. There was the mighty battleship *Tirpitz*, the battle cruiser *Scharnhorst*, and the cruiser *Lützow*, backed by a collection of destroyers that numbered nine or ten.

The presence of these formidable warships haunted the British Admiralty. They not only posed a distinct threat to Allied shipping in the Atlantic, but also to what was called the Murmansk run, in which convoys carrying tanks, airplanes, and other war matériel to the Soviet Union sailed north of Norway and anchored above the Arctic Circle at Murmansk. This critical lifeline to Russia was only a relatively short distance from Alten Fjord, the lair of the *Tirpitz*, *Scharnhorst*, and *Lützow*.

To meet the threat of these German heavy warships, the Allies had a formidable force of their own heavies, including aircraft carriers, hovering in and near the great British naval base at Scapa Flow, surrounded by the Orkney Islands off the northern coast of Scotland. These Allied ships were to prevent the *Tirpitz* and the remainder of its squadron from breaking out into the North Atlantic shipping lanes.

With the arrival of spring 1943, the British Admiralty concocted a series of schemes to neutralize or destroy the German warships at Alta Fjord. All of the plans, however, had to be rejected. The ships could not be attacked by surface vessels, for their lair was considered to be impenetrable. Nor would heavy bombings get the job done, because the German vessels were beyond the range of any British or U.S. aircraft then available.

Consequently the British admirals decided on getting the job done by unconventional means—a secret mission attack by midget submarines called X-craft. These underwater miniatures were fifty-one feet long, weighed some thirty-four tons, and traveled at six and a half knots on the surface and five knots beneath it. An X-craft crew consisted of three officers and one engine room artificer. Its weapons were two detachable mines, each containing two tons of explosives.

Planning for the audacious raid on the big German warships was carried out in conditions of extreme secrecy. The mission of six X-craft to be involved was to penetrate the minefields, antisubmarine nets, and boom defenses that guarded Alta Fjord from sea attack. Once inside the German ships' lair, the crews were to position the mines under the keels of the *Tirpitz, Scharnhorst,* and *Lützow* and set fuses to blow up the vessels. Then the X-craft were to get out of the fjord as rapidly as possible.

For two months in the summer of 1943, the crews of six X-craft trained for the delicately timed secret mission on Loch Cairnbawn in Aryllshire. Under cover of night on September 11–12, conventional submarines began towing the small craft in the direction of a point 150 miles off Alta Fjord. There they were to slip their tows, make their attack, then return to the mother submarines. Three X-craft were assigned to mine the *Tirpitz,* two the *Scharnhorst,* and one the *Lützow.*

A series of mishaps resulted in only the X6 and the X7 reaching the fjord. It was then determined that the *Scharnhorst,* although regularly shadowed by the British Royal Air Force, had slipped out of its lair. So X6 and X7 set out to attack the main prize, the 38,000-ton *Tirpitz.*

On the night of September 20–21 the two miniature subs, traveling beneath the surface, negotiated the elaborate minefields, thanks to intelligence that had been received by the British from the Norwegian underground. Then troubles beset the X6, and it had to drop out of the operation. The X7, however, continued to bore farther into the fjord—and became badly entangled in the sturdy antisubmarine nets.

In a frenzy to release itself from the steel grip, the X7 went out of control and inadvertently broke the surface. Crewmen, piercing the blackness with their eyes, suddenly felt a surge of deep concern. In front of them, only 75 feet away, was the great dark hull of the mighty *Tirpitz.*

Without a loss of moments, the X7 dived—and struck the big battle-wagon's hull. The four Britons held their breaths: the clanging against the much larger ship must surely have alerted the Germans on guard duty on deck. However, the crewmen on the little sub managed to plant one of its mines.

Then the X7 snaked its way aft along the *Tirpitz*'s keel and planted a second explosive charge.

The X7 immediately made a run for the fjord's entrance, but again it became entangled in the same nets, lost control, and came to the surface, where it was raked by heavy gunfire and sank. Miraculously, two of the crew survived, but the two others lost their lives.

A short time later, Alta Fjord was rocked by an enormous explosion, followed by another blast. The *Tirpitz* heaved several feet out of the water. All three major turbines were put out of operation by the explosions. The *Tirpitz* was immobilized, and Norwegian patriots soon reported to London by radio that the battleship was no longer seaworthy.

The cost of the covert operation's success had been heavy. None of the midget subs returned to England.[9]

A French Boy and His Music Teacher

A HUNDRED MILES NORTHWEST of Paris along the English Channel in Normandy, a French underground *reseau* code-named Centurie was keeping a close watch on the Atlantikwall, part of Adolf Hitler's megalomaniacal scheme to encase all of Europe in a solid girdle of concrete. Centurie's eyes and ears were hundreds of men and women who lived along the coast.

Although the possibility of Allied landings in Belgium, the Netherlands, Norway, or elsewhere in France had not been ruled out, the führer and his generals concluded that when the Anglo-Americans struck across the English Channel they would hit somewhere along the coast of northwestern France. Apart from the two greatest ports in that region, Cherbourg and Le Havre, the most important harbor was Port-en-Bessein, where the Germans based a minesweeper flotilla and five swift E-boats that regularly prowled the Channel for shipping targets.

The harbor at Port-en-Bessein was sheltered by two long breakwaters like curved concrete arms. The town itself lies in a deep cleft between two high hills. More than a year after construction had started on the Atlantikwall, the Germans had converted Port-en-Bessein into a miniature fortress.

Early in 1943 the Centurie underground in Normandy, headed by Marcel Girard, a forty-one-year-old, graying cement salesman who lived in Caen, had taken on the gargantuan task of creating a detailed master map of the Atlantikwall that would depict the entire coast extending from the Cap de la Hague at the northwestern tip of the Cherbourg Peninsula all the way to Ouistreham, 125 miles to the east.

Obstacles to the huge mapping job seemed insurmountable, but Centurie agents recruited hundreds of ordinary French men and women living along the Channel coast to serve as the eyes and ears for the project. They would smuggle bits and pieces of information on the fortifications to collecting points in Caen.

From Caen, the ancient capital of Normandy, the Atlantikwall information was taken by courier to a dingy suite of rooms in an old building in a run-down section of Paris. This was Centurie's headquarters in its Battle of the Wall.

Lysander aircraft, which could land and take off in a short distance, flown by Royal Air Force pilots, landed under a blanket of darkness at predesignated pastures outside Paris. The planes taxied up to signaling flashlights held by French underground agents, collected the Centurie data on the wall, sped down the grassy field, and lifted off for England.

Eventually this mountain of scraps of information reached a closely guarded and supersecret facility known as the Martian Room, outside London. There a remarkably detailed master map of 125 miles of the Atlantikwall was being pieced together, using the Centurie data.

As the Martian map grew ever more detailed there was a major deficiency of information about fortifications within Port-en-Bessein. The big coastal guns with their thick concrete covers, bunkers, machine gun posts, barriers, and other defenses were disposed roughly in the form of a triangle, with especially strong positions on the heights to the east and west. This entire triangle was known to the Germans as a *Stuetzpunkt* (strong point), a forbidden zone entirely sealed off from the French population.

Now the major problem facing Centurie leaders was how to get an agent inside the Port-en-Bessein triangle to obtain the microscopic details of the fortifications needed by the Martians in London. When the underground chiefs were about to admit defeat, fifteen-year-old François Guerin, a student living in nearby Bayeux, came up with an idea.

François, a bright-eyed youngster with a crop of curly black hair, enlisted the help of his friend and music teacher Arthur Poitevin, a heavily built man some fourteen years François's senior. There had been Poitevins in the region since William, duke of Normandy, massed his fleet in the Port-en-Bessein harbor before sailing across the Channel to conquer England in 1066.

Both François and Poitevin knew their planned caper would be a hazardous one, but each accepted that fact. As though on a casual morning stroll to breathe in the refreshing sea air, the pair had just entered the stuetzpunkt when a loud shout rang out: *"Halten!"* The two intruders froze. Moments later, a *Feldgrau* dashed up. Excitedly waving his arms and shouting, he demanded that the intruders leave the restricted area immediately.

Then the German did a double-take. He looked at the white cane that Arthur Poitevin was carrying and moved his hand rapidly in front of the Frenchman's eyes. Poitevin did not blink; he had been blind since birth.

François, cool and collected beyond his tender years, explained to the sentry that his sightless friend loved to breathe the sea air and hear the seagulls scampering around nearby. The German relented. After all, what harm to the Third Reich could be caused by a blind man and a wisp of a boy who was lovingly guiding his friend's footsteps?

François held tightly to Arthur's arm as they walked along the waterfront, where no Frenchman had been permitted for more than a year. They halted.

"Tell me what you see," Poitevin said.

"There's a gun, a really big gun, sticking out of a concrete casemate on the height above us on the left."

"In what direction is the gun sited, François?"

"Northeast, it looks like."

"What else do you see?"

"There's a path leading up to it near where we're standing. It must be at least 150 feet up to the gun. Hold on to my arm. I'm going to start counting our steps from here at the breakwater to where the path begins."

Arthur and François were careful not to draw suspicion by remaining for too long a time in the forbidden fortified zone. But all the while they were there, the boy was talking, explaining in detail the defense works that abounded.

After leaving the strong point François asked, "Arthur, can you really remember all that?"

The music teacher replied, "When you're blind, François, other faculties are sharpened, especially the memory."

Back at the studio the music teacher used, François took out a tablet and scribbled furiously to get down every word that flowed effortlessly and accurately from Arthur's lips. It was an amazing recitation of everything the boy had said during their time in the stuetzpunkt.

For the next month, the French man and boy, inseparable companions, strolled about the forbidden zone of Port-en-Bessein. Eventually the Martians in London had a highly detailed layout of the fortifications—including such tiny matters as the names of German squad leaders at each machine-gun post.

When British Tommies would storm ashore near Port-en-Bessein on D-Day, perhaps hundreds would survive because a blind man and his music student had pinpointed the German big guns on the heights, permitting bombers and naval guns to demolish the weapons prior to H-Hour.[10]

An Atomic Alert on New Year's Eve

DR. HAROLD C. UREY, a Nobel Prize recipient and discoverer of heavy water, and other American scientists had grown worried that the Germans, although they may not have perfected an atomic bomb, might devise means to contam-

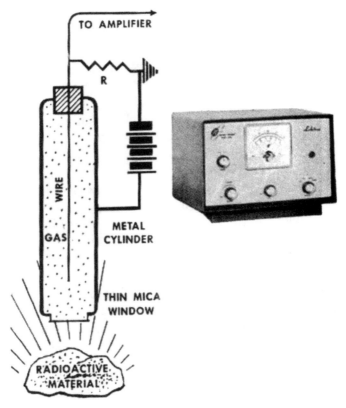

Geiger counters to detect radiation were distributed in anticipation of a German atomic attack on the United States. (Author's collection)

inate U.S. cities with large amounts of radioactivity. In the fall of 1943 Urey urged General Leslie Groves, the director of the Manhattan Project, to warn the American people that they should be prepared for a possible atomic attack.

Groves was aghast over the suggestion, knowing that such an announcement would give away to the Germans and Japanese the supersecret of the Manhattan Project. However, he, too, was deeply concerned about the possibility of German atomic attacks. He called on General George Marshall, the silver-haired, astute army chief of staff in the new Pentagon across the Potomac from Washington, and warned that the United States might receive large quantities of radioactive materials. Marshall merely nodded his understanding but made no reply.

Back at his office elsewhere in the huge Pentagon, Groves sent for five trusted military officers. Warning that they must not breathe a word to anyone about what they were doing, he provided each man with a Geiger counter, an instrument used to detect radioactive radiation, such as that given off in the release of atomic energy. "Under the highest secrecy," the military couriers were to take the instruments to the Manhattan Project offices in San Francisco, Boston, Chicago, Washington, and New York.

Army and navy officers in those cities were given secret instructions in the use of the device, a thin metal cylinder enclosed in a glass tube, which was named after a German physicist, Dr. Hans Geiger, who had developed it in 1908 and improved its design in 1920. Scientists designated by General Groves were put on a standby basis to rush to the scene of any suspected radiation contamination by German sources.

At an installation given the cover name Metallurgical Laboratory, housed in a cluster of buildings on the University of Chicago campus, scores of scientists had been conducting experiments in large-scale self-sustaining chain reactions. Many of those at Metlab (the shortened term) had become convinced that Adolf Hitler had targeted Chicago for his first atomic broadside.

Perhaps recalling that the Japanese sneak attack at Pearl Harbor had hit on a Sunday, the Metlab scientists decided that the most likely time for the führer to strike would be Christmas Day 1943, only a few weeks away. Several of the family men sent their families to the country for the holidays.

Christmas came and went in Chicago. It was quite peaceful. Now the Chicago staff decided that the Nazis planned an atomic surprise on New Year's Eve. In England, where Allied armies were massing to invade Normandy in the spring, commanders were warned secretly about the suspected atomic attack at a time when most soldiers, presumably, would be imbibing and therefore less able to respond to the new conditions.

In the event of a radioactive emergency in England, Dr. Norman Hilberry, the principal aide to Dr. Arthur Holly Compton, a Nobel Prize recipient in physics and now head of Metlab, was to rush several scientists to Europe aboard Army Air Corps planes that would be fueled and standing by at the Chicago airport.

At his Chicago apartment on New Year's Eve, Hilberry nervously paced about. He knew he would be unable to sleep, so he decided to stay up until the wee hours of the morning, when it would be daylight in Europe. If anything drastic were to have happened there, he would be called by the duty officer at Metlab.

Finally, at about 3:00 A.M., Hilberry and his wife decided to go to bed. Just then the telephone jangled, shattering the stillness. The instrument sat at the end of a long hallway. Hilberry felt his heart thumping. It seemed to skip beats. Certain that an atomic attack was in progress, he dashed down the hall. After breathlessly picking up the telephone, Hilberry was greeted by long moments of silence.

Then an unknown drunk, who presumably had dialed the wrong number, shouted in a slurred voice: "Happy New Year!"[11]

"Ghost Voices" over Europe

FOR FOUR YEARS the British and the Germans had been locked in a sophisticated, intricate, and ceaseless battle of the airwaves over Europe. The enormous speed of air combat made both sides critically dependent on wireless communications and radiotelephones, which were necessary to assemble and direct bomber fleets as well as to guide intercepting fighter planes to enemy bombers. Consequently the objective of the ether war was to disrupt the other side's radio communications.

Seeking new wavelengths that were not jammed by the British, the Germans regularly replaced or modified their electronic system to aid Luftwaffe fighter planes to locate and shoot down Royal Air Force bombers. Each time the Germans altered the fighters' communication equipment, the British would develop a way to jam the new wavelength. One of these jammers was code-named Airborne Cigar, an instrument so light it could be placed in Royal Air Force bombers, and it was activated on missions over Europe.

Airborne Cigar proved to be so successful that the Germans had to install a high-powered transmitter on the ground to "talk" their night-fighter pilots to approaching bombers by radiotelephone. In turn, the British countered by setting up an equally high-powered transmitter on the same frequency used by the Germans.

Code-named Operation Corona, the new British technique was tried for the first time on the night of October 22–23, 1943, in a Royal Air Force raid against Kassel, a large city on the banks of the Fulda River in western Germany. Ground controllers in England and those in the Third Reich were manning the new ground transmitters.

As soon as Luftwaffe night fighters scrambled to intercept the approaching bomber stream, "ghost voices," speaking idiomatic German, began to fill the airwaves over northwestern Europe, heckling the Luftwaffe ground controllers. These ghost voices from the British transmitter issued orders contrary to those given by the German ground controllers.

In the dark sky the Luftwaffe pilots quickly became aware that the British were doing something to snarl radio communications. But which voice was actually the German ground controller?

Finally the German controller called out, "Beware of another voice!" Moments later he called out in frustration, "Don't be led astray by the enemy! Follow my directions!"

The ghost voice from Great Britain continued to give fake orders.

Growing steadily more angry, the German controller shouted, "Get off the air, you *Schweinhund!*"

"The Englishman is swearing," came the German-speaking ghost voice of the British ground controller. "Pay no attention to him!"

"No, no!" the German shouted. "It's not the Englishman who is swearing, it's me!"

"Don't let him confuse you," the German-speaking Briton exclaimed. "It's the Englishman swearing."

Now the confused and confounded Luftwaffe pilots began shouting curses at the German ground controller, at each other, and at the ghost voice—whichever one was the ghost voice.

Meanwhile, the city of Kassel was pulverized by a cascade of RAF bombs.[12]

Close Call in a Secret Room

STOCKHOLM in neutral Sweden was a hotbed of espionage during the war. It was said that if a person were to accidentally bump into another individual in the darkness, chances were 50–50 that one or the other would be a spy for one of the warring countries.

One of the most successful Allied espionage rings operating in Sweden was composed of German refugees who hated Adolf Hitler and his Nazi regime. Leader of the covert network was a man named Kurt Englich, who had become renowned within the ring for his audacity and coolness in tight situations.

Through diligent research, Englich learned that the center of German espionage in Sweden was in a huge, vaultlike room of the Nazi air attaché's office in Stockholm. The room served as a clearinghouse of incoming intelligence, which was segregated into categories, interpreted, bundled, and sent to the appropriate agency in Berlin. It was November 1943.

More snooping by Englich disclosed that the room was always empty of personnel at night, when it was guarded by only a lone German, always the same one. In a neutral nation there was no need for heavy security. Besides, it was doubtful if hostile persons even knew of the secret room.

Discreet inquiry by Englich established that the guard was not happy with his assignment in Stockholm, that he felt he was being denied promotions and a more worthwhile task, and that he was far from being a booster of the Nazi regime. The adroit Englich found out where the guard lived, where he ate, and where he went for recreation. Then he "happened" to be at those places periodically, found an excuse to make friends with the guard, and the two discussed "politics" over schnapps at a Stockholm restaurant.

Bit by bit, the guard, his tongue loosened by the strong spirits he was consuming, let slip his antagonism toward the Nazis. Englich bored in on this chink in the guard's armor and managed to convince him that Germany was a cinch to lose the war.

Soon Englich felt the time was ripe to put the crucial question to his new friend: would the guard permit him to enter the air attaché's office at night to copy important documents that were left lying on the desks and counters in the locked room? If the guard said no, Englich was in big trouble, for no doubt the man would tip off the air attaché and "remedial action" would be taken against the spy ring leader. However, the German agreed.

Night after night, Englich worked in the room, furiously photographing papers, maps, charts, and anything else that looked as though it concerned espionage. Outside the door, his friend, the guard, relaxed, read newspapers, and smoked. There was no danger. In the year he had been guarding the secret room, no one from the air attaché's office had ever shown up at night.

During one document-copying session, the guard heard heavy footsteps coming down the hall and a Luftwaffe lieutenant, who was an aide to the attaché, appeared moments later. With a cursory nod to the ashen-faced guard, the young officer walked to the vaultlike room, took out his key, and opened the door. There had been no time for Englich to escape. The spy leader seemed to be trapped.

Quick-witted as always, Englich continued copying the document on which he was working, as though he belonged in the place legitimately. He knew that espionage and government officials from Berlin often traipsed in and out of the building on business, and he was banking that the lieutenant would not question an unknown man—especially one who appeared to be totally unconcerned about a German officer being in the room.

Clearly, the lieutenant had arrived to take care of some crucial matter. After giving Englich a terse *"Guten Abend"* (Good evening), the newcomer strolled rapidly across the room, opened one of the large safes, and removed a bottle of Scotch whisky. Then he locked the safe again, put the precious container under one arm, and walked out of the room.

Kurt Englich and his friend the guard resumed breathing.[13]

Masking the "Chicago Skyline"

As the year 1943 drew to a close, strange new devices of war were being developed in England for the invasion of Normandy, set for the first week in May 1944. There were tanks that could swim and others that carried great rolls of lath to be used in antitank ditches or as stepping-stones over concrete barriers. Yet other tanks were equipped with great chain flails that beat the ground in front of them to explode mines.

New kinds of landing craft, including the awkward DUKW (Duck, to the Americans), would disembark troops and heavy vehicles close to shore. There were flat, block-long ships, each carrying a forest of pipes for the mass launching of warfare's newest weapons, rockets. For a time the British had even considered constructing an enormous aircraft landing platform of frozen seawater and sawdust.

A portion of Mulberry in operation off Normandy. Trucks are on Spud pierhead.
(National Archives)

The most ingenious new devices were two artificial harbors—one for a British beach called Gold and the other for an American beach known as Omaha. These two engineering miracles were code-named Mulberry. When in place, the two harbors would assure a steady flow of troops, tanks, guns, artillery pieces, vehicles, and supplies into the Allied beachhead until the port of Cherbourg could be captured, perhaps two weeks after D-Day.

The principal units in the man-made harbors were 145 huge concrete caissons called Phoenix. The largest of these caissons would have crew quarters and antiaircraft guns. When being towed across the Channel, they would look like a five-story building lying on its side. These Phoenixes would be sunk butt to butt offshore to make inner breakwaters.

A short distance outside the Phoenix barrier would be a line of 70 old merchant vessels and four obsolete warships, code-named Gooseberries. These would be jettisoned end to end to form a secondary breakwater.

Inside the bodies of water sheltered at the two beaches from the heavy Channel waves by the Phoenixes and Gooseberries would be pierheads code-named Spuds—great floating platforms with steel legs at each corner that would sink into the Channel floor. From these piers, metal roadways would run over a succession of floating barges to the shore, where the roadways were securely anchored.

At these pierheads offshore, landing craft and small ships would be able to discharge their cargoes into various vehicles that would be driven over the metal roadway onto shore. Within the calm waters of these artificial harbors good-sized freighters could unload into barges ferrying back and forth to the beaches.

The Mulberries would be the linchpins of the Normandy invasion. So vital were these portable harbors that Prime Minister Winston Churchill was briefed daily on progress and problems. Should Adolf Hitler's intelligence agencies discover the true purpose of the Mulberries, the führer could alter strategy and prepare to confront the Allies, not in a port, but on the open beaches.

The artificial harbors were being constructed in segments along the Sussex coast of southeastern England. When completed, the components would be towed across the Channel in the wake of the assault troops by a large fleet of tugs, including every available one in England and on the eastern seaboard of the United States.

As D-Day grew closer, the huge caissons, stretching for miles at intervals along the Sussex shore, presented an amazing sight. "It looks as though someone has picked up Chicago and put it down on the beach," remarked Royal Navy Rear Admiral William Tennant, who was coordinating Mulberry construction.

That dazzling "Chicago skyline" presented a haunting problem for Admiral Tennant and British security forces: how could this mass of strange shapes be "hidden" from the Germans? It was a given that Luftwaffe reconnaissance planes would take photographs of the monstrous caissons. What about Nazi spies in southern England? Could the twenty thousand men in the Mulberry labor force keep the secret? Surely some of them might talk, especially when tongues were lubricated late at night in pubs, and their comments could fall on hostile ears.

To conceal the secret of the Mulberries, the British launched a misinformation campaign. A bevy of undercover operatives spread word among the workers and the Sussex coastal population that the weird-looking caissons were floating grain silos that would be towed across the Channel after D-Day to help feed the hungry population.

Britain's supersecret XX Committee (Double-Cross Committee) joined in the scenario to hoodwink Hitler about the artificial ports. Early in the war, seven Nazi spies captured in England had been hanged, and several more were to be executed. Then Major Thomas A. "Tar" Robertson of MI-5, the British secret service, convinced his superiors that a living Nazi double-crosser would bolster the British war effort far more than would a dead German spy.

Thereafter, captured Nazi agents in England, instead of being hanged, buried, and forgotten, were given a choice: they could use their own transmitters to send phony information back to their controllers in Hamburg as though they were free, or they could be hanged. All chose to cooperate.

Now two "turned" German spies, with XX Committee men sitting at their elbows, began transmitting information on the caissons to their former masters in the Third Reich. The messages had been carefully scripted by members of the XX Committee. The caissons, the spies reported, were being built to replace docks that would be badly damaged or destroyed when the Allies launched a frontal assault against a major port.

As the work progressed on the Mulberries, tens of thousands of Britons were tuned to Radio Berlin to hear Lord Haw-Haw make his daily propaganda broadcast. Born William Joyce in Brooklyn, New York, to an English mother and an American father, he had moved to England in 1921 and settled in Berlin shortly before war erupted in Europe in late 1939.

Lord Haw-Haw held a fascination for many in Great Britain. Now he said on the air:

> We know exactly what you intend to do with those concrete units [on the Sussex coast]. You think you are going to sink them on our coasts in the assault. Well, we are going to help you out. We'll save you the trouble. When you get under way [on D-Day], we're going to sink them for you in the middle of the English Channel.

No German propaganda broadcast during the war caused greater consternation and alarm among Allied leaders. It seemed as though the elaborate secrecy and machinations to mask the purpose of the Mulberries had been in vain. Lord Haw-Haw's broadcast was widely interpreted as indicating Hitler and his generals had deduced that the invasion would hit, not frontally from a port, but over open beaches nearby.

In this climate of near-panic, General Eisenhower urged Washington to rush fifty Coast Guard picket boats to be used to guard against any attacks against the Mulberries.

Had German intelligence really uncovered the secret of the Mulberries? The anxious Allied high command turned to Ultra and the supersecret American Signals Intelligence Service (ASIS) for an answer to that haunting question. Curiously, the main listening post of the ASIS was in an unlikely locale—Asmara, in Ethiopia—where a staff of some three hundred technicians toiled under clandestine conditions.

The primary function at Asmara was to eavesdrop on wireless messages flowing between Tokyo and the Japanese ambassador in Berlin, General Hiroshi Baron Oshima. Because Adolf Hitler and the Japanese warlord General Hideki Tojo had joined in a mutual assistance pact shortly after Pearl Harbor, Oshima was regularly briefed by the Germans on weapons, economics, and politics throughout the Nazi Empire.

A squat, outgoing individual, Oshima transmitted the most important intelligence to imperial headquarters in Tokyo over a high-speed radiotelephone link from Berlin. Intercepted by the ASIS at Asmara, Oshima's reports to Tokyo were sent on a radioteleprinter to a mansion at Arlington Hill, a few miles outside Washington, D.C., which housed the Signals Security Agency (SSA).

When the raw intercepts had been decoded by the SSA, they were sent by wireless to an underground American signals center in London, from where the intelligence was circulated on a restricted basis to U.S. and British officials. Only perhaps ten men in all of London knew how the intelligence had been obtained.

While thousands of German agents around the world were trying feverishly to learn where and when the Allies would strike across the English Channel, General Hiroshi Oshima was given a tour of the Atlantikwall and then briefed in detail by Field Marshal Karl Rudolf Gerd von Rundstedt, the *Oberbefehlshaber West* (Commander in Chief, West), whose headquarters was in a Paris suburb.

Rundstedt, a brilliant officer known in the Third Reich as the Last of the Prussians, secretly hated Hitler and had had numerous arguments with him. Few had ever engaged in disputes with the führer and survived for long. What does that "Bohemian corporal" know about high command? the field marshal would state to confidants. And Rundstedt had long held the conclusion that Germany had already lost the war.

During his lengthy briefing of Oshima, Rundstedt referred to the existence of the concrete structures off the coast of Sussex in England. However, he assured the ambassador that he had high-grade intelligence that they were being constructed to replace docks that might be destroyed at whatever port was assaulted by the Allies.

When a long summary of Rundstedt's briefing was telegraphed to Tokyo by Oshima, it was intercepted by the monitoring station at Asmara, which shuttled it to the SSA mansion outside Washington. In London, news of Oshima's report resulted in collective sighs of relief.

In the time ahead, Ultra kept especially vigilant for any indication that Field Marshal von Rundstedt was shuffling his forces around because of intelligence about the Mulberries. Such actions would indicate he knew the Allies would land on the open beaches. Security officers in London realized that Rundstedt could have been lying to General Oshima about the caissons on the Sussex coast being built to replace damaged or destroyed docks.

However, no dramatic change in troop deployment was uncovered. Aging Rundstedt, who could have retired years earlier, merely remained in his headquarters outside Paris, drank champagne, talked with aides about the "good old days" in the Wehrmacht—and waited for the defeat he thought to be inevitable.[14]

Part Six

The Lights Go On Again

A U.S. Colonel's Private Airline

LATE IN JANUARY 1944, Norwegian-born Bernt Balchen, an American citizen, arrived in Stockholm, Sweden, and checked into a suite at the Grand Hotel. Although wearing civilian clothes, Balchen was a colonel in the U.S. Army Air Corps, and he had slipped into Stockholm incognito on an important covert mission.

Sweden, a neutral country sharing an eight-hundred-mile border with German-occupied Norway to the west, was a haven for war refugees from all over Europe—some two hundred thousand of them. Dozens of Swedish agencies, both private and government-operated, provided the displaced persons with food, shelter, clothing, and medical care.

Among the refugees were thirteen thousand Norwegian men of military age who had escaped from their country and had volunteered for training in secret camps established throughout Sweden. All hoped to join the Allies in the fight against Nazi Germany. Clad in Swedish uniforms with Norwegian shoulder patches and armed with Swedish weapons, the volunteers were formed into infantry battalions.

When the German ambassador to Sweden protested, the Swedes assured him that the Norwegians were merely training in "health camps" to "keep them out of mischief."

Meanwhile, a few hundred miles away, London was gripped by "invasion fever." Clearly, a powerful military machine in England was preparing to strike across the English Channel against Nazi-held France, Belgium, or the Netherlands. So the Norwegian government-in-exile in London wanted a part in the shooting war. Consequently, the British government agreed to arrange advanced training facilities in Canada for the young Norwegians in the Swedish "health camps."

Throughout the war the Swedish government had been walking a tightwire to maintain its neutral status. On occasion it secretly "appeased" the Germans; at other times it made covert concessions to the Americans and British. Now, in early 1944, the tide had clearly turned against Nazi Germany, so the Swedes agreed to permit the release of two thousand of the Norwegian trainees, although taking such a step was a gross violation of neutrality.

Now British authorities were stumped by a major obstacle: how to get the two thousand men out of Sweden. After discussions with U.S. officers in London, it was decided that Colonel Bernt Balchen would be given that clandestine task. Hence he arrived in Stockholm a few days later.

Balchen had one of the strangest underground assignments of the war. With five old and battered B-24 four-engine bombers, veterans of countless missions over Europe, he was to organize a secret air transport service to fly the two thousand Norwegians out of Sweden, through the skies above Nazi-occupied Norway, and on to London. Then the volunteers would be taken to Canada for training and return in a few months to join in the fight against Adolf Hitler.

Balchen's decrepit B-24s landed at a secret airfield in an especially remote region in Sweden. Although cooperating in the illegal venture, the Swedes sometimes irked Balchen with what he interpreted to be legalistic mumbo jumbo. The Air Ministry, for example, demanded that the five bombers comply with Swedish regulations by displaying official registration numbers on their sides. Balchen knew that he would have to comply with the strict order. So he had the airplanes painted dark green; then the black numerals were visible only from a distance of a few yards.

Balchen, from his command post in a suite in Stockholm's Grand Hotel, soon had his private outfit in operation. He even gave it a name: Ve-do-it Airline. Plucking the Norwegian volunteers out of Sweden proved to be a slow maneuver. Each bomber could carry only thirty-five passengers at a time. And Balchen was hit by another maddening restriction by Swedish authorities: no more than three flights could be made on any given night.

Despite the plethora of roadblocks, Ve-do-it Airline had transported all two thousand of the Norwegians to England by late May 1944. Ve-do-it did not go out of business, however. Rather, several more four-engine bombers were assigned to the clandestine operation.

Meanwhile, German scientists at Peenemünde, on a secluded island just off the Baltic Sea coast, were conducting research and development activities for both the V-1 buzz bomb, a pilotless aircraft packed with explosives, and the V-2, a forty-six-foot, thirteen-ton rocket that had a range of more than two hundred miles and a one-ton, high-explosive warhead.

These were the two secret weapons with which Adolf Hitler was convinced he could pound Great Britain into submission. A rain of buzz bombs (also known to the Allies as doodlebugs) began falling on England on June 13, 1944, and some forty-six hundred of them would explode, mainly on London, during the next three months.

On the same day the buzz-bomb assault was launched, German scientists at Peenemünde fired the experimental Wasserfall antiaircraft rocket equipped with a revolutionary radio mechanism that allowed the rocket to be steered by remote control. This Wasserfall soared high into the blue heavens, but it went awry. Instead of splashing into the Baltic Sea, it flew too long and landed almost

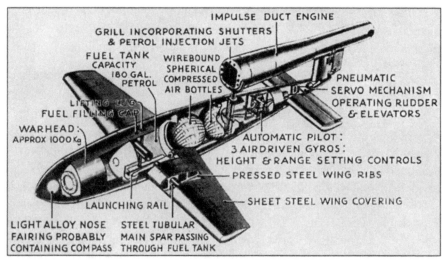

Adolf Hitler's secret weapon, the buzz bomb. (U.S. Army)

intact near Malmö, in southern Sweden. Swedish authorities promptly put armed guards around the impact site and the rocket.

Nearly a month later, on July 10, Stewart Menzies, chief of MI-6, Great Britain's secret service agency in London, received a report from a spy that the Wasserfall had landed in Sweden and that the Germans were desperately trying to recover it. One group of Germans already had tried to enter the sealed-off area behind a slowly moving hearse, posing as mourners. The Swedish guards turned them away.

British officials promptly engaged in clandestine negotiations with the Swedes. At this time of the war, with powerful Allied forces having crossed the English Channel and being in Normandy, the neutral Swedes were inclined to secretly lean toward the British and Americans. So a deal was struck. In return for the rocket, Britain would secretly ship two squadrons of tanks to the Swedish Army.

Now Stewart Menzies was confronted by a daunting problem: how to get the Wasserfall out of Sweden. That obstacle was resolved when several British ordnance officers were flown to Sweden on Colonel Bernt Balchen's Ve-Do-It Airline. At the impact site, the ordnance men dismantled the Wasserfall, loaded it onto one of Balchen's bombers, and the precious cargo was flown to England.

This intelligence coup permitted British scientists at the Royal Aircraft Establishment (a government research facility) at Farnborough, outside London, to inspect a complete German missile. The conclusion reached from the intense research was frightening: there would be no defense against the supersonic V-2 onslaught that Hitler was preparing to launch against England.

Recovery of the Wasserfall on the Ve-Do-It Airline provided the British government with time to evacuate hundreds of thousands of persons, mainly children, before the V-2 bombardment began devastating London on September 8, 1944.[1]

Kidnapping a German General

EARLY ON THE MORNING of February 4, 1944, a Wellington bomber of the Royal Air Force lifted off from the Egyptian airport at Bardia amid great secrecy. On board were twenty-year-old British Major Patrick Leigh-Fermor and eighteen-year-old British Captain Stanley Moss, along with two Greek agents, Georgi Tyrakis and Manoli Paterakis.

This clandestine group was embarking on an especially audacious mission, one that promised only the slimmest chance of success: the kidnapping of Generalmajor Friedrich Wilhelm Müller, the German commander on the large Aegean Sea island of Crete. British cloak-and-dagger officers had planned the abduction not only to strike a heavy blow at the morale and prestige of Wehrmacht forces on Crete but also to help hoodwink Adolf Hitler and his high command into believing that the Balkans, not northwestern France, was to be the next invasion target of the Western Allies.

Crete lies about eighty miles from the Greek mainland. Oblong in shape, it measures about 160 miles in length and from 7 to 35 miles in width. Towering mountain ranges run from one end of Crete to the other.

The island, cradle of Zeus and scene of Icarus's legendary flight, had seen many conquerors in the course of its long and stormy history: Dorians, Romans, Arabs, Venetians, and Turks. But none of these invaders had struck with the fury, power, and suddenness as did 13,000 German paratroopers and glidermen who had jumped or glided onto the island back in May 1941.

After six days of bloody fighting, the relatively small force of Germans, led by Generalleutnant Wilhelm Seussman, who had landed in the first glider, had defeated 42,500 British, Greek, Australian, and New Zealand troops. Under cover of night, some 23,000 of the defenders, a large number of them wounded, had been evacuated to Egypt by ship.

Although capturing Crete entirely by an airborne force had been one of the most daring exploits of the war, victory had a high price tag: a total of 5,140 of the 13,000 German paratroops and glidermen had been killed or wounded.

Now, nearly three years after the German seizure of Crete, the Wellington bomber carrying the four British and Greek secret agents arrived over the Lassithi plain, long known to Cretans as "the valley of the twenty thousand windmills." Bad weather conditions made it difficult for the pilot to locate the drop zone, but he finally did so, and out leaped Major Patrick Leigh-Fermor. Moments after the young Briton crashed to the ground with a heavy thud, mist closed in over the valley. After circling several times in an effort to drop the other three agents, the pilot had to give up and return to Barida.

Leigh-Fermor, meanwhile, had been taken in tow by several men in the Greek underground and escorted to a small but comfortable shepherd's hut to await the arrival of the three agents the next night. But the bad weather and ground fog resulted in having to abort several more attempts to drop Leigh-Fermor's companions.

After two seemingly endless months of being the only armed Allied soldier on an island held by thousands of German soldiers, Leigh-Fermor received word that Captain Stanley Moss and the two Greek agents, Paterakis and Tyrakis, would land by sea at night on Crete's southern coast on April 4. After two days of arduous climbing up and down mountains and dodging German patrols, Leigh-Fermor and a few Cretan partisans reached the designated beach.

In the hush of the night, while Leigh-Fermor and the partisans listened for an approach of Germans, the soft purr of a motor launch was heard in the blackness offshore. A narrow slit of light was flashed from the beach. Minutes later, Leigh-Fermor and the newcomers were exchanging enthusiastic greetings. Moss, Tyrakis, and Paterakis were told that the kidnapping target, General Müller, had departed from Crete only forty-eight hours earlier. His successor was Generalmajor Heinrich Kreipe, who had been transferred from the Eastern Front after receiving several high decorations for bravery.

This unexpected switch of commanders presented no undue alteration in the kidnapping plan. The target would merely be changed to General Kreipe.

Leigh-Fermor, Moss, Tyrakis, and Paterakis began a strenuous march across the heights toward Kastamonitza, a small town nestled at the foot of a mountain. Stealth would be crucial; Germans were everywhere. Two days later, the four men reached the town just as dawn started to break. They were welcomed with open arms by a Crete family. Soon word spread of the newcomers' arrival, and nearly the entire village descended on the hideout to greet the guests.

Because of the hubbub, the doors and shutters of the safe house were kept closed, and partisan guards were posted to warn of any hostile activity. There was ample reason for these precautions: a convalescent home for German soldiers had recently been opened on the edge of the town.

The next day, Mickey Akaumianos, a man in his midtwenties and chief agent for the British secret service on Crete, arrived in Kastamonitza. He came by regular commercial bus from Heraklion, Crete's capital, on the northern coast. After a strategy powwow among the four insurgents and the Cretan underground head, it was decided that Akaumianos would return to Heraklion, taking Leigh-Fermor with him. There the two men would try to obtain information about German forces on the island.

Disguised as peasants, Leigh-Fermor and Akaumianos took the bus to Heraklion, from where they walked four miles to the heavily guarded Villa Ariadne, the island's most luxurious mansion, which had been built by Arthur

Evans, a famous British archaeologist. Peering at the large structure from a clump of bushes only two hundred yards away, Leigh-Fermor felt his heart pounding furiously: Villa Ariadne was where General Kreipe lived.

After slipping back out of the region, Leigh-Fermor and Akaumianos agreed that it would be suicide to try to kidnap the general from his villa, which was surrounded by strands of barbed wire and numerous guardposts sprouting machine guns. At night, floodlights illuminated the premises, and soldiers with ferocious dogs stalked around the perimeter of the enclosure.

Meanwhile, back in Kastamonitza as planned, Captain Moss and a small partisan band climbed into the mountains to locate a headquarters site and settled on a cave on a slope high above the town. A stream only a few yards from the entrance provided fresh water. Each morning a partisan scrambled down the mountain to bring back freshly baked bread.

Word of the secret cave hideout spread like wildfire throughout Kastamonitza, and a large number of villagers began climbing up to the cave bringing wine, cheese, and meat—and unintentionally creating an enormous racket that no doubt could be heard for miles around.

At the same time, outside Heraklion, Leigh-Fermor and Mickey Akaumianos had availed themselves of an excellent observation post to keep an eye on General Kreipe's goings and comings—an upstairs bedroom of a farmhouse in which Akaumianos's parents lived on the grounds of Villa Ariadne. The two secret agents remained for ten days, during which German soldiers visited the farmhouse and became friendly with the two young men introduced as the Akaumianoses' sons, that description being only half correct.

After scrutinizing the general's movements and habits, the two secret agents concluded that the best time to kidnap him was when he would be returning at night from his headquarters some ten miles away. They became so familiar with the general's chauffeur-driven car that they could easily recognize its outline in the dark, or even the sound of its engine.

On some nights Leigh-Fermor and Akaumianos slipped out of the house and prowled around the region to test every detail of their abduction plan. They were not unduly concerned about the possibility that they would be halted by roving German patrols. Akaumianos earlier had forged papers created for the two Britons and the two Greek agents.

Leigh-Fermor and his Cretan comrade decided that the best place to perform the kidnapping was in a hairpin bend in the road leading halfway between Kreipe's headquarters and his living quarters. There the driver would have to slow almost to a crawl. The bend had steep upward slopes on each side, and there were roadside ditches to hide in while awaiting the car's approach.

Returning southward to Kastamonitza, Leigh-Fermor and Akaumianos climbed up to the hideout cave and briefed Captain Moss and the Greeks, Paterakis and Tyrakis, on the abduction plan. Then a courier was sent to another mountain, some twenty miles away, to bring back a guerrilla leader named

Boudzalis and his men. The new arrivals were armed to the teeth, carrying rusty rifles perhaps used by their ancestors in battles against the invading Turks decades earlier.

Boudzalis, a fierce-looking warrior with a handlebar mustache, was given his instructions. He and his guerrillas were to conceal themselves in the brush to either side of the bend in the road at the kidnapping site and emerge only if anything went awry.

That night, Leigh-Fermor, Moss, Paterakis, and Tyrakis left the cave and headed over the mountains for Skalani, a hamlet only three miles from the road bend chosen for the kidnapping. Taking refuge in a peasant's house in Skalani, the four men verbally rehearsed the operational plan.

The two Englishmen, dressed in authentic uniforms of the German military police, were to wait beside the road at the bend. Both men were diplomatic enough not to ask Mickey Akaumianos how he had managed to acquire the German uniforms. When General Kreipe's car approached, the pair would move into the center of the road, waving red lamps, and halt the vehicle. Leigh-Fermor was to take charge of the general, while Moss handled the driver.

On the night of the planned kidnapping, April 26, 1944, all the participants were in place. Up the road, Mickey Akaumianos, from a small hillock, gave the signal that General Kreipe's auto was approaching the hairpin bend. Moss and Leigh-Fermor walked into the middle of the road. Both men spoke fluent German.

As the new Opel automobile slowed for the sharp turn, the driver slammed on his brakes at the sight of the waving red lights. The two men in German uniforms stepped up to the car. Leigh-Fermor demanded to see the general's travel document, which was not required on Crete. Then the Briton demanded the password.

Kreipe was thoroughly angry. These two buffoons didn't even recognize their commanding general, even though the car had a pennant identifying his rank. Now Kreipe made a serious mistake. Instead of telling his chauffeur to drive on, he got out of the Opel and soundly upbraided the two "Germans" for not recognizing him.

"Oh, we know you, General," Leigh-Fermor said. "You are a prisoner of war in British hands!"

For whatever his reasons, one of Boudzalis's guerrillas rushed from his place of concealment and lunged at the general, who promptly knocked him down with a powerhouse punch. Others wrestled Kreipe to the ground, trussed him up, and gagged him. Then he was thrown into the backseat of his Opel.

Mickey Akaumianos pointed a pistol at the general's driver and asked him how much fuel was in the car's tank. He replied that it was full. The driver was handed over to the guerrillas, who by now were swarming all over the road bend.

The two "German military policemen," Moss and Leigh-Fermor, climbed into the front seat and drove away in the Opel with the general, bound and helpless, lying on the backseat, with two guerrillas sitting on him. Kreipe was aware that the car was headed in the direction of Heraklion and that it had passed at least three German checkpoints. Much to the general's anger, the soldiers manning the roadblocks hadn't even bothered to stop the Opel (the general's pennant had been removed).

Near the northern coast, Moss, who was driving, stopped the car at a secluded locale, and everyone got out. A partisan drove the Opel on to the coast, where it was abandoned. Left inside the vehicle was a note Leigh-Fermor had written earlier. It stated, "General Kreipe is on his way to Cairo." To avoid retaliation against the civilian population, a British military beret, British cigarette stubs, and a British detective novel also were left in the car.

For the next several nights the kidnappers and their captive trudged southward over extremely rugged terrain. During the day they holed up in caves or in thick woods. There were no paths, no roads.

In the meantime, all of the thirty thousand German soldiers on Crete had been scouring the island for their missing general. Airplanes crisscrossed the countryside in search of the kidnappers.

Then British operatives in London got into the act to inject more confusion into the already muddled situation on the island. Radio Calais, a station operated by the British deception agencies but projecting itself as being German, broadcast a report that General Kreipe had been disillusioned with Adolf Hitler and had gone over to the British. Kreipe, the radio stated, had covertly asked to be taken out of Crete by British Commandos.

After marching for four days, the escaping party received alarming news from a partisan courier. Anticipating that the general would be evacuated by submarine, which indeed was the plan, the Germans had deployed thousands of soldiers all along the southern coast.

Now the kidnappers were only four hours from their rendezvous point on the beach. While they were on the side of a mountain, another underground courier arrived with even more disturbing news. German troop units had moved into the valleys on either side, and some two hundred Germans had taken up positions at the precise point of the submarine rendezvous. The marchers were almost encircled.

General Kreipe, in his mid-fifties and not accustomed to such arduous endeavors, was near exhaustion, so a mule was acquired for him to ride. Then a decision was made to try to break through the forming German noose, and a partisan scout was sent to the coast to try to find a beach sector that had not yet been occupied by German soldiers. The Cretan returned a day later with more bad news: Germans were everywhere along the beaches.

Major Leigh-Fermor and Captain Moss then reached a critical decision. They would resume the trek in the direction of the village of Rodakino, where the coast was so rugged and inaccessible that the Germans, hopefully, had not manned it. A few hours earlier, Leigh-Fermor had managed to locate a British secret agent with a radio transmitter who was only one hour's marching time away. The agent sent a message to Cairo telling of a change of plans and requesting a motor launch to meet the escaping party at the Rodakino beach. Cairo had replied that the new vessel would be at the new rendezvous on the night of May 14–15.

The march had been resumed for less than an hour before the mule stumbled and General Kreipe was pitched to the ground, breaking his shoulder. He remounted the mule, however, and the arduous trek continued. Two hours later, the party—minus the mule—was huddled along a black beach, concealed in bushes. Suddenly the silence was broken by the faint purr of an engine. The sound grew louder, and moments later the dim silhouette of a British launch could be discerned.

Two rubber dinghies carrying several British commandos were paddled ashore, and subdued but exuberant greetings were exchanged.

Thirty-six hours later, Major Leigh-Fermor, Captain Moss, and their prize prisoner, the highly decorated General Heinrich Kreipe, boarded a plane and flew to Cairo. Thus concluded one of the war's most audacious secret operations.[2]

Blasting a Japanese Headquarters

FOR A YEAR AND A HALF, U.S. General Douglas MacArthur had been conducting what he called a "hit 'em where they ain't" campaign, leapfrogging westward along the rugged northern coast of primitive New Guinea, a fifteen-hundred-mile-long island, on the jungle road to Tokyo. His technique was to skirt Japanese strongholds to keep U.S. casualties down and to speed his advance.

All the while, PT boats, among MacArthur's favorite weapons, were dashing up and down the New Guinea coast, looking for trouble. They usually found it. They tangled with Japanese warships, sank cargo vessels, and blasted barges filled with troops and supplies for the Japanese garrisons that had been cut off and left to wither on the vine by MacArthur's leapfrog tactics.

The seventy-eight-foot-long mighty midgets, armed with four .50-caliber machine guns and four torpedoes, came to be called devil boats by the Japanese, who hated and feared them. The swift, highly maneuverable craft were manned by a new breed of American fighting men, a combination of seagoing cavalry, commando-type raiders, and Indian scouts out of the Old West.

In February 1944 MacArthur's intelligence received word from friendly native coast-watchers deep behind forward Japanese positions that the enemy had occupied a mansion at a place called Higgins Point on Rooke Island and had established a major headquarters that directed much activity in the region.

Consequently, Lieutenant Fred Calhoun, a PT-boat skipper who had just returned to duty after having been seriously wounded by strafing Japanese aircraft, was handed the job of infiltrating enemy-occupied waters and wiping out the headquarters, which sat on a hill overlooking the sea. The daunting task would require stealth, seamanship, gunnery expertise—and luck.

Just before sundown, Calhoun and his crew shoved off in their boat and headed for Higgins Point. With them was a middle-aged Australian who was to navigate the craft through treacherous reefs just off the target. The Aussie had volunteered for the dangerous mission.

Soon after daylight, the PT boat reached the objective and idled to a halt two hundred yards offshore. Then the gunners began blasting away at the sturdy mansion with the deck-mounted machine guns and a flat-trajectory, high-velocity gun brought along especially for knocking down the building. Much to the chagrin of Calhoun and his men, the shells and bullets bounced off the target.

"Raise your gunfire a little, because the lower floor is of thick concrete," the Aussie suggested to Calhoun.

The gunners complied, and in minutes the mansion collapsed into a large pile of masonry and wood splinters.

Then the Aussie pointed to a clump of trees. "You might want to send a few bursts in there," he stated casually. "There's a building hidden in among those trees, and the Nips are probably using that, too."

As a torrent of bullets and shells defrocked the trees of their leaves, the building became visible. It also was blasted into smithereens.

As the PT boat set a course for home, the curious Lieutenant Calhoun asked the Aussie, "How in the hell did you know the layout so well back there?"

With no display of emotion, the Aussie replied, "Because I built the place with my own hands over a two-year period and lived there with my family till the bloody Japs showed up."[3]

Mad Dash in an Explosive-Laden Car

SOON AFTER Adolf Hitler sent his jackbooted legions plunging into nearly defenseless Norway in the spring of 1940, the Norwegian underground had developed into one of the most productive in Europe. Unlike in France, Italy, and Yugoslavia, the resistance was motivated solely by patriotic concerns, not tainted by partisan political maneuvering.

In April 1944, after Norway had been under the Nazi yoke for four years, Milorg, the underground's intelligence organization, received startling information from Colonel Theodore Steltzer, who was with German Army headquarters in Oslo. Steltzer was a member of the Schwarze Kapelle, the clandestine group of prominent German military, government, and civic leaders who had been plotting for several years to eliminate Adolf Hitler and his regime.

Steltzer disclosed that the Wehrmacht planned to withdraw large numbers of German troops from Norway and send them to northern France to reinforce the garrison there against a threatened invasion from England by the Allies. Milorg promptly notified Allied intelligence sources in London and said the underground urgently needed shipment of a powerful explosive to insert in limpets for attacking German ships when they were ready to depart with the withdrawing army units from the ports of Oslo, Stavanger, and Narvik.

The limpet was a special weapon of the saboteur. It contained a small amount of explosives and had a magnet that caused it to adhere to a ship's surface below the waterline. The saboteur approached the target, usually at night, in a kayak and put the limpet in place by means of a long pole. The device was so fashioned that withdrawing the pole activated the explosive. A magnesium alloy window on the limpet was slowly etched away by salt water after several hours, giving time for the saboteurs to be far away when the blast erupted.

Although the hole blown by the explosion was small in itself, the enormous recoil of the ocean caused a twenty-foot aperture, usually large enough to cause a ship to sink.

Now, with D-Day in Normandy rapidly approaching, Allied intelligence in London contacted the headquarters of the Office of Strategic Services in Washington, asking if the urgent request to supply Torpex, a special explosive, to the Norwegian underground could be fulfilled. The problem fell into the lap of fifty-four-year-old Stanley P. Lovell at the OSS office at Twenty-fifth and E Streets.

Lovell, a noted chemist and holder of scores of patents, was the OSS director of research and development, known by insiders as the Dirty Tricks Department. In 1942 he had been recruited into the cloak-and-dagger agency from a high-paying post in industry. In a time span of only two years Lovell had been credited with spearheading the development of many devious devices for killing or bedeviling the enemy.

About a year earlier, Lovell had a memorable confrontation with Torpex when he had found about a hundred pounds of it stashed in his personal office. He telephoned an expert to come and fetch it—pronto. Not to worry, Lovell was told. Simply flush it down the toilet.

Lovell and his assistant, Allen Abrams, set about the task. Moments after Lovell returned to his office, the explosives expert's boss was on the telephone.

"Whatever you do, Lovell," the other man said excitedly, "don't flush that explosive down the toilet. The organic matter in the sewer will react with it and blow the entire Washington sewer system sky high, along with every building over it."

One sewer line, Lovell knew, ran diagonally from the OSS headquarters across to Sixteenth Street, near the White House. For nearly an hour, Lovell and Abrams debated over whether to inform the OSS security chief, the District of Columbia chief engineer, the U.S. Army, OSS boss William Donovan—or no one at all. They decided to keep mum.

In the hours ahead, Lovell and Abrams instinctively jumped each time a truck backfired or a door slammed. That night they dined at the Cosmos Club and were just beginning to breathe a little easier, helped by a few drinks of liquid courage. Then a waiter dropped a loaded tray of dishes on the tile floor right next to the two men's table. Lovell and Abrams dashed frantically into the outside garden, returning sheepishly to their meal moments later as the other patrons stared at them.

At dawn, Lovell and Abrams were across the street from the White House, greatly relieved to see the stately building still standing. The Potomac River, they agreed, had long since sent the hundred pounds of delicate explosives on a course to the sea.

With that haunting episode long faded from his memory, Lovell pondered over the request for explosives from the Norwegian underground. He was beset by a major problem. The Torpex supply was half a country away—in the small city of Hastings, Nebraska. How could the Torpex be brought to Washington, then shipped to England, then to Norway?

Commercial airlines were ruled out. So were the railroads. The entire project was wrapped in tight security, and there might be a leak. Besides, the explosive was highly temperamental, and Lovell didn't want to be thrust into a position of explaining his role if an airplane blew up high above Ohio or West Virginia.

Finally, Lovell decided he would send an automobile to make a mad dash to Nebraska, pick up the explosive, and race back to Washington. He asked for volunteers, and a Captain Frazee and a Sergeant Walker in his office agreed to the perilous task, one that might blow them into confetti. Lovell provided them with his personal automobile, and they were off, hell-bent for Hastings.

After driving almost continuously for nearly twenty-four hours, the two OSS operatives arrived at their destination, loaded the explosive into the car, and began their return trip to Washington. It proved to be an epic task. Their nerves, already frayed from lack of sleep, were on edge. The cargo weighed the car down onto the axles, making each of the countless holes and bumps in the roads a real peril. They could be blown sky high at any moment.

Compounding their anxieties was the fact that Frazee and Walker, for security reasons, had been told only that their task could save many Allied lives. They conjectured if that were truly the case, or if some overeager operative in the Washington headquarters had dreamed up a crackpot scheme that would never be fulfilled and they were risking their lives for nothing.

Before the captain and sergeant had left Washington, Stanley Lovell realized that they might be halted along the way by a law enforcement officer. They were driving an unmarked car and wearing civilian clothes. If the two men were to be arrested with their unseemly cargo and the episode given wide publicity, as no doubt it would be, the entire venture would have to be scuttled.

On two occasions the OSS men were stopped by suspicious local police who noticed the heavily weighted automobile. Each time the pair produced a letter that resulted in abject apologies from the policemen. Typed on White House stationery, the letter stated:

Captain Frazee and Sergeant Walker are on a secret mission for me as Commander-in-Chief. Any assistance given these two officers will be helping to win the war. Any interference with their vital mission, any search, questioning, or delay of any sort will be followed by my severest disciplinary action. This is a Top Secret operation.

Had President Franklin Roosevelt ever seen the letter, he would have sworn that he had signed it. Actually, the OSS Documentation Branch had both created the stationery and the letter and forged Roosevelt's signature.

There was one final touch of authenticity to the manufactured document: an official seal. A seal always connotes something highly important. The Documentation Branch craftsmen had been extremely careful to make certain the seal was almost, but not quite, legible.

Halfway back to Washington, the explosive-laden automobile stalled on a railroad track. Despite desperate efforts by the occupants, the motor failed to start. After almost ten minutes, a train's warning whistle could be heard in the distance. Could they halt the onrushing train before it hurtled into the stalled automobile? The explosion would be monumental. Moments later, the motor came to life. Both men issued sighs of relief. By the time the train raced past the crossing, the vehicle was a half mile away.

As soon as the vital load of Torpex reached Washington, Stanley Lovell, the research and development chief, arranged with the British to rush the cargo to Norway. Within a week the explosives were in the hands of the Norwegian underground and being encased in limpets.

A few weeks later, after the Allied invasion of Normandy, Major General Colin McV. Gubbins, chief of Britain's highly effective cloak-and-dagger agency the Special Operations Executive (SOE), informed Lovell that the Torpex timing had been perfect.

The Germans had begun pulling troops out of Norway, and the Norwegian resistance warriors paddled out at night in their kayaks and installed the limpets. At a time when Adolf Hitler desperately needed reinforcements to halt the Allied drive deeper into France, the fjords of Norway became the final resting places for several German ships, which took their troops to watery graves.

The mad dash of Captain Frazee and Sergeant Walker across half of the United States to fetch the Torpex from Hastings, Nebraska, had paid off.[4]

A Special Job for "Scarface Otto"

IN THE DARK SKIES over southern Germany on the night of April 28, 1944, a fierce shoot-out erupted when several squadrons of Luftwaffe fighter planes pounced on a British Royal Air Force bomber stream. During the confused battle, a three-seat Me-110 fighter, piloted by Leutnant Wilhelm Johnen, strayed into the airspace of neutral Switzerland.

SS Colonel Otto Skorzeny (left) was a favorite of Adolf Hitler.
(National Archives)

Swiss antiaircraft-gun crews at Dübendorf Air Base bathed the German plane with powerful searchlight beams; then they fired red and green flares, signals for it to land. The plane approached the runway, and the searchlights were extinguished. Suddenly the Me-110 gained speed as if to escape, and the searchlight beams again caught the aircraft. The dazzling glare temporarily blinded Johnen and forced him to land.

Moments after the Me-110 rolled to a halt and the pilot shut off the engine, there was a tapping on the cockpit. A voice in German told the crew, "Please get out. You are in Switzerland. You are interned." Glancing around, the Luftwaffe men saw that they were surrounded by twenty Swiss soldiers holding weapons aimed at the airplane.

Leutnant Johnen and his two crewmen promptly realized that they would have to take quick action to destroy secret devices on the Messerschmitt. The plane was equipped with the new night-flying radar, the Luchtenstein SN-2, which could track U.S. and British bombers from a distance in excess of four miles.

Also on board was an important new weapon that the Germans had given the nickname Slanted Music. It was a pair of top-mounted cannon that could fire directly upward and was designed to attack the vulnerable underside of Allied bombers.

Perhaps even more devastating to the German war effort should it fall into the hands of Allied intelligence was a set of top-flight Luftwaffe code books. Joachim Kamprath, the radio operator, had violated strict orders and brought the codes with him.

Before heeding the order to emerge from the Me-110, Kamprath tried futilely to badly damage the radar by kicking it. Paul Mahle, who manned the twin guns that fired upward, tried desperately, but failed to destroy them.

The tapping on the cockpit grew more insistent, so the Germans quickly stashed the secret code books into the pockets of their flight suits and climbed down onto the tarmac. After smoking a cigarette and chatting with the affable Swiss soldiers, Paul Mahle, the gunner, said he had to get back into the plane to retrieve some personal items. Without waiting for an approval, he scrambled into the cockpit.

Several Swiss soldiers were right on his heels, and they pulled the struggling gunner by one leg as he tried to reach a switch that would have touched off a delayed-action explosive device and blown up the aircraft.

Then the three interned men—the Swiss didn't regard them as captives—were escorted to the air base canteen, where they were given food and wine. After the Germans excused themselves to go to the men's room, two Swiss soldiers followed, saw them flushing pages from the secret code books down the toilet, and snatched the remainder of the sheets from them.

Twenty-four hours later, the German high command in Berlin erupted in near-panic. Swiss officials refused to return the Me-110 that had violated their tiny nation's airspace. Berlin feared that the secret equipment and the code books might be slipped to Allied intelligence by the Swiss.

Suspecting that the three Luftwaffe men had committed treason, the Gestapo immediately arrested their families. Reichsführer Heinrich Himmler, once a chicken farmer and now Gestapo chief and head of the elite Schutzstaffel (SS), probed the possibility of using Nazi espionage agents already in Switzerland to murder the three downed German airmen.

At his battle headquarters at Wolfsschanze behind the Russian Front, Adolf Hitler flew into a rage on being told of the Swiss episode by his longtime trusted chief of staff, Generaloberst (four-star general) Alfred Jodl. However, the führer rejected Himmler's murder plan and also a scheme by the Luftwaffe chief, rotund Reichsmarschall Hermann Goering, to heavily bomb Dübendorf Air Base.

Instead, Hitler sent for one of his favorites, SS Sturmbannführer (Major) Otto Skorzeny, a folk hero on the German home front, a sinister figure known as "Scarface Otto" to the Allies. A burly 6 feet, 3 inches tall and weighing 250 pounds, the "commando extraordinary," as he came to be known in the Third Reich, was handed a seemingly impossible assignment: locate and destroy the Me-110 being held by the Swiss.

The mission would require exceptional stealth, cunning, and courage, traits that Skorzeny had in abundance. As an engineering student in his native Vienna, he had fought fifteen of the ritual saber duels popular among some Teutonic types. In one encounter, young Skorzeny's left cheek to the tip of his jaw had been laid open. It was sewn up on the spot—without anesthetic—and the duel resumed.

After joining the SS in 1940, Oberleutnant (First Lieutenant) Skorzeny fought in the Balkans and later in Russia, from where he was invalided home with severe head wounds. He commanded a desk until late July 1943, when the führer assigned him the daunting task of rescuing Hitler's crony Benito Mussolini, who had been in almost absolute control of Italy for twenty-one years.

Mussolini had been taken prisoner by Italian partisans after having been booted out of his office by shy, diminutive King Victor Emmanuel III, and was being held prisoner in a peacetime tourist hotel on a towering peak in the Appenines known as Gran Sasso. After spending two weeks prowling around Italy in civilian clothes, Skorzeny had discovered where Mussolini was incarcerated.

On September 12 Skorzeny and a handful of *Fallschirmjäger* (paratroopers) swooped down on Gran Sasso in gliders, snatched the deposed dictator from under the noses of more than two hundred Italian guards, and bundled the famous prisoner into a light Storch aircraft that had just made a dangerous landing near the hotel.

The bulky Skorzeny wriggled into the little plane designed to carry two passengers and, along with Mussolini and a Luftwaffe pilot, Hauptman (Captain) Heinrich Gerlach, lifted off from a short, boulder-strewn plateau. On reaching the edge of the plateau, the Storch plunged downward into a yawning valley and Gerlach was able to right the aircraft just before it crashed. Flying at treetop level, the pilot set a course for Rome, which was still in German hands.

Now Otto Skorzeny had been given an equally "impossible" task—finding and blowing up the Me-110. As he had done in his search for Mussolini's whereabouts, Skorzeny, a conspicuous figure because of his great bulk and ugly dueling scar, put on civilian clothes and slipped across the border into Switzerland at night.

Skorzeny ambled around the perimeter of Dübendorf Air Base, seeking some sign of the German aircraft, asking questions of natives living nearby and of civilian employees as they left the facility. Swiss authorities had moved the Me-110 deep within the mountainous country, the commando learned. Finding it would be akin to discovering the proverbial needle in a haystack. So Skorzeny, for one of the few times in his life, had to admit defeat.

Now behind-the-scenes diplomatic maneuvering took place, and a strange deal was worked out between Nazi Germany and Switzerland. On the morning of May 17, 1944, Hitler's military attaché watched intently as the Messerschmitt, which had been brought back to Dübendorf, with its secret equipment, was doused with gasoline and burned to a crisp.

For its part in the arrangement, the Swiss government was permitted to purchase from Germany twelve high-performance Me-109G fighter planes, a major concession since the seriously depleted Luftwaffe needed every available aircraft to combat the almost daily and nightly raids by British and U.S. bombers against targets in the German homeland.

As a component of the secret agreement, Leutnant Wilhelm Johnen, radar operator Joachim Kamprath, and gunner Paul Mahle were released from custody and returned to Germany. The three airmen were held blameless once the true details of the Dübendorf episode became known to German intelligence, and their families were released from prison.

Perhaps the airmen's fate would have been different had the Gestapo learned about the Luftwaffe secret code books, most of which presumably were in the hands of Swiss authorities—or maybe being scrutinized by U.S. and British intelligence.[5]

Sneaking onto Utah Beach

NEPTUNE, the assault phase of Operation Overlord, the invasion of Normandy, would be unmatched in scope and complexity in the annals of warfare. The printed plan was 5 inches thick, and even the typed list of American units— 1,400 of them—required 31 pages. On D-Day alone, the equivalent of 500 trainloads of troops—57,506 American and 75,215 British and Canadian— along with their weapons, vehicles, ammunition, and supplies, would be put ashore in Normandy. Thousands of Allied paratroopers and glidermen would jump and land behind the beaches.

There would be landings by five great naval task forces in the Bay of the Seine, which was divided into the American assault area on the west (Utah and Omaha Beaches) and the British and Canadian assault area on the east (Gold, Sword, and Juno Beaches).

Early in May 1944, about a month before the mighty endeavor would take place, U.S. Navy Commander John D. Bulkeley was summoned to a headquarters not far from Dartmouth, on the English Channel. Bulkeley, who had been awarded the Congressional Medal of Honor and a chestful of other decorations for his exploits as a PT-boat skipper in the Pacific early in the war, had arrived in England only two weeks earlier. His PT-boat squadron had been engaged in sneaking spies into Nazi-occupied France.

Now at the headquarters, a British Navy captain gave Bulkeley orders for a bizarre mission. He was to cross the Channel under cover of night in a PT boat and, together with two of his men, sneak onto a beach Allied planners had code-named Utah. Bulkeley was told only that he was to go ashore at a precise stretch of the Normandy coastline and bring back buckets of sand scooped up at fifty-yard intervals.

"Any questions?" the Briton queried.

"No, sir," replied Bulkeley.

Jeeping back to Dartmouth, Bulkeley mulled over the mission. This was the most ridiculous order he had ever received, he concluded. Perhaps the

Nazi propaganda depicted disaster for American and British troops if they tried to invade northern France. (Author's collection)

pressure-cooker tension had gotten the best of the British officer. Moreover, this was a classic suicide mission if there ever was one, Bulkeley decided, because the Germans knew that the big invasion would hit soon and they would be on the alert all along the Channel coast.

"It's astonishing that our brass would risk a valuable PT boat and the lives of its crew to bring back some damned French sand," Bulkeley told a confidant. "Whoever dreamed this one up was a harebrained twit!"

Thirty-two hours later, in the eerie stillness at 2:10 A.M., Bulkeley's PT boat dropped anchor on the Bay of the Seine some five hundred yards off the designated Normandy beach. Slipping noiselessly into a rubber dinghy, he and two men began rowing. Their faces and hands had been blackened with grease. They wore all-black clothing.

Reaching the beach, the three Americans paused and listened: the only sound was the soft lapping of the surf.

None of the nocturnal intruders carried a weapon, for their "cover" was that they were on a rescue mission searching for downed pilots. But Bulkeley and his companions knew that if captured, they would be turned over to the Gestapo, charged with being spies, and shot.

Stealing along the wet beach in the blackness, Bulkeley began scooping sand into the two buckets he was carrying; then he took the containers back to the dinghy. Retracing his steps, he repeated the process. When about one hundred yards away from the rubber raft, he filled a final bucket with sand. Suddenly a dark figure, wearing a steel, bucket-shaped helmet and armed with a rifle, leaped in front of Bulkeley and flashed a light beam in his face.

Bulkeley knew that this was a German sentry and that his comrades were, no doubt, nearby. Either Bulkeley would have to dispose of the German or face a Gestapo firing squad. The husky skipper, who had been a boxer on the U.S. Naval Academy team, pitched the wet sand in the bucket he was holding into the face of the German. Then, catlike, he sprang on the sentry and threw him onto his back.

Leaping astride the German, Bulkeley began strangling him with his hands. When the sentry went limp, the American leaped to his feet and ran like a jackrabbit back to the dinghy. After quickly checking to make certain that all the buckets of sand were aboard, Bulkeley and his two men paddled furiously out to the waiting PT boat. Minutes later, the powerful craft leaped forward and headed back to Dartmouth.

"Now I know that British captain is crazy!" Bulkeley muttered to his crew.

It would be months before Bulkeley learned the reason for the bizarre mission from which he thought he would never return. Long after the landing beaches had been selected, a scientist who had escaped from France and claimed to have knowledge of the region dropped a blockbuster on invasion planners: the shoreline known as Utah Beach consisted largely of peat, with only a thin covering of sand. If that shocking revelation were true, it would mean that tanks and vehicles would bog down while crossing the beach on D-Day. Bulkeley's sand samples had relieved worried minds in Allied headquarters.[6]

X2 Agents in Cherbourg

SHORTLY AFTER DAWN on June 6, 1944, Operation Neptune, the assault phase of the invasion of Normandy, struck behind a mammoth deluge of ten thousand tons of explosives dropped from twenty-five hundred bombers and fired from the guns of six hundred warships. Under Major General J. Lawton "Lightning Joe" Collins, the U.S. VII Corps stormed ashore at Utah Beach and launched a drive toward the port of Cherbourg, twenty-five miles to the north.

Cherbourg, where the majestic luxury liners *Queen Elizabeth*, *Normandie*, and *Queen Mary* had discharged passengers in peacetime, was crucial to the success of the invasion. Although two artificial harbors (Mulberries) would be established, that engineering feat would be a stopgap measure. Should Cherbourg not be seized in timely fashion, the invading Allies would be in danger of withering on the vine and then cut to pieces by German field marshal Erwin Rommel's panzers converging around the Normandy bridgehead from throughout Europe.

Nazi flag waves over Cherbourg prior to Normandy D-Day. (Author's collection)

Adolf Hitler's hopes for an Allied invasion debacle and a subsequent negotiated peace with the Americans and British focused on the heavily fortified port of Cherbourg. Hard-pressed German troops under hulking Lieutenant General Karl Wilhelm von Schlieben resisted stubbornly, but the prized port fell to the Americans on D-Day plus 24.

While German diehards were still being mopped up in Cherbourg, it became starkly evident to the Americans that Hitler's orders had been carried out by General von Schlieben with great skill and thoroughness. "Leave the Allies not a port but a field of utter destruction!" the führer had ordered.

Major General Cecil R. Moore, the chief engineer of SHAEF (Supreme Headquarters, Allied Expeditionary Force) told Eisenhower that the Germans had "knocked hell out of the harbor."

Other U.S. engineers were aghast by what they found. Colonel Alvin G. Viney, who had prepared the original plan for the rehabilitation of Cherbourg's harbor facilities, declared: "The demolition was masterful, beyond a doubt the most complete, intensive, and best-planned demolition job in history."

These assessments triggered nervous tics at SHAEF. Estimates based on a similar experience at the harbor in Naples, Italy, a year earlier had been that Cherbourg's port facilities could be made operational three days after the city's capture. Now it appeared that it would take several months, perhaps a year, before the first Allied ships could be unloaded.

Tensions at SHAEF were not eased when air reconnaissance and reports from the French underground disclosed that Field Marshal Rommel was already rushing troops and panzers to Normandy from southern France and Germany.

Prior to the invasion, Colonel Dick Goldsmith White, a peacetime school principal and head of the secret SHAEF Counterintelligence War Room, had warned that the Abwehr and the Gestapo, which had been entrenched in France for four years, would leave behind in territory captured by the Allies a large number of spies, mostly French pro-Nazi men and women. Hard on the heels of the first U.S. troops, White's agents slipped into Cherbourg. Within two hours the first stay-behind agent was detected transmitting to Abwehr headquarters in Paris by radio.

Stealthily, White's men surrounded a house used by the spy, burst open a door, and captured the turncoat Frenchman, whose code name with his Abwehr controllers was George. Also seized were the radio set, operating codes, and a transmission schedule.

George confessed that his undercover mission was to report to Paris on the amount of destruction in Cherbourg's harbor and whether the Allies would be able to use it to bring in massive amounts of war accoutrements and troops.

X2, the branch of the U.S. Office of Strategic Services (OSS) designed to confuse and mislead the enemy, realized that all the ingredients to conduct a wireless game with the Abwehr had been captured. So George was given a choice: He could be shot immediately as a spy, or continue to send his scheduled reports to Paris—with a slight modification. X2 operatives would create phony scripts for him, and they would sit at his elbow during the transmissions. George chose to become what is known in the espionage trade as a double agent, one "turned" to send misleading information to the other side.

X2 agents concocted George's messages with utmost skill, combining harmless truths (which the Abwehr already knew or suspected) with the desired falsehoods. And the "doubled" operator had to send them himself, for the Paris receiver, knowing his "fist," would immediately detect an impostor. Also, the turned agent had to be watched intently, lest he slip in a prearranged code word that warned: "This stuff is phony. They're making me send it!"

Within twenty-four hours of Cherbourg's capture, George's controller in Paris made the cat-and-mouse wireless game easier: The Abwehr officer sent repeated and frantic requests for George to send reports on Allied progress in restoring the port. No doubt the controller could feel the hot breath of Adolf Hitler flowing down his neck.

George's wireless reports assured the Abwehr in Paris that the Allies were appalled by the extent of the destruction—which was true—and that they were about to give up on rebuilding the destroyed port facilities—which was an X2 lie. The goal of the wireless machination was to impress on Adolf Hitler and Field Marshal Rommel that the Allies would not be able to use Cherbourg as a port until winter—if ever.

Three weeks after the first U.S. soldier had entered Cherbourg, the first Allied ship was unloaded at the port. American engineers had performed a near-miracle. Somehow George failed to report this crucial fact to his masters in Paris. Instead, he sent an urgent message stating that U.S. agents were closing in on him and that he would have to shut down and flee for his life.[7]

Covert Targets: Germany's Atomic Scientists

IN EARLY JUNE 1944 most of the world's focus was on England, where powerful Allied forces were coiled to strike across the Channel against Adolf Hitler's Festung Europa (Fortress Europe). At the same time, General Leslie Groves, the hulking human dynamo directing the atomic bomb project in the United States, was gripped by the nightmare of the still-mysterious status of the Nazi effort to construct the ultimate weapon. Ominous intelligence obtained by Allied sources indicated that German atomic scientists might be on the brink of a major breakthrough.

British undercover agents heard that a Swiss scientist was working in an abandoned building in the Black Forest of southern Germany, creating an explosive a thousand times more powerful than TNT. Operatives working for the U.S. Office of Strategic Services (OSS) in Bern, Switzerland, reported that Werner Heisenberg, regarded by many in his field as the world's foremost theoretical physicist, had moved to the small town of Hechingen, also in southern Germany. American censors had intercepted a letter from a prisoner of war who said he was assigned to work in a secret research laboratory in Hechingen. Undercover agents in France said that some of the huge bunkers in the Atlantikwall along the French coast might contain atomic warheads to be used against the Allies when they invaded.

Heading the Nazi atomic effort along with Heisenberg, who, in 1932, had been awarded the Nobel Prize in physics for developing an advanced theory about the hydrogen atom, was the equally brilliant scientist Carl Freidrich von Weizsäcker.

Throughout the decade of the 1930s, while the führer was rearming Germany and preparing for war, Heisenberg had rejected many lucrative job offers in the United States. Even though he claimed to despise Hitler and the Nazi regime, he refused to leave the Third Reich. "I was born in Germany," the physicist told friends. "Now Germany needs me."

Only a handful of people in the Allied camp were even aware that the United States had been laboring to construct an atomic bomb. Fewer still knew that Germany was working diligently at the same task. So it was coincidental when operatives in the OSS in Washington hatched a bizarre scheme in early 1944 to kidnap Werner Heisenberg and spirit him out of Germany.

Werner Heisenberg headed the German effort to make the atom bomb. (National Archives)

Selected for the covert mission was Major Carl Eifler, a bear of a man weighing 280 pounds. A graduate of the Los Angeles Police Academy, Eifler had worked as an undercover agent for the U.S. Customs Service, and had engaged in several shoot-outs while tracking smugglers through the mountains of Mexico.

Eifler had been told only that a German scientist was developing a devastating new weapon and he had to be "stopped," meaning "eliminated," "neutralized," or kidnapped.

Rugged and rough, Eifler was delighted with his new assignment. He would kidnap Heisenberg, either in Berlin or at his home in southern Germany. Then he would smuggle the physicist into neighboring Switzerland, where the two men would board an airplane and fly out over the Mediterranean Sea. Far from land, Eifler and Heisenberg would parachute, land in the water, and be picked up by a waiting submarine.

Eifler departed in May on the first leg of his trek, and he happened to run into the OSS boss, "Wild Bill" Donovan, in Algiers, North Africa. Donovan loved crazy machinations, but he was far from impressed when Eifler briefed him on the kidnapping scheme. Perhaps the million-to-one odds for success influenced Donovan, who promptly called off the caper.

A short time later, on June 4, 1944, huge throngs of Romans packed the streets of the ancient Italian capital to cheer the arrival of General Mark Clark's

U.S. Fifth Army after the Wehrmacht had suddenly pulled northward out of the sprawling metropolis. On the heels of the American spearheads was a secret team of scientists and military officers code-named Alsos (Greek for grove). Headed by Colonel Boris Pash, the team had been created a few months earlier by General Groves. Its mission was to find out how close the Germans were to developing an atomic bomb.

Werner Heisenberg was the main target of Pash's investigation. In discussions with intellectuals who had fled Europe in recent years, including Italian physicist Enrico Fermi and Hungarian scientist Edward Teller, Groves had been told that Heisenberg was the most likely German to develop an atomic bomb.

Soon after reaching Rome, Colonel Pash, who had been born in Russia, learned from the Italian underground the address of the home of Edoardo Amaldi, the country's foremost physicist. Amaldi was the only physicist at the University of Rome who had not fled from the country during the war. Although he professed to have hated Benito Mussolini, who had been Italy's dictator for more than two decades until being ousted in 1943, Amaldi had stayed behind to "help my country."

Colonel Pash hurried to 50 Via Parioli, the ornate home of Amaldi, who had known Heisenberg and Carl von Weizsäcker for many years. Yes, Amaldi stated while smoking a pipe, Germany was making an all-out effort to develop an atomic bomb.

Twenty-four hours after Pash's grilling of Amaldi, Allied armies in England charged across the Channel and went ashore along a sixty-mile stretch of beach in Normandy. Pash was instructed to hurry to France and follow on the heels of the invaders. Six weeks after D-Day, the Allies broke out of their narrow enclave and liberated Paris.

A primary aim of the Alsos group was to find France's leading atomic scientist, Frédéric Joliot-Curie, son-in-law of Marie Curie, who had received the Nobel Prize in chemistry in 1911 for her work in the discovery of radium and polonium and the isolation of pure radium. Because the Nazis had taken over and used Joliot-Curie's laboratory, the Alsos group believed that he must know much about their work.

Colonel Pash was concerned that the Nazis might kidnap Joliot-Curie when advancing Allied forces approached Paris, so Pash and two army sergeants wielding tommy guns charged into the French capital on one of the leading tanks. Joliot-Curie was soon located and said that German scientists had taken over his laboratory for experiments in nuclear physics. However, Joliot-Curie told Pash, he did not believe that Germany had the knowledge to build a bomb.

Within days, the Alsos team pushed on to just-liberated Strasbourg, a French city noted for its medieval buildings and a majestic Gothic cathedral. Strasbourg is some 250 miles east of Paris and on the German border. It was known that Carl von Weizsäcker had taught physics at the University of Strasbourg before going back to Germany when the Allies neared.

This time the investigation was headed by Dr. Samuel A. Goudsmit, who had been born in the Netherlands. Friendly and witty, Goudsmit had been appointed scientific director for Alsos because he was an outstanding nuclear physicist, spoke fluent Dutch, German, and English, and had been on close terms in prewar years with most of the leading scientists in Europe.

Among his good friends was the target of his investigation, Werner Heisenberg, who had been his house guest at the University of Michigan prior to the outbreak of war in Europe. Goudsmit had not been involved in the U.S. atomic bomb project, so if he were to be captured, he could reveal no technical secrets.

Goudsmit and several members of his team went to Weizsäcker's office in Strasbourg. They were delighted that the German had left behind voluminous files containing correspondence, diaries, notes, and computations. Goudsmit spent long, tedious hours riffling through these papers. Then he struck a bonanza.

For many months, Allied intelligence had been trying to pin down Heisenberg's precise address in Hechingen. Now, among Weizsäcker's papers, there it was: Heisenberg's home address and also his unlisted telephone number. If the Alsos team wanted to contact Heisenberg, Goudsmit said with a chuckle, all they had to do was to call him on the telephone.

One Alsos team found a nuclear laboratory in a wing of a Strasbourg hospital. In it were seven German physicists and chemists who tried to pose as physicians and refused to talk about their work. Goudsmit rushed to the hospital and, as the Germans shelled the city and knocked out the power that night, he pored over the "physicians'" papers and correspondence. Letters from scientists in Germany complained bitterly in highly technical language about the enormous problems they were encountering. A copy of a letter to Heisenberg criticized the total lack of progress of the German uranium pile.

All of these papers in Weizsäcker's office and in the hospital laboratory created to Goudsmit's knowing eye a comprehensive portrait of the entire German atomic bomb effort.

"Germany has no atomic bomb and is not likely to have one in the near future," the physicist told Colonel Pash.

That conclusion was flashed to General Groves in Washington, but he remained skeptical. Could Goudsmit prove that the documents were not cleverly crafted "plants"? No, he replied, he could not give that assurance.

In late November the focus of the counterintelligence attack against German atomic bomb secrets shifted to mountainous Switzerland, adjacent to the Third Reich. Allen Dulles, the cagey OSS spymaster in Bern, informed Washington that Heisenberg had accepted an invitation to give a lecture in Zurich, Switzerland, on or about December 15.

In Paris, forty-two-year-old Morris "Moe" Berg, an OSS agent and a former major league baseball catcher with the Boston Red Sox and Chicago White Sox, received an astonishing order from Washington. He was to attend Heisenberg's lecture, which would be open to the public, in Zurich.

Berg had been recruited by the OSS two years earlier and already had carried out three perilous covert missions, including parachuting into German-occupied Norway to ferret out secrets in a heavy-water plant operated by the Nazis. Heavy water is required to build an atomic bomb.

Berg had graduated with honors from Princeton and attended the prestigious Sorbonne in Paris. He spoke seven languages and could converse on scientific topics on a par with academics.

In preparation for his *coup de main*, Berg was given a crash course in advanced physics and instructed to listen for "certain things"—meaning those related to atomic energy—during Heisenberg's lecture. If the German physicist said anything that convinced Berg that the Nazis were close to creating an atomic bomb, Berg was to shoot him as he stood at the podium.

How Berg was to escape capture by the Swiss police, who no doubt would be present, was left rather vague.

On the appointed date, Berg arrived at the lecture hall in Zurich masquerading as a Swiss physics student. With him was another OSS agent, Leo Martinuzzi, who was disguised as a French businessman. They joined a modest gathering of some twenty university professors and graduate students who had come to hear one of the world's foremost physicists discuss his latest theories. None knew that the German had been and was a leading light in Hitler's atomic bomb project.

Berg was mesmerized by Werner Heisenberg, a warm, affable man in his early forties, and wondered if he would have to kill him within the hour. Although Berg did not fully grasp the thrust of Heisenberg's remarks, the spy played his role to the hilt by taking copious notes, most of which was doodling.

Casting an occasional glance around the room, Berg thought he recognized one man in the audience. Minutes later, the other's identity struck him: he was Carl von Weizsäcker.

When the lecture appeared to be nearly over, Berg wasn't certain about what he had heard. Had Heisenberg hinted that Germany was on the brink of developing an atomic bomb? Berg leaned over to a Swiss professor next to him and asked in a whisper what he thought of the lecture. "Very interesting," was the reply. Berg decided he could not murder a man, even an enemy, because he was an entertaining speaker.

The fully loaded pistol with a silencer remained in Berg's pocket, as did the lethal cyanide pill to be used in case he needed to kill himself in the event he was about to be captured after having shot Heisenberg.

Back in the United States, General Groves was beginning to feel easier about the prospect of Germany's being close to creating an atomic bomb when Radio Berlin loosed a blockbuster: "All German citizens west of the Rhine River should flee because atomic power is about to be released. Human beings caught in this hurricane will be shattered to smithereens."

As Allied armies overran most of western Germany, Colonel Boris Pash and his Alsos mission inspected scientific laboratories in several locales. The Germans had not even been near to developing the ultimate weapon.[8]

Alias Gregor and Igor

IN THE SUMMER OF 1944, Allied armies had broken out of the Normandy beachhead and were racing across France toward the border of the Third Reich. At the same time, the Soviet Army had advanced westward, into Poland. Germany was about to be caught in a vice.

In Berlin, the Oberkommando der Wehrmacht suspected that the Soviets were preparing to launch an all-out offensive that could carry them to the Third Reich. Consequently, forty-one-year-old Major General Reinhard Gehlen, chief of the Fremde Heere Ost (Foreign Armies East), an intelligence branch of the army, was instructed to find out details of when, where, and with which forces the Soviets would strike.

Gehlen, who had a reputation within the German Army of being a remarkable forecaster of Soviet military strategy, devised a daring and imaginative scheme to collect the necessary information from behind Red Army lines and labeled the mission Drossel. For the task, he designated two of his most capable officers, Captain Albert Müller and Lieutenant Vassilij Skriabin.

Müller had been born in Leningrad thirty-five years earlier and spoke fluent Russian. He was skilled as a radio operator and electrical engineer. Müller's code name for Drossel would be Gregor.

Skriabin, twenty-three years of age, had been born in Gorki and had been a lieutenant in the Russian Army. But he had become disillusioned with communism and deserted to the Germans in August 1941, two months after Adolf Hitler had launched Barbarossa, the invasion of the Soviet Union. Skriabin's code name for Drossel would be Igor.

Gregor and Igor were immediately put through a crash course in espionage techniques to be used in the mission behind Russian lines. They rehearsed their assumed identities until, in the words of Gehlen, they could "recite them in their sleep." Each would be dressed in brown Russian uniforms with officers' epaulets and military decorations. Gregor would be a major on the Soviet General Staff, and Igor would masquerade as a lieutenant in the Red Air Force.

The two spies had to learn by heart the codes for the messages they would radio back from behind Russian lines, and they learned to use the radio receiver/transmitter they would take with them. They had to know everything a Red Army officer would know, from the size of the civilian cigarette ration to the latest Soviet movies.

General Reinhard Gehlen, ace German spymaster. (Author's collection)

Just past midnight on August 10, 1944, a Luftwaffe transport plane lifted off from a German airfield, flew deep behind Russian lines to a remote region, and the two Germans bailed out into the black unknown. They crashed onto the earth, shaken but unharmed. Unbuckling their harnesses, they buried their parachutes in a nearby woods and settled down to await daylight.

At 9:00 o'clock in the morning, the bogus Soviet major—alias Gregor—brushed the grass and dirt from his Red Army uniform and walked to a military post. There he asked for and was provided with a vehicle and driver to take him to the headquarters of the 11th Guards Division.

Arriving at his destination, he immediately demanded to see General Koslow, the division commander, and presented him with a large envelope marked top-secret in bold letters. The envelope contained an order from the Soviet high command identifying Gregor as Major Posjuchin and stating that he was to be given maximum assistance to investigate conditions at the front. The phony papers had been painstakingly crafted by General Gehlen's operatives in Berlin.

"Major Posjuchin" spent the next two days inspecting General Koslow's records, looking over his tactical plans, and trouping up and down the sector held by the 11th Guards Division. When it was time for "Posjuchin" to depart, Koslow gave a dinner in his honor. The wine flowed freely and the "major" had no trouble in extracting valuable intelligence from the loose-tongued commanders.

Koslow offered his personal car and driver to take the "major" to Vitebsk, where it had been arranged earlier that he was to meet Igor. Stealing out of town that night, the two German spies headed for a wooded area where, at the predesignated time of 9:30 P.M., Igor began tapping out a lengthy coded message that indicated that the 11th Guards Division was getting ready to launch a major attack. By midnight General Gehlen was poring over the decoded intelligence report in Berlin.

Now that the first phase of Operation Drossel had been completed, Gregor, as senior officer, opened a large envelope that held orders for his next venture. The envelope contained a set of new false identity papers and changes of rank. Gregor had been "demoted" to a first lieutenant whose name was Frassin. Igor now became a second lieutenant named Kruilow.

Also in the large envelope were phony Soviet documents, appropriately stamped and validated by signatures, that stated the two men had been discharged from active duty because of combat wounds. They were to be assigned to a Moscow labor office to work as technical specialists in the armament industry.

Reaching Moscow on a military train, Gregor and Igor went to the labor office, where they easily obtained the jobs that General Gehlen wanted them to have. Gregor went to work as an inspector in an electrical factory, and Igor was assigned to the central industrial planning organization. Because of their expertise and alleged service in the Red Army, Igor and Gregor shared a furnished apartment, a rare benefit in overcrowded Moscow for only two persons.

In mid-September, five weeks after parachuting behind Russian lines, the two agents tried to transmit a second intelligence report—and nearly were exposed as spies. The transmitter batteries had run down, so the radio had to be connected to the main electrical line.

When Igor began sending a coded message, the lights in the apartment—and elsewhere in the neighborhood—began flickering in rhythm with the Morse code he was tapping out. Minutes later, there was a sharp knock on the door. The dreaded Soviet secret police? Gregor, his heart thumping furiously, opened the door to an attractive young woman who said her name was Marfa and that she lived on the same floor.

Both men noticed that she was staring intently into the room: they had carelessly left the radio transmitter in plain sight. She said that she was having trouble with her oven, had heard one of the men was an electrical engineer, and asked if they could help out. The two agents soon had her oven in working order.

After a few discreet questions, the spies were convinced that Marfa, too, was anti-Communist and therefore sympathetic to their mission. They felt certain enough about her to ask her to buy a new set of batteries for the radio transmitter, which she did. Now the Russian woman joined the German agents. For the next six weeks Igor sent intelligence messages several times each week while Marfa served as a lookout.

Meanwhile, at the central industrial planning organization where he worked, Igor made friends with one of the chief clerks who coordinated the railroad operational schedules. For forty thousand rubles, the man agreed to let Igor have in his possession for one night the microfilm of plans for the impending deployment of all the trains in the entire Russian railroad system.

Igor was ecstatic. With this information on train movements, the experts in Berlin would be able to determine the possible moves of the Red Army along the entire battlefront, because the extremely limited and primitive Russian road system forced the generals to rely mainly on the railroad lines for the supply of their advancing armies. On the other hand, Igor was frightened. His friend might be an informer for the NKVD (the Soviet secret police), in which case the spy would be hideously tortured and then executed.

It was a chance Igor decided to take. He arranged with the chief clerk to bring the railroad plans to his apartment. In the meantime, Gregor sent, by wireless, word of the astonishing coup to Gehlen, who gave the green light to proceed.

Working all night, Gehlen's undercover agents photographed every page of the voluminous report as Marfa lingered outside the apartment building to warn of impending danger. There was a stern rule against taking notes, but Gregor decided to jot down information on all of the plan's important points.

General Gehlen was informed by radio of the total success of the operation. Based on this information, the intelligence chief set into motion plans for flying the three agents—and their precious microfilm—to Germany.

Igor and Gregor notified Gehlen's headquarters that a field in a remote region outside of Moscow had been selected for the evacuation. This pasture was large enough for a twin-engined plane to land and take off.

The designated night for the rescue was miserable: cold, rainy, and windy. Shivering violently from the weather and the tension, Igor, Gregor, and Marfa huddled under a large tree and listened. When they heard the distant murmur of an airplane's engine, they lighted a small fire—the predetermined landing signal.

Five minutes later, the dim silhouette of an airplane could be seen gliding to a landing on the lumpy ground. The pilot shut off the engine, and the three conspirators began dashing toward the aircraft, which had halted about a hundred yards away.

Suddenly the relative stillness was shattered as a cacophony of machine-gun fire erupted from the darkness. Clearly, someone had tipped off the NKVD about the escape rendezvous. With torrents of bullets hissing past them, Igor, Gregor, and Marfa kept running. Their eyes were focused on the aircraft's open hatch.

Much to their horror, the three agents saw that the plane was starting to roll forward. But before it could pick up speed, Gregor, who was in front of the others, reached the hatch and was pulled inside. He was bleeding profusely from a bullet in an arm.

Igor and Marfa, staring in wild disbelief, flung themselves to the ground and watched their lifeline to freedom gain speed, lift off, and disappear into the darkness. As bullets continued to whip around them, Igor and Marfa leaped to their feet and together ran into the nearby woods to escape the secret police they knew would be scouring the region for them after daylight.

Twenty-four hours later, Captain Albert Müller, alias Gregor, now wearing his German uniform, told a colonel in Gehlen's department that he did not have the microfilm, that Igor had the valuable Russian railroad deployment plan. However, Müller said, he did have the notes he had taken.

Nothing was heard from Igor and Marfa for ten days. Then, at the usual hour of 9:30 P.M., a wireless message was received from them. They had escaped their pursuers, hidden in the woods for several days until the NKVD had given up the search, then caught a train to Moscow. After sending that message, Igor and Marfa were never heard from again.

The railroad transport plan and other intelligence Gregor and Igor had furnished, along with information from other German agents, permitted General Gehlen to forecast the looming offensive by the Red Army. His report included maps and charts that gave the strength of Soviet forces and where each would attack.

General Heinz Wilhelm Guderian, the German Army chief of staff, had stood up to Adolf Hitler on occasion, and they had had several notable donnybrooks. Now Guderian, who had gained fame earlier in the war as "Hurrying Heinz" because of the slashing attacks by his panzer force, was greatly impressed by General Gehlen's detailed assessment of the Red Army's intentions.

Guderian promptly presented the analysis to Hitler, who barked: "This is the greatest bluff since Genghis Khan. . . . Who dug up this garbage?" The führer demanded that "the author of this report be locked up in a madhouse."

Two weeks later, thousands of Soviet guns belched on the Eastern Front. The Red Army was launching its all-out offensive to capture Berlin, striking at the precise sectors that Gehlen, based on the intelligence provided by Igor and Gregor, had said it would hit.[9]

Dodging the Gestapo in the Ruhr

A VEIL OF DARKNESS hovered over Western Europe when a Royal Air Force bomber lifted off from a remote airfield outside London and set a course for Germany. Soon the lone passenger, a man dressed in shabby wartime civilian clothing and known to the crew as Wilhelm Leineweber, fell into a fitful sleep. It was September 2, 1944.

Two hours later, the civilian sat on the rim of the hole in the floor, checked his parachute one final time, then bailed out. The moon was shining brightly, and he could discern houses, buildings, roads, and rivers as he floated earthward. The night was eerily silent. Moments later, he crashed onto a pasture.

Suddenly, Leineweber felt a surge of terror. He was utterly alone in Nazi Germany and had long been on the Gestapo's most wanted list. His true name was Jupp Kappius, and he was the first U.S. agent to parachute into the Third Reich.

As a boy in his native Germany, Kappius had been caught up in the tumultuous turmoil that followed the nation's crushing defeat in World War I. A structural engineer by training, he had given up that profession to become a full-time militant in the Socialist Party and a labor union organizer.

In 1937, more than four years after Adolf Hitler seized power, Kappius had been sought by the Gestapo for offenses punishable by death. He knew his days were numbered in Germany. So he and his wife, Anne, who had been working with him as a labor organizer in the Socialist Party, fled to England, where the couple spent the next seven years.

In the spring of 1944, just prior to the Normandy invasion, Kappius was recruited by the OSS Labor Division, which had been organized and was directed by Colonel George Pratt, in peacetime the general counsel for the National Labor Relations Board in Washington, and by Major Arthur Goldberg, a Chicago labor lawyer (who later would become a U.S. Supreme Court justice).

The clandestine mission that had been handed to Kappius was gargantuan in scope, especially for a lone agent. His task was also fraught with peril. He was to parachute into Germany near Sögel, create an underground organization, and launch a sabotage campaign aimed at crippling the Third Reich's war production in the Ruhr, a vast region in northwestern Germany that held the massive Krupp arms works, along with chemical, iron, and steel industries.

Moreover, Kappius was to use his underground network to promote internal resistance to Hitler and the Nazi regime, and to spread rumors designed to create rifts between leaders of the Wehrmacht and politically oriented organizations such as the Gestapo and the Waffen SS.

A painstakingly devised cover implementing elements in his background was created for Kappius. He became Wilhelm Leineweber, a structural engineer in the Todt Organization, which had built the Siegfried Line, the Atlantikwall, and was in charge of highways, power plants, and navigable waterways. He had traveled from France to Sögel to try to find his mother, who had been bombed out of her home and whose whereabouts were unknown. Then, according to his cover, he would travel to the Ruhr for a new assignment by Todt.

Kappius was given nine forged documents that would be essential for remaining free for any period of time in the police state that was Nazi Germany. These phony papers included an ID card, food rationing coupons, and blank official travel orders, which he himself would fill in as needed.

A wiry man of medium height in his late thirties, Kappius underwent vigorous physical and espionage training all summer in London. His tutors were impressed by his intelligence, moral strength, and devotion to the holy cause of eliminating Adolf Hitler and his regime. He refused to take the customary

OSS pay for his work and accepted only £5 (about U.S. $25) monthly for living expenses.

Now, after dropping into a dark German pasture, Kappius buried his parachute in a nearby wood, then waited for daylight. He hoped that the Royal Air Force navigator knew his trade and had landed him near Sögel. With the arrival of dawn, Kappius found a road, walked along it past numerous farmers and schoolchildren, and boarded a train in Sögel without incident.

Soon the conductor came down the aisle and approached Kappius, who handed him his ticket and said in English, "I guess you want this." That blunder could have been the spy's death warrant. A chill raced along his spine. Without changing expression, the conductor punched his ticket, handed it back to Kappius, said, "Heil, Hitler!" and moved on down the aisle.

Late that night, Kappius reached his destination, Bochum, in the Ruhr. Making his way through the blacked-out city, he knocked on the door of a couple who had been notified to expect a visitor. In their late twenties, the man and woman had already served prison terms for their involvement in the outlawed Socialist Party movement in Germany.

Despite the danger of Gestapo detection, the couple warmly welcomed Kappius; they knew of his reputation in the Socialist Party years earlier. It was agreed that the spy would remain indoors and out of sight at all times, and that the husband would do the necessary legwork to make contact with potential underground recruits.

Kappius's host, who was exempt from military service because he had tuberculosis, proved to be quite adept at clandestine operations. He managed to secure genuine official papers for his guest identifying him alternatively as an employee of Krupp, an employee in a Bochum factory, and a miner.

Meanwhile, in England, a U.S. C-47 transport plane took off from a remote airport outside London and headed for Thonon-les-Bains, a town on the shores of Lake Geneva in southeastern France. On board the aircraft were two women, Anne Kappius and Hilde Meisel. Both were OSS spies.

After landing at Thonon-les-Bains, Hilde was to travel to German-occupied Vienna and organize an underground sabotage network. Anne was to cross the border into neutral Switzerland, then travel to the Ruhr disguised as a Red Cross nurse. There she was to serve as a courier for her husband, Jupp.

During the final week of September, Anne Kappius was reunited with her husband in Bochum. Although Jupp had been in the Third Reich for only about a month, he already had recruited a cadre for an anti-Nazi underground network. His agents lived or worked in Bochum, Witten, Essen, and other Ruhr cities, as well as in the major cities of Berlin, Frankfurt, Breslau, Cologne, and Hanover.

In a few more weeks, Kappius sent his wife back to Switzerland to relay a message to Allen Dulles, the OSS chief in Berne, for transmittal to London. Kappius had acquired more than two hundred rifles, and he planned to take advantage of the chaos when Allied armies reached the Ruhr to blow up bridges, rail lines, and retreating German Army vehicles.

What Kappius needed, his wife was to tell the OSS, was an air drop of some two hundred hand weapons, incendiary grenades, and explosives. The field where the parachutage was to take place was pinpointed. A seemingly gibberish message, along with scores of others, to be broadcast over BBC in London would mean that the air drop would be made within twenty-four hours.

As days stretched into weeks, Kappius listened intently on his small radio for the message stating *"Grossmutter hat drei Kinder"* (Grandmother has three children), code for the anticipated parachutage. The message never came. Kappius had no way of knowing that his request had been scrubbed because the Germans had an antiaircraft battery positioned near the designated drop zone.

It was mid-January 1945 before Anne Kappius, again masquerading as a Red Cross nurse, was able to make her way back to Bochum. After a few days, she set out again for Switzerland. Concealed on her person was a message from her husband. It was highly risky business. Should the document be discovered by the Gestapo, it would be like signing her death warrant and that of her husband, along with most of his underground members.

In his message, Kappius pointed out that a generating complex near Cologne, on the Rhine River, which furnished nearly all of the electricity to the Ruhr, had suffered virtually no bomb damage. Moreover, the mammoth I. G. Farben plant, which made war matériel and had twenty-six thousand employees, also had escaped damage and was operating on around-the-clock shifts. Within a week, both key facilities were pulverized by Allied heavy bombers.

A week after Frau Kappius left for Switzerland, her husband learned through a contact in an area police station that the Gestapo had grown suspicious of him. So he left the young couple's home where he had lived for nearly five months and traveled almost constantly to other cities in the Ruhr, never staying in one for more than two days.

At about the same time that Jupp Kappius was forced to go on the run in the Ruhr, Hilde Meisel had created an underground intelligence chain in Vienna. One day she left for Switzerland to report her activities and the intelligence she had gained to the OSS. She was preparing to steal across the Austrian border when a German patrol spotted her and opened fire. Bullets struck her in both legs. By the time the Germans rushed to her, she had bitten into a cyanide capsule and died.

Meanwhile, the Western Allies had stormed over the Rhine River, and numerous spearheads began racing deep into the Third Reich. The German Army was in chaos. Some units stood fast and fought tenaciously; others gave up without firing a shot.

On April 9, 1945, Kappius was walking along a Ruhr road that was ominously empty of traffic. Rounding a sharp curve, he came face to face with a parked tank, the muzzle of its deadly gun pointed directly at him. Then he heard a booming voice from a helmeted head stuck out of the iron monster's open hatch: "Hey, Mac, where in the hell do you think you're going?!"

Kappius felt a deep surge of relief: that voice was unmistakenly American.[10]

A Murder Job for Two "Specialists"

OBERGRUPPENFÜHRER KARL WOLFF, the military governor of German-occupied northern Italy, had become convinced that the Third Reich had lost the war. During February 1945 Wolff, known in the Wehrmacht as "Little Karl," had been conducting covert peace negotiations with Allen W. Dulles, the head of the U.S. Office of Strategic Services (OSS) in Berne, Switzerland, to surrender all German forces in Italy. The SS general had been introduced to Dulles by a Major Waibel of the Swiss Army and Italian industrial tycoon Luigi Parilla.

At the same time, U.S. Major General Lyman Lemnitzer and British Major General Terence Airey had slipped into Switzerland disguised in civilian clothes to take part in the discussions with Wolff and Dulles.

Meanwhile, at Rosignano, a city on the western coast of Italy some 150 miles northwest of Rome, Colonel Monro MacCloskey, commander of the U.S. 885th Bombardment Squadron, accepted an invitation to lunch with the British liaison officer at an air base. The Briton had told MacCloskey that he wanted to present a highly important mission that he wished the American himself would fly.

The term "bombardment squadron" was actually a cover for the true function of MacCloskey's B-24 and B-17 four-engine bombers. The actual function of the 885th was to drop supplies and spies into German-occupied Europe in support of underground movements. Other airmen referred to MacCloskey and his men as "the cloak-and-dagger boys."

Everything about the 885th was unique. Each aircraft was painted a dull black, because nearly all the secret missions were conducted at night. Flame dampeners were attached to engine exhausts to make the low-flying plane less visible. The ball turret in the nose was replaced to give the nighttime bombardier wider visibility.

A special hatch was installed in the waist, and through the opening were dropped by parachute a cache of rifles, tommy guns, and bazookas, together with corresponding ammunition, along with explosives, caps, and fuses. Food, clothing, blankets, and boots were packed in bundles and shoved out of the hatch for a free fall without parachutes.

Now, when Colonel MacCloskey arrived at the Royal Air Force mess, the British liaison officer was already seated at a table with two men in uniform, who were introduced as Major Keith Bevan and Sergeant Frederick Alexander. Both men were in their early thirties; each was articulate and personable.

MacCloskey soon found himself listening to the British liaison officer explain that the two Britons were "specialists" and had been carefully selected for their clandestine task. "Their mission is so secret that even I am not being fully informed," the liaison officer stated.

Major Bevan then said he would explain as much as he was allowed to do. He said that hard-pressed German forces in the vast Po Valley of northern Italy, aware that the Third Reich was crumbling and the final outcome of the war was inevitable, were trying to surrender.

"The surrender is being blocked by a high-ranking German general whose name I cannot tell you," Bevan stated. "This general refuses to capitulate even though he has been ordered to do so by his superior [possibly SS General Karl Wolff]." This recalcitrant general was in a position to seriously delay the northward offensive of the Allies and cause considerable loss of life, the major added.

Then Bevan unfolded a map, pointed a finger at a specified locale, and said that if MacCloskey could drop him and Sergeant Alexander there, they would try to persuade the balking German general to change his mind. Mac-Closkey was quite aware that the true meaning of "persuade" was "kill."

Two nights later, MacCloskey and his crew were standing near their black bomber on the dark runway at Rosignano. It was nearly midnight. A British staff car, its cat's-eye headlights barely visible, pulled up and two shabby men in civilian clothes emerged and walked toward the colonel. They greeted him in fluent Italian, then switched their brief discussion into perfect German—neither language of which MacCloskey understood. These were the two "specialists" MacCloskey was to drop behind German lines—Major Bevan and Sergeant Alexander.

Soon the airplane was flying generally northeast. After about an hour, the bomber's power was reduced and its flaps lowered to reduce speed and noise. A green light flashed on in the cabin and out went the two Joes, as the airmen called all the secret agents they carried.

Neither Bevan nor Alexander was an experienced parachutist, but each landed without injury. After burying their 'chutes they started walking in the blackness toward their destination, the town of Mantova. They had been briefed in detail and knew that the German general's routine was for him to be driven from his headquarters to his comfortable villa at seven o'clock each night for a leisurely supper. Two hours later, he would be driven back to his office.

Each night, while the general would be dining, his chauffeur headed straight for a nearby small restaurant operated by an extremely attractive young Italian widow. She could have had her pick of the eligible bachelors in town but preferred the company of the German *Feldwebel* (sergeant).

Wanting to avoid attention to his frequent visits to the widow, the chauffeur always parked his limousine directly behind the restaurant. On the night the two Britons parachuted, the widow apparently was especially attentive to the

German, because he stayed almost the entire two hours before he had to rush to pick up the general.

What the sergeant did not know was that the restaurant was the headquarters of the Italian partisan band in the region and that the lady was one of its most productive agents. All were working against the Germans, whom they hated.

Forearmed with knowledge of the chauffeur's routine, the two British agents, Major Bevan and Sergeant Alexander, had sneaked into hiding in the darkness behind the restaurant and near the general's car. When the German approached, the two Britons, like giant cats, leaped upon him from the shadows and cracked him over the head with a blunt object.

Alexander rapidly took off his civilian clothes and put on the German's uniform. Then several partisans emerged from the restaurant and buried the sergeant in the nearby woods.

Both of the Britons, with Bevan still wearing his Italian civilian garb, got into the car. Alexander was at the wheel, Bevan hunched down in the backseat. After driving about two miles, Bevan leaped out where the road made a sharp turn and rolled into a ditch. There he remained motionless while the "chauffeur" drove on to the general's villa.

At 9:00 P.M., precisely on schedule, the general strolled out of his quarters and climbed into the backseat of the limousine without saying a word. During the customary nighttime routine, the general had dispensed with the need of his sergeant driver jumping out to hold open the rear door.

As the car neared the sharp turn in the road, Alexander managed to make the engine sputter and cough, then go dead right opposite where Major Bevan was prone in the ditch. The "chauffeur" emerged from the vehicle and opened the hood, then bent over as though trying to start the engine.

Moments later, the general, restless, got out of the auto and stood beside it in the darkness. Bevan sprang from the nearby ditch holding each end of a rawhide thong and cast it over the general's head and around his neck. Bevan, a husky man, pulled tightly until the German went limp and collapsed in a heap.

The two Britons lifted the lifeless body into the backseat of the vehicle; then they got into the front and drove about two miles. They abandoned the car and its dead general and set out walking cross-country to a previously designated safe house.

A few weeks later, with the help of Italian partisans, Bevan and Alexander made it back to Allied lines and then to the air field at Rosignano. There they were greeted warmly by Colonel MacCloskey, who had felt that the pair would never return from their perilous mission.

MacCloskey warmly congratulated the two Englishmen on their clandestine accomplishment. By now, General Heinrich Baron von Vietinghoff, the German commander in Italy, following Karl Wolff's surrender arrangements, had signed a document that ended hostilities on May 2, 1945.

"You saved countless lives," MacCloskey told the two men. "I presume you'll be going to London now for decorations and a vacation."

"No," replied Alexander. "We're going to Devonshire."

"Why are you going there?" the colonel asked. "All I ever knew about Devon is that there is a gloomy old prison there—Dartmoor, or something like that."

"You hit the target right on the nose once again," Bevan replied with a smile. "Dartmoor is where we're going. There were some youthful indiscretions which we haven't finished paying for—a little matter of murder."

MacCloskey was taken aback. Now he knew why the British liaison officer had kept referring to the two men as "specialists." They were murder "specialists" who had been promised a commutation of their prison term if they agreed to perform a perilous task of vital interest to the Allies—"eliminating" the balking German general.[11]

T Force Hunts for Chemical Weapons

IN EARLY MARCH 1945 Nazi Germany was hemmed in on all sides by hostile forces and was teetering on the brink of collapse. Soviet armies were hammering at the gates of the Third Reich in the east. General Dwight Eisenhower's American, British, French, and Canadian armies were arrayed for 450 miles along the western border of Germany.

Eisenhower was ready to unleash his forces over the broad, swift-flowing Rhine River, the ancient barrier to invasion of the German homeland. At his headquarters outside Paris, the Allied supreme commander was gripped by a nagging worry: in a last-ditch effort to snatch a negotiated peace out of the jaws of defeat, would Adolf Hitler unleash poison gas or some other chemical weapon against the Allies when they stormed the Rhine?

Consequently, Eisenhower's staff assigned a clandestine outfit called T Force to infiltrate German positions and investigate any poison gas stocks or chemical weapons Hitler might use to end the war in Europe in a tidal wave of lung deaths and blindness. T Force, in turn, created a small, mobile unit known as Section 6, whose members were largely British scientists and technicians. They had been "drafted" from their occupations and put into uniform with ranks approximating their civilian plateau.

No doubt Section 6 was the most rank-heavy outfit of the war. Never, perhaps, had so many commanded so few. The lowest grade was captain; colonels and generals abounded. It had been necessary to put them into uniform because, operating behind enemy lines, they were prime candidates for capture, in which case the Germans might shoot them as spies if they wore civilian clothing.

Information on targets for Section 6 came from two primary sources: the Combined Intelligence Subcommittee (CIS), which drew up what was called the black list, a series of suspected secret chemical warfare facilities; and the Inter-Services Topographical Unit (ISTU), which largely had the same function.

After the Allies, paced by the largest single airborne assault in history, plunged over the Rhine and advanced deeper into Germany in late March 1945, Section 6 received word that there was a suspected chemical warfare facility at Münsterlager. Rushing to the site, the unit found several laboratories that seemed to have been vacated in a hurry. Numerous notebooks containing chemistry symbols and related data were scattered about the premises.

Most of the laboratory employees had fled when the Allied spearheads approached, Section 6 officers were told by a German who was friendly and tried to be helpful. He said that he had been a U-boat commander in World War I, but had taken up forestry and was now chief forester in the region. Speaking fluent English, the forester said he did not know where the commander of the laboratory was: he had simply disappeared.

A short time later, the laboratory commander was caught by American soldiers. While being interrogated, he said that the "chief forester" was in fact the *Gauleiter* (Nazi political leader) of the region and it had been his function to sabotage the chemical warfare laboratory if the Allies drew near. The gauleiter was soon in an Allied prisoner-of-war camp.

While snooping around the laboratory premises, a Section 6 officer found a barn that had a concrete floor with a trap door in the center. After pulling open the door, he climbed down a stairway that led to an underground chamber filled with furnaces, tubing, and condensers. There were filing cabinets crammed with slides, which the Section 6 officer identified as showing the effects of chemical warfare materials on human organs.

The Section 6 scientists immediately identified the subterranean operation as a pilot plant for the production of Tabun, a colorless, odorless, and tasteless nerve gas that could kill or horribly cripple human beings.

If the Germans had manufactured large amounts of Tabun, which apparently had been their intention, the gas could have been disastrous for Allied forces. Their masks were designed to protect the wearer from breathing harmful gases into the lungs, but the respirators were no protection against Tabun.

To many in Section 6, it appeared that the Allies were about to win the war in Europe—and not a day too soon.[12]

Notes and Sources

Part One—A Gathering Tempest

1. **Black-Bag Jobs and Madam X**
   Toshiyuki Yokoi, *Nihon no kimitsu shitsu* ("The Japanese Version of the Black Chamber"), English trans., 1953, pp. 6–7, 9, 12. Washington, D.C.: National Archives.
   Edwin T. Layton, *And I Was There* (New York: Morrow, 1985), pp. 44–46, 48.

2. **Hitler's Crony a U.S. Secret Agent**
   Ernst Hanfstaengl, *The Missing Years* (London: Eyre & Spottiswoode, 1957), pp. 78, 136–137, 205.
   Louis L. Snyder, *Encyclopedia of the Third Reich* (New York: McGraw-Hill, 1976), p. 137.
   Hugh Thomas, *The Spanish Civil War* (New York: Harper & Brothers, 1961), pp. 316–317.

3. **"Me No Here, No Movies!"**
   Illustrated Encyclopedia of World War II (New York: Cavendish, 1966), pp. 1385–1386.
   Edwin T. Layton, *And I Was There* (New York: Morrow, 1985), pp. 50–51.

4. **Hitler's "Mystery Spy" in London**
   Harold C. Deutsch, *Hitler and His Generals* (Minneapolis: University of Minnesota Press, 1974), pp. 414–415.
   Illustrated Story of World War II (Pleasantville, N.Y.: Reader's Digest Association, 1969), pp. 52–53.
   Ladislas Farago, *The Game of the Foxes* (New York: McKay, 1971), pp. 103–104.

5. **Stealing a Supersecret Bombsight**
   Ladislas Farago, *The Game of the Foxes* (New York: McKay, 1971), p. 43.
   David Kahn, *Hitler's Spies* (New York: Macmillan, 1975), p. 321.
   Burke Wilkinson, ed., *Cry Spy!* (Englewood Cliffs, N.J.: Bradbury, 1969), pp. 71, 73.
   Author's archives.

6. **Espionage Target: The Panama Canal**
   FBI interrogation reports, data on convictions for espionage (1937–1945), and assorted documents relating to World War II era espionage and sedition, copies in author's files.
   Leon Turrou, *The Nazi Spy Conspiracy in America* (Freeport, N.Y.: Books for Libraries Press, 1969), pp. 191–193.
   Ladislas Farago, *The Game of the Foxes* (New York: McKay, 1971), pp. 59–60.

7. **The Gestapo Comes to New York**
   Leon Turrou, *The Nazi Spy Conspiracy in America* (Freeport, N.Y.: Books for Libraries Press, 1969), pp. 211–213.
   Burke Wilkinson, ed., *Cry Spy!* (Englewood Cliffs, N.J.: Bradbury, 1969), pp. 82–83.
   Author's archives.

8. **Practicing "Nazi Psychology" in the United States**
   Ladislas Farago, *War of Wits* (New York: Funk & Wagnalls, 1954), pp. 19–20.
   Author's archives.

9. **A Gentleman Farmer Flies to London**
Ian Colvin, *Master Spy* (New York: McGraw-Hill, 1951), pp. 67, 72, 75.
John W. Wheeler-Bennett, *Nemesis of Power* (New York: Macmillan, 1953), pp. 411–412.
Eddy Bauer, ed., *Illustrated Encyclopedia of World War II*, Vol. 1 (New York: Cavendish, 1966), pp. 5–7.
Adam B. Ulam, *Expansion and Coexistence* (New York: Praeger, 1968), p. 251.

10. **An "Unsportsmanlike" Murder Scheme**
Der Spiegel, Hamburg, July 1971.
David Dilks, ed., *The Diaries of Sir Alexander Cadogan* (New York: Putnam, 1972), pp. 141, 143.
New York Times, August 5, 1971.

Part Two—Outbreak of War

1. **"Take Possession of the [British Captives]"**
Stephen Howarth, *Great Naval Captains of World War II* (New York: St. Martin's Press, 1993), p. 495.
Winston S. Churchill, *The Second World War*, Vol. 1 (Boston: Houghton Mifflin, 1948–1953), pp. 562–563.
Eddy Bauer, ed., *Illustrated Encyclopedia of World War II*, Vol. 1 (New York: Cavendish, 1966), p. 125.

2. **Agent X Conspires with the Pope**
"Pius XII and Germany," *American Historical Review*, 1964, p. 70.
Harold C. Deutsch, *The Conspiracy Against Hitler in the Twilight War* (Minneapolis: University of Minnesota Press, 1968), pp. 113–114, 117, 121.
Der Spiegel, Hamburg, October 15, 1953.
Daily Telegraph, London, January 2, 1971.
The Columbia Encyclopedia (New York: Columbia University Press, 1950), p. 47.

3. **The Spy Was a Clip Artist**
"Hearings Before the Joint Committee on the Investigation of the Pearl Harbor Attack, Congress of the United States," 1946. Part 35, p. 555. Washington, D.C.: National Archives.
Ibid., Part 1, pp. 229–230.
Ibid., pp. 262–263.
Gordon W. Prange, *At Dawn We Slept* (New York: McGraw-Hill, 1981), p. 71.

4. **Denmark's Patriotic Burglar**
Der Spiegel, Hamburg, October 15, 1953.
Winston S. Churchill, *The Second World War*, Vol. 2 (Boston: Houghton Mifflin, 1948–1953), p. 30.
Reader's Digest, May 1946.
Anthony C. Brown, *Bodyguard of Lies* (New York: Harper & Row, 1975), p. 518.

5. **Deceit in the Desert**
"Cover and Deception," memorandum to the U.S. Joint Chiefs of Staff, May 14, 1945. Washington, D.C.: Modern Military Records, National Archives.
Anthony Cave Brown, *Bodyguard of Lies* (New York: Harper & Row, 1975), pp. 54–55.
Author's archives.

6. **The Jewish Pal of the Nazis**
M. R. D. Foot, *SOE in France* (London: Her Majesty's Stationery Office, 1966), pp. 369, 371, 377.

Charles Franklin, *The Great Spies* (New York: Hart, 1967), pp. 182–183.
Author's archives.

7. **The FBI Undercover in South America**
Don Whitehead, *The FBI Story* (New York: Random House, 1955), pp. 212–213, 216.
Declassified FBI documents in author's files.

8. **"War of Nerves" against England**
Author's archives.

9. **The Führer's Concrete Crocodiles**
Author's archives.

10. **Tuned in to the Luftwaffe**
Aileen Clayton, *The Enemy Is Listening* (New York: Ballantine, 1982), pp. 47, 76, 115.
Anthony Cave Brown, *Bodyguard of Lies* (New York: Harper & Row, 1975), p. 42.
Author's archives.

11. **Hosting a Boy Scout Official**
Winston S. Churchill, *The Second World War*, Vol. 2 (Boston: Houghton Mifflin, 1948–1953), pp. 134–135.
Secrets and Spies (Pleasantville, N.Y.: Reader's Digest Association, 1964), p. 137.
Author's archives.

12. **"We Came to Blow Up America!"**
William L. Shirer, *The Rise and Fall of the Third Reich* (New York: Simon & Schuster, 1960), p. 684.
Documents on German Foreign Policy, 1918–1945. Washington, D.C.: Thomsen messages, National Archives.
Ladislas Farago, *The Game of the Foxes* (New York: McKay, 1971), p. 437.
Max Lowenthal, *The Federal Bureau of Investigation* (New York: Sloane, 1950), pp. 425–426.

13. **The Bogus Traitor of Flekkefjord**
Per Hansson, *The Greatest Gamble* (New York: Norton, 1967), pp. 20–21, 31, 40.
Sverre Kjeldstadli, *Hjemme Styrkene* (Oslo: Aschenhoug, 1959), pp. 76, 94, 105.
E. H. Cookridge, *Set Europe Ablaze* (New York: Crowell, 1966), pp. 314, 317–318.

14. **A One-Man Cloak-and-Dagger Agency**
New York Times, December 6, 1940.
Business Week, December 8, 1940.
Chicago Tribune, December 17, 1940.
William F. Troy, *Donovan and the CIA* (Washington, D.C.: Center for the Study of Intelligence, 1981), pp. 37, 42.
Robert E. Sherwood, *Roosevelt and Hopkins* (New York: Harper & Brothers, 1948), 231–232.
Richard Dunlop, *Donovan* (New York: Rand McNally, 1982), pp. 233, 245, 248–249.
William L. Langer and S. Everett Gleason, *The Undeclared War* (New York: Harper & Brothers, 1953), p. 365.

Part Three — Conflict Spreads to the Pacific

1. **One Briton's Revenge**
Details of Major Grant Taylor's action were provided the author by Major G. G. Norton (Ret.), curator of the Airborne Forces Museum in Aldershot, England, in the late 1980s. Some came to the author by correspondence from British Major K. H. M.

O'Kelly (Ret.), who had known Grant Taylor well during the war. U.S. colonel Carlos C. Alden, who had taken and passed with flying colors Taylor's "killer school," was interviewed by the author in 1992, and told of the techniques the Britons taught.

2. **Spies inside a U.S. Embassy**
   Ladislas Farago, *The Game of the Foxes* (New York: McKay, 1971), pp. 423–424.
   Anthony Cave Brown, *Bodyguard of Lies* (New York: Harper & Row, 1975), pp. 155, 175.
   Author's archives.

3. **The "Evangelists" of New York Harbor**
   Edwin P. Hoyt, *U-Boats Offshore* (New York: Stein & Day, 1978), pp. 72–73.
   Arch Whitehouse, *Subs and Submariners* (Garden City, N.Y.: Doubleday, 1964), p. 142.

4. **Confrontation at a Montana Airport**
   Robert E. Sherwood, *Roosevelt and Hopkins* (New York: Harper & Brothers, 1948), pp. 136–138.
   Sanche de Gramont, *The Secret War* (New York: Putnam, 1962), pp. 56–57.
   C. L. Sulzberger, *Picture History of World War II* (New York: American Heritage, 1966), p. 132.
   Author's archives.

5. **Clandestine Payoffs in Mexico**
   John Toland, *The Rising Sun* (New York: Random House, 1970), pp. 163–164.
   Robert E. Ward, "The Inside Story of the Pearl Harbor Plan," *U.S. Naval Institute Proceedings*, December 1951.
   Author's archives.

6. **Urgent: Hide the Suez Canal**
   Eddy Bauer, ed., *Illustrated Encyclopedia of World War II*, Vol. 3 (New York: Cavendish, 1966), p. 414; Vol. 7, pp. 855–856.
   Anthony Cave Brown, *Bodyguard of Lies* (New York: Harper & Row, 1975), pp. 102, 150–152.
   Geoffrey Barkas, *The Camouflage Story* (London: Cassell, 1952), pp. 202–203.
   "Organization and Function of 'A-Force.'" Washington D.C.: Modern Military Records, National Archives.
   David Fisher, *The War Magician* (New York: Coward-McCann, 1983), pp. 119, 127–128, 130–131.

7. **A Covert Cruise in the Pacific**
   Author interview with former FBI Assistant Director W. Raymond Wannall, 1997.
   Walter Lord, *Day of Infamy* (New York: Henry Holt, 1957), pp. 15, 18.
   Don Whitehead, *The FBI Story* (New York: Random House, 1956), pp. 190–192.
   Author's archives.

8. **Four Frogmen against Two Battleships**
   Janusz Piekalkiewicz, *Secret Agents, Spies, and Saboteurs* (New York: Morrow, 1969), pp. 63, 71, 73–74.
   Eddy Bauer, ed., *Illustrated Encyclopedia of World War II*, Vol. 3 (New York: Cavendish, 1966), pp. 438–439.

9. **The Superspy at Pearl Harbor**
   "Papers Relating to the Foreign Relations of the United States: Japan, 1931–1941," Vol. 11, pp. 165–167. Washington, D.C.: National Archives.
   "Hearings Before the Joint Committee on the Investigation of the Pearl Harbor Attack, Congress of the United States," 1946. Part 29, pp. 2072–2073. Part 35, p. 82. Washington, D.C.: National Archives.

David Kahn, *The Codebreakers* (New York: Macmillan, 1967), pp. 234–235.
John Toland, *The Rising Sun* (New York: Random House, 1970), p. 189.

10. An American Turncoat in Washington
Viscount Alanbrooke, *Diaries*, Vol. 1 (London: Collins, 1957–1959), pp. 292–293.
Winston S. Churchill, *The Second World War*, Vol. 3 (Boston: Houghton Mifflin, 1948–1954), p. 540.
John Toland, *The Rising Sun* (New York: Random House, 1970), p. 257.
Author's archives.

Part Four—The Turning Tide

1. The World's Richest Spymaster
Leon Turrou, *The Nazi Spy Conspiracy in America* (Freeport, N.Y.: Books for Libraries Press, 1969), pp. 232–233.
FBI press releases: March 12, 1942; July 9, 1942; October 16, 1943.
Declassified FBI files on Nazi espionage activities in the United States, December 1941 through October 1942.

2. The Plot to Blow Up the Pan Am Clipper
Author's archives.

3. Lady Luck Flies with the Führer
Peter Hoffmann, *The History of the German Resistance* (Cambridge, Mass.: Massachusetts Institute of Technology Press, 1977), p. 271.
John Erickson, *The Road to Stalingrad* (New York: Harper & Row, 1975), p. 267.
Saturday Evening Post, July 20, 1946.
Author's archives.

4. Rommel's Secret Informant
Anthony Cave Brown, *Bodyguard of Lies* (New York: Harper & Row, 1975), p. 111.
Winston S. Churchill, *The Second World War*, Vol. 4 (Boston: Houghton Mifflin, 1948–1953), pp. 464, 467–468.
Leonard Mosley, *The Cat and the Mice* (New York: Harper & Row, 1959), pp. 167–168.

5. The Scientist Who Knew Too Much
After the war, Jack Nissenthall shortened his name to Nissen. The author is indebted to him for providing, in a 1990 interview, many details on his role and actions at Dieppe.
James Leasor, *Green Beach* (New York: Morrow, 1975), pp. 39–40.
Files of Canadian General Staff Historical Section, Ottawa.
Winston S. Churchill, *The Second World War*, Vol. 4 (Boston: Houghton Mifflin, 1948), pp. 467–468.

6. The Dogs of Torigni
Quentin Reynolds, *The Man Who Wouldn't Talk* (New York: Random House, 1953), pp. 57, 59.
Jerrard Tickel, *Moon Squadron* (Garden City, N.Y.: Doubleday, 1958), pp. 121, 124.
Author's archives.

7. Conspiracy in Casablanca
Author interview with General Mark W. Clark (Ret.), 1984.
Lucian K. Truscott, Jr., *Command Missions* (New York: Harper & Brothers, 1950), pp. 72–73.
Samuel Eliot Morison, *The Two Ocean War* (Boston: Little, Brown, 1961), pp. 127–128.
George F. Howe, *Northwest Africa* (Washington, D.C.: Chief of Military History, 1957), pp. 88–89.

8. **Outfoxing the Desert Fox**
   Winston S. Churchill, *The Second World War*, Vol. 4 (Boston: Houghton Mifflin, 1948–1953), pp. 464, 467–468, 489.
   Leonard Mosley, *The Cat and the Mice* (New York: Harper & Row, 1959), pp. 94–95, 136–137.
   Erwin Rommel, *The Rommel Papers* (New York: Harcourt, 1953), pp. 277, 284.
   Anwar Sadat, *Revolt on the Nile* (New York: Viking, 1960), pp. 112–113.

9. **Smuggling Two Men out of Morocco**
   Mark W. Clark, *Calculated Risk* (New York: Harper & Brothers, 1950), pp. 149–150.
   Richard Dunlop, *Donovan* (New York: Rand McNally, 1982), pp. 372–373.
   OSS archives.
   Author interview with General Mark W. Clark (Ret.), 1983.

10. **The Creeps and the Atomic Scientists**
   Stephane Groueff, *Manhattan Project* (Boston: Little, Brown, 1967), pp. 50–51.
   Leslie R. Groves, *Now It Can Be Told* (New York: Harper & Row, 1962), pp. 33–36.
   Reader's Digest, November 1947.
   Gordon Thomas and Max Morgan Witts, *Enola Gay* (New York: Stein & Day, 1977), p. 76.
   Author's archives.

Part Five—Beginning of the End

1. **The Spy Who Refused to Die**
   Anthony Cave Brown, *Bodyguard of Lies* (New York: Harper & Row, 1975), pp. 172–173.
   E. H. Cookridge, *Set Europe Ablaze* (New York: Crowell, 1966), pp. 200–202.
   Author's archives.

2. **Blowing Up a Locomotive Works**
   C. L. Sulzberger, *Picture History of World War II* (New York: Crown, 1966), pp. 417–418.
   E. H. Cookridge, *Set Europe Ablaze* (New York: Crowell, 1966), pp. 173–174.
   Author's archives.

3. **The Mystery Man of Algiers**
   U.S. Air Force Historical Group, *The Army Air Forces in World War II*, Vol. 2 (Washington, D.C.: U.S. Government Printing Office, 1962), p. 20.
   Eric Linklater, *The Campaign in Italy* (London: His Majesty's Stationery Office, 1951), p. 20.
   Bernard Fergusson, *The Watery Maze* (New York: Holt, Rinehart, & Winston, 1961), pp. 238–239.

4. **Top Secret: Parachuting Mules**
   Author interviews with Major Mark J. Alexander (Ret.), 1984, and with Lieutenant General James M. Gavin (Ret.), 1988.

5. **America's Fifteen Thousand Secret Snoopers**
   Author interview with Dr. Bradley Biggs, a World War II veteran of the 555th Parachute Infantry Battalion, 1990.
   Washington Post, February 3, 1946.
   Arch Whitehouse, *Espionage and Counterespionage* (Garden City, N.Y.: Doubleday, 1964), pp. 149–150.

6. **Coercing Surrender of the Italian Fleet**
   Author interview with Richard H. O'Brien, who led PT boats on McGregor mission, 1997.

Winston S. Churchill, *Closing the Ring* (Boston: Houghton Mifflin, 1951), pp. 114–115.
Author's archives.

7. **Deception Role for the Panjandrum**
Author's archives.

8. **Bedeviling the Gestapo in Toulouse**
Charles Franklin, *The Great Spies* (New York: Hart, 1967), pp. 181–182.
Nebur Gulbenkian, *Pantaraxis* (London: Hutchinson, 1965), pp. 97–99.
Winston S. Churchill, *The Second World War*, Vol. 2 (Boston: Houghton Mifflin, 1949), pp. 68–70.

9. **An X-Craft Calls on the *Tirpitz***
Eddy Bauer, ed., *Illustrated Encyclopedia of World War II*, Vol. 7 (New York: Cavendish, 1972), p. 945; Vol. 17, p. 2286; Vol. 18, p. 2490.
Stephen Roskill, *The War at Sea 1939–1945*, Vol. 3 (London: Her Majesty's Stationery Office, 1954–1961), pp. 64, 68.
Admiral Karl Doenitz, *Memoirs* (London: Weidenfeld & Nicolson, 1959), pp. 325, 332, 341.

10. **A French Boy and His Music Teacher**
Eddy Bauer, ed., *Illustrated Encyclopedia of World War II*, Vol. 12 (New York: Cavendish, 1966), p. 1637.
Richard Collier, *Ten Thousand Eyes* (New York: Dutton, 1958), pp. 160–161.
Author's archives.

11. **An Atomic Alert on New Year's Eve**
Peter Wyden, *Day One* (New York: Simon & Schuster, 1984), p. 106.
Leslie R. Groves, *Now It Can Be Told* (New York: Harper & Row, 1962), p. 112.
Stephane Groueff, *Manhattan Project* (Boston: Little, Brown, 1967), pp. 312–313.
Author's archives.

12. **"Ghost Voices" over Europe**
Reader's Digest, October 1946.
Anthony Cave Brown, *Bodyguard of Lies* (New York: Harper & Row, 1975), p. 45.
Author's archives.

13. **Close Call in a Secret Room**
Virgil Busch, *Modern Arms and Free Men* (New York: Henry Holt, 1949), pp. 174–175.
Arthur Moorhouse, *The Traitors* (New York: Macmillan, 1952), p. 1.
Author's archives.

14. **Masking the "Chicago Skyline"**
Gerald Pawle, *The Secret War* (New York: Sloane, 1957), pp. 263–264.
Dwight D. Eisenhower, *Crusade in Europe* (Garden City, N.Y.: Doubleday, 1948), p. 235.
Edward Ellsberg, *The Far Shore* (New York: Dodd, Mead, 1960), p. 155.
A. B. Stanford, *Force Mulberry* (New York: Morrow, 1952), pp. 112–113.

Part Six—The Lights Go On Again

1. **A U.S. Colonel's Private Airline**
Author correspondence with Professor Reginald V. Jones of Aberdeen, Scotland, who was a scientific adviser to Prime Minister Winston S. Churchill in World War II, 1992.
Wilhelm M. Carlgren, *Swedish Foreign Policy During the Second World War* (New York: St. Martin's Press, 1977), various passages.
Bernt Balchen, *Come North with Me* (New York: Dutton, 1958), pp. 57–58, 72–73.

2. **Kidnapping a German General**
    Winston S. Churchill, *The Second World War*, Vol. 3 (Boston: Houghton Mifflin, 1948–1953), p. 194.
    Janusz Piekalkiewicz, *Secret Agents, Spies, and Saboteurs* (New York: Morrow, 1969), pp. 356, 359, 366.
    Eddy Bauer, ed., *Illustrated Encyclopedia of World War II* (New York: Cavendish, 1966), pp. 486–487.
    Gerard M. Devlin, *Silent Wings* (New York: St. Martin's Press, 1985), p. 45.

3. **Blasting a Japanese Headquarters**
    Author interview with wartime Pacific PT boat skipper L. Rumsey Ewing, who served with Lieutenant Fred Calhoun in the Pacific, 1997.

4. **Mad Dash in an Explosive-Laden Car**
    Reinhard Gehlen, *The Service* (New York: World, 1972), p. 99.
    Stanley P. Lovell, *Of Spies and Stratagems* (Englewood Cliffs, N.J.: Prentice-Hall, 1963), pp. 52–53.
    Author's archives.

5. **A Special Job for "Scarface Otto"**
    Denis J. Fordor, *The Neutrals* (New York: Time-Life Books, 1962), p. 52.
    Charles Franklin, *The Great Spies* (New York: Hart, 1962), pp. 181–82.
    Charles Foley, *Commando Extraordinary* (Costa Mesa, Calif.: Noontide Press, 1988), pp. 127–128.

6. **Sneaking onto Utah Beach**
    Author interviews with Vice Admiral John D. Bulkeley (Ret.), 1990–1993.
    U.S. Navy records of episode, 1944. Washington, D.C.: National Archives.

7. **X2 Agents in Cherbourg**
    Martin Blumenson, *Breakout and Pursuit* (Washington, D.C.: Chief of Military History, 1961), pp. 176–177.
    Military Review, March 1951.
    "Utah to Cherbourg," U.S. Department of the Army, 1949.
    "U.S. VII Corps Operations in Europe." Privately printed, 1945.

8. **Covert Targets: Germany's Atomic Scientists**
    Author correspondence with Professor Reginald V. Jones of Aberdeen, Scotland, who was a scientific adviser to Prime Minister Winston S. Churchill in World War II, 1988.
    Stephane Groueff, *Manhattan Project* (Boston: Little, Brown, 1967), pp. 107–108.
    Leslie R. Groves, *Now It Can Be Told* (New York: Harper & Row, 1962), pp. 136–137.
    Boris Pash, *The Alsos Mission* (New York: Award House, 1969), pp. 36, 95, 178.
    Samuel A. Goudsmit, *Alsos* (New York: Henry Schuman, 1947), pp. 72, 86.

9. **Alias Gregor and Igor**
    General Heinz Wilhelm Guderian, *Panzer Leader* (New York: Dutton, 1954), pp. 314, 316.
    Heinz Hoehne and Hermann Zolling, *The General Was a Spy* (New York: Coward, McCann, & Geoghegan, 1972), p. 5.
    Reinhard Gehlen, *The Service* (New York: World, 1972), pp. 61, 72.
    Louis Hagen, *The Secret War for Europe* (New York: Stein & Day, 1969), pp. 26–27, 29–30.

10. **Dodging the Gestapo in the Ruhr**
    Albert Speer, *Inside the Third Reich* (New York: Macmillan, 1970), pp. 191–193.
    Joseph E. Persico, *Piercing the Reich* (New York: Viking, 1979), pp. 2, 74–75.

"Memorandum of Information for the Joint U.S. Chiefs of Staff: OSS Penetration of Nazi Germany." Washington, D.C.: Office of Strategic Services, June 1945. Washington, D.C.: National Archives.

William J. Casey, "Final Report on OSS Operations in Germany," July 24, 1945. Washington, D.C.: National Archives.

11. A Murder Job for Two "Specialists"

John R. Angolia, *On the Field of Honor* (San Jose, Calif.: Bender, 1979), p. 82.

Mark W. Clark, *Calculated Risk* (New York: Harper & Brothers, 1950), pp. 248–249.

Monro MacCloskey, *Secret Air Missions* (New York: Rosen, 1966), pp. 129, 135–136.

Author's archives.

12. T Force Hunts for Chemical Weapons

Philip Warner, *Secret Forces* (Chelsea, Mich.: Scarborough House, 1985), pp. 224–225.

Dwight D. Eisenhower, *Crusade in Europe* (Garden City, N.Y.: Doubleday, 1948), p. 386.

Author's archives.

Index

Abrams, Allen, 197, 198
Achilles (British cruiser), 33
Airborne Cigar, 177
Airey, Maj. Gen. Terence, 221
Ajax (British cruiser), 33
Akagi (Japanese aircraft carrier), 95, 96
Akaumianos, Mickey, 191, 192
Alexander, Sgt. Frederick, 221–24
Alexander, Gen. Harold R. L. G., 118
Alexander, Maj. Mark J., 153, 154
Altmark (German ship), 33, 34, 35
Amaldi, Edoardo, 210
Amé, Gen. Cesare, 118
American Signals Intelligence Service
    (ASIS), 182
Ark Royal (British aircraft carrier), 33, 69
Atlantic Clipper (airplane), 72
Auchinleck, Gen. Claude, 117
Axelssen, Viggo, 68, 69

Balchen, Col. Bernt, 187–188
Barkas, Maj. Geoffrey, 91
Barnes, Lt. Cmdr. Stanley, 159
Beck, Gen. Ludwig, 10–11, 26, 27, 36
Beck, Prof. Walter, 24–25
Berg, Morris "Moe," 211–12
Bergmann, Julius, 62, 64
Bermuda Clipper (airplane), 71
Bevan, Maj. Keith, 221–24
Bianchi, Seaman Emilio, 97, 99
Bismarck (German battleship), 69
Black Code, (U.S.), 119, 120
Blaum, Wolfgang, 20
Blomberg, Gen. Werner von, 9–11
Blue Code (Japanese), 4, 5
Boetticher, Gen. Friedrich von, 14
Böning, Wilhelm, 17–18, 19
Brandt, Col. Heinz, 116, 117

Brauchitsch, Gen. Heinrich von, 39, 40,
    41
Brazos (U.S. tanker), 8
Bremen (German ship), 13, 16, 84
Bruce, David K., 134
Brückner, Rev. Hermann, 83, 84
Bulkeley, Cmdr. John D., 203–05
Burke, Lt. Michael, 160, 161, 162, 163
buzz bomb, 188
Byers, William, 50–52

Cadogan, Alexander, 30
Calhoun, Lt. Fred, 195–96
Canaris, Adm. Wilhelm, 17, 36, 73, 81
    French plans stolen by, 9
    order to blow up *Clipper* given to, 113,
    114
    U.S. embassy spy planted by, 80
Capone, Al, 79
Cárdenas, Gen. Lázaro, 88
Carstenn, SS Maj. Eric, 81–82
Centurie (French underground unit),
    172–73
Chamberlain, Prime Minister Neville,
    28–29
Churchill, Prime Minister Winston, 28,
    46, 55, 106, 117–18
Clark, Lt. Gen. Mark W., 128
Clarke, Col. Dudley W., 45, 129, 132
Clayton, Lt. Aileen, 58, 59
Collins, Maj. Gen. J. Lawton, 205
Combined Intelligence Subcommittee
    (CIS), 225
Combined Operations Experimental
    Establishment (COXE), 165, 166
Compton, Dr. Arthur H., 176
Conant, Dr. James B., 137
Condor Legion, 6

Consodine, Maj. William A., 137
Cossack (British destroyer), 34, 35
Crandall's Navy, 51
Creeps, 137, 138, 139
Crockett, Brigadier Norman R., 167
Croyden Airport (London), 25, 27
Cunningham, Adm. Andrew B., 96
Czar Boris III, 73

Dau, Capt. Heinrich, 34, 35
Directive 40 (Hitler order), 164
Directorate of Miscellaneous Weapons
    Development (DMWD), 165
Doenitz, Adm. Karl, 83, 169
Donovan, OSS Director William J.,
    70–75, 208
Dorner DO-X (German airplane), 23
Driscoll, Agnes Meyer, 4, 5
Dufour, Jacques, 145, 146
Dulles, Allen W., 219, 221
DuPre, George, 124, 125

Earle, George H. III, 73, 75
Ebell, Dr. Wolfgang, 111, 112
Eddy, Lt. Col. William A., 126, 128
Effingham (U.S. ship), 64
Eifler, Maj. Carl, 208
Einstein, Albert, 24
Englich, Kurt, 178–79
Eppler, John, 130, 131
Europa (German ship), 21, 24
Exeter (British cruiser), 33

Fahmy, Hekmeth, 130, 131
Feder, Gottfried, 57
Federal Bureau of Investigation (FBI),
    19, 20, 49–52, 53, 79, 104, 109–11,
    155, 157
Fellers, Col. Frank B., 118, 120
Fermi, Dr. Enrico, 210
Fiske, Col. Norman E., 118
Foch, Field Marshal Ferdinand, 46
Foley, Maj. Francis, 30
Foxworth, FBI Agent Percy S., 83
Franco, Generalissimo Francisco, 60
François-Poncet, Ambassador André, 11

Frick, Frau, 81
Fritsch, Gen. Werner von, 10–11
Fuchido, Capt. Mitsuo, 93, 95, 96

Gamelin, Gen. Maurice, 12
Garrow, Capt. Ian, 167
Gauraud, Father Emile, 124, 125
Gavin, Col. James M., 153
Gehlen, Maj. Gen. Reinhard, 213, 215,
    217
Geiger, Dr. Hans, 176
German-American Bund, 18
German Armistice Commission, 127,
    128
Gestapo (Geheime Staatzpolizei), 21, 22,
    66, 68, 163, 168, 169, 218
Girard, Marcel, 172
Girosi, Lt. Marcello, 160
Girosi, Adm. Massimo, 160, 163
Goebbels, Josef, 5, 24–25, 55–57
Goerdeler, Karl-Friedrich, 114, 115
Goering, Field Marshal Hermann, 5, 6
    bombing Swiss airport proposed by,
    201
    "Eagle Day" proclaimed by, 59
Goldberg, Maj. Arthur, 218
Goodeve, Lt. Cmdr. Charles F., 165
Gooseberry (code name), 180–81
Goudsmit, Dr. Samuel A., 211
Graf Spee (German battleship), 33
Gray Code (U.S.), 3, 4
Graziano, Marshal Rudolfo, 45, 46
Groscurth, Col. Helmuth, 36
Groves, Maj. Gen. Leslie R., 136, 138,
    175, 208
Gubbins, Maj. Gen. Colin McV., 199
Guderian, Gen. Heinz, 217
Guerin, François, 173–74
Guingand, Col. Francis W. de, 129, 132
Gulbenkian, Nubar, 167
Gutmann, Ingeborg, 21

Hanfstaengl, Ernst Franz, 5–7
Hapag-Lloyd Steamship Company, 21
Harwood, Commodore Henry H., 33
Hausberger, Walter von, 62, 64

Heisenberg, Werner, 208–10
Herrmann, Karl, 21
Hess, Rudolf, 5, 46
Heydrich, SS Gen. Reinhard, 81
Hilberry, Dr. Norman, 176
Himmler, Reichsfuehrer Heinrich, 5, 201
Hitler, Adolf, 5, 6, 7
    assassination attempts against, 115–17
    England invasion ordered by, 54
    England invasion planned by, 57
    Rhineland occupation planned by,
      9–13
    Stalingrad debacle infuriates, 116
Hoesch, Leopold von, 12, 13
Hood (British cruiser), 69
Hoover, FBI Director J. Edgar, 49, 50,
    112, 158
Hopkins, Harry, 85

Independence Hall (U.S. ship), 64
Inter-Services Topographical Unit
    (ISTU), 225

Japanese Citizens Patriotic Society, 7, 8
Jervis Bay (British ship), 100
Jodl, Gen. Alfred, 53, 54, 55
Johnen, Lt. Wilhelm, 199, 200, 203
Joliot-Curie, Frédéric, 210
Jordan, Maj. George R., 86–87

Kaas, Monsignor Ludwig, 37, 38
Kaiser Wilhelm, 9
Kamprath, Sgt. Joachim, 200, 201, 203
Kappius, Anne, 218, 220
Kappius, Jupp, 218–20
Keitel, Field Marshal Wilhelm, 46, 53,
    54, 55, 113
Kempeitai (Japanese secret police), 3
Kerner, Capt. Rudolf, 68
Kieffer, SS Col. Hans, 147
King Christian X, 42
King Edward VIII, 12–13
King George V, 12
King Haakon, 66
King Victor Emmanuel III, 202
Kita, Consul Nagao, 104–05

Kleist-Schmenzin, Edwald von, 25–29
Klope, Carl V., 134–35
Kluge, Field Marshal Hans von, 114, 115
Knox, Navy Secretary Frank, 126
Kondor Mission, 130, 132
Kreipe, Maj. Gen. Heinrich, 191, 193–95
Kuhn, Bundesfuehrer Fritz, 109, 110
Kuhrig, Ernst, 20–21
Kunze, Bundesfuehrer Gerhard, 110, 112

"L" (Japanese overseas intelligence net-
    work), 88
Lang, Hermann W., 16, 17
Langsdorff, Capt. Hans, 33
Lansdale, Lt. Col. John, Jr., 137, 138,
    139
Lavelle, Georges, 124, 125
Layton, Lt. Cmdr. Edwin T., 7, 8, 9
Lehmitz, Ernest F., 155, 156, 158
Leiber, Father Robert, 38, 39
Leigh-Fermor, Maj. Patrick, 190–95
Lemnitzer, Maj. Gen. Lyman, 221
Lend-Lease Act, 85
Liewer, Philippe (aka Charles Staunton),
    143, 145, 146
Lindberg, Karl, 20
Lindemann, Prof. Frederick, 89
London Controlling Section (LCS), 165
Lord Haw-Haw (William Joyce), 182
Lord Lloyd of Dolobran, 27, 28
Lovell, Stanley P., 197, 198
Lützow (German cruiser), 170, 171

MacArthur, Gen. Douglas, 195
MacCloskey, Col. Monro, 221–24
Madam X (*see* Driscoll)
Maejima, Cmdr. Toshihide, 94, 95
Mahle, Sgt. Paul, 201, 203
Malavergne, Jules, 134–35
Manhattan Engineer District, 87
Manhattan Project, 137, 138, 175, 176
Manville, Mrs. Thomas, 22, 24
Marceglia, Capt. Antonio, 97, 99
Marino, Sgt. Mario, 97, 99
Marshall, Gen. George C., 136, 175
Martellotta, Capt. Vincenzo, 97, 99

Martian Room, 173

Martinuzzi, Leo, 212

Maskelyne, Lt. Jasper, 89–93

Mason-MacFarlane, Gen. Frank, 30

Meisel, Hilde, 219, 220

Menzies, Stewart, 189

Merritt, Lt. Col. Charles C., 121–22

Metallurgical Laboratory (Metlab), 176

Metaxas, Premier John, 73

MI-5 (British counterintelligence service), 181

MI-6 (British intelligence service), 26, 60, 189

MI-9 (British escape service), 167

Milorg (Norwegian underground), 196–97

Miramar Hotel (Casablanca), 127

Molzahn, Rev. Kurt, 111

Monkaster, Peter, 130, 131

Moore, Maj. Gen. Cecil R., 206

Morgan, Capt. Charles, 100

Morgan, Lt. Gen. Frederick E., 163–64

Morhange (French resistance group), 167–68

Mortier, Robert, 143, 144, 145, 146

Moss, Capt. Stanley, 190, 191, 192, 193, 195

Mueller, Josef, 37–39

Mullberry (code name), 180–81, 182, 183

Müller, Capt. Albert, 213–17

Müller, Maj. Gen. Friedrich, 190

Munthe, Maj. Malcolm, 67

Mussolini, Benito, vii, 44, 202

Nasjonal Samling (Norwegian Nazi Party), 65

Nazi Socialist German Workers' Party (Nazis), 5

Nissenthall, Flight Sgt. Jack, 120–23

Njaa, Tor, 67, 68

NKVD (Soviet secret police), 216, 217

Norden, Carl T., 14

Norfolk (British cruiser), 69

Normandie (French ship), 205

North, John R., 160, 161, 163

O'Brien, Lt. Richard H., 160, 162, 163

Okuda, Otojiro, 41–42

Operations:
    Alsos (Allied search for German atomic scientists), 210
    Corona (British radio jamming), 177
    Drossel (German spy plan in Russia), 213, 215
    Jubilee (Dieppe raid), 120–24
    Neptune (assault phase in Normandy), 205
    Overlord (Normandy invasion), 203
    Schulung (German plan to occupy Rhineland), 9, 13
    Sea Lion (planned German invasion of England), 45, 54, 57
    Torch (North Africa invasion), 126, 135
    Winteruebung (German occupation of Rhineland), 13
    Z (Pearl Harbor attack), 101

Oppenheimer, Dr. J. Robert, 138, 139

Oppenheimer, Katherine, 139

Ordnung Dienst (U.S. Nazi group), 17

Osborne, Ambassador D'Arcy, 38–39

Oshima, Gen. Hiroshi, 182, 183

Osten, Capt. Murray, 121–22

Oster, Maj. Gen. Hans, 36, 37, 38

Pareyre, Michel, 167

Pash, Lt. Col. Boris T., 139, 210–13

Paterakis, Manoli, 190, 191, 193

Patton, Gen. George S., Jr., 127

Pavasi, Vice Adm. Gino, 153

Payton, Col. Bernard L., 81

Penne, Lt. Luigi Durand de la, 97, 98–100

Pennsylvania (U.S. battleship), 7

Pétain, Marshal Henri, 143

Petersen, Hans, 42–44

Phoenix (code name), 180–81

Poitevin, Arthur, 173–74

Pope Pius XII, 37, 38

Pratt, Col. George, 218

Prince of Wales (British battleship), 69

Prinz Eugen (German cruiser), 69

Pritchard, Lt. Col. Vernon S., 72
Project 14 (German plan), 20
Prosper (French underground unit), 48, 49

Queen Elizabeth (British battleship), 96, 99, 100, 205
Queen Mary (British ship), 205
Quisling, Vidkun, 65, 66

Radio Berlin, 56, 182
Ramm, Ernst, 20
Rankin, Hans (see Ritter)
Rebecca (novel), 131, 132
Reeves, Adm. Joseph M., 8
Renown (British battleship), 33
Ribbentropp, Joachim von, 61, 62
Richardson, Adm. James, H., 41
Ridgway, Maj. Gen. Matthew, 153
Ritchie, Gen. Neil, 117
Ritter, Nicholaus, 14–17
Robertson, Maj. Thomas A., 181
Rochefort, Lt. Cmdr. Joseph J., 7
Rommel, Gen. Erwin, 90, 117–18, 129–33
Rommel, Lucie Maria, 133
Roosevelt, President Franklin D., 7, 49, 106, 158
Rorvig, Sofie, 68
Rossberg, Fritz, 18, 19, 20
Royal Aircraft Establishment, 189
Rundstedt, Gen. Karl von, 183
Ruth, Babe, 3

S-19 (Japanese code), 104
Saguna (British ship), 100
St. George Hotel (Algiers), 150
St. Louis (German ship), 19, 20
Savoldi, "Jumping Joe," 160, 161
Savoy-Plaza Hotel (New York), 22, 24
Schackow, Hans, 21
Scharnhorst (German cruiser), 170, 171
Schellenberg, SS Gen. Walther, 113
Schlabrendorff, Maj. Fabian von, 115, 116, 117
Schlieben, Lt. Gen. Karl von, 206

Schutzstaffel (SS), 27
Schwarze Kapelle (Black Orchestra), 26–29, 36, 38, 39, 115, 196
Scire (Italian submarine), 96, 97, 98
Section 6, 224, 225
Seland, Johannes, 68
Shaheen, Lt. John, 159, 161, 162, 163
Shell Oil Company, 7
Sibony (German ship), 155
Sicherheitsdienst (SD) (German intelligence branch), 27, 41, 81, 113
Signals Security Agency (SSA), 183
SIM (Italian secret service), 118
Simpson, Wallis Warfield, 12
Skorzeny, SS Maj. Otto, 201–02
Skriabin, Lt. Vassilij, 213–17
SNCF (French National Railways), 149
Soehn, Heinrich, 15, 16
Somervell, Gen. Brehon B., 136, 137
Special Operations Executive (SOE), 143, 199
Sperry, Elmer, 14
Spud (code name), 180–81
Stalin, Premier Josef, 85
Starheim, Odd, 67
Stark, Adm. Harold R., 41
Starzincy, Josef, 52–53
Steltzer, Col. Theodore, 196
Stephens, Mr. Marion, 109
Stieff, Gen. Helmuth, 116, 117
Stimson, War Secretary Henry L., 70, 136, 137, 138
Strassmann, Antonie, 22, 23, 24
Strong, Maj. Gen. George V., 72
Sulfolk (British cruiser), 69
Supreme Headquarters, Allied Expeditionary Force (SHAEF), 206–07
Suttill, Maj. Francis, 47, 48
Suzuki, Lt. Cmdr. Suguru, 94, 95, 96
Szabo, Violette, 145, 146, 147

Taft Hotel (New York), 15
Taillandier, Capt. Marcel, 166, 167, 168, 169
Tait, Vice Marshal, Victor H., 120
Taiyo-maru (Japanese ship), 93, 94, 95

Taylor, Maj. Grant, 79–80
Tedder, Air Chief Marshal Arthur, 152
Teller, Dr. Edward, 210
Tennant, Rear Adm. William, 181
T Force, 224
Thomsen, Hans, 61, 62, 70
Tirpitz (German battleship), 170, 171,
   172
Todt Organzation, 218
Tojo, Gen. Hideki, 182
Tomstad, Gunvald, 65–69
Tomstad, Mother, 65
Touchette, Pierre, (*see* DuPre)
Tresckow, Gen. Henning von, 115, 116
Trotobas, Michel, 147–50
Turner, Bradwell, Lt. Cmdr., 35
Tyrakis, Georgi, 190, 191, 193

Ultra, 59, 75, 79, 133
U.S. Forest Service, 159
U.S. Office of Censorship, 155, 158
U.S. Office of Naval Intelligence (ONI),
   4, 5, 7
U.S. Office of Strategic Services (OSS),
   49, 126, 132, 159, 197
Unkel, John Baptiste, 17, 18, 19, 20
Urey, Dr. Harold C., 174

Valiant (British battleship), 96, 99, 100
Ve-do-it Airline, 188, 189, 190
Vian, Capt. Philip L., 34, 35

Victorious (British aircraft carrier), 69
Vietinghoff, Gen. Heinrich von, 223
Viking (Norwegian boat), 67
Vonsiatsky-Vonsiatsky, Count Anastase,
   109–12
V-2 (rocket), 188, 190

WAAF (Women's Auxiliary Air Force),
   58, 59
Wachi, Cmdr. Isunezo, 88, 89
Warnecke, Richard, 83
Weil, Jacques, 46, 47, 49
Weizsäcker, Carl von, 208, 210
Wenner-Gren, Axel, 160
White, Col. Dick, 207
Wilhumeit, Dr. Otto, 111, 112
Windsor Castle, 61
Wolff, SS Gen. Karl, 221
Wolfsschanze (Wolf's Lair), 201
Worms, Jean, 47

X2 (branch of U.S. OSS), 207
XX Committee, 72, 75, 181, 182

Y Service (British wireless monitoring),
   58, 59, 60
Yamamoto, Adm. Isokuru, 101, 104
Yorktown (U.S. carrier), 161
Yoshikawa, Takeo, 100–05

Zuckerman, Prof. Solly, 150, 152